Somewhere in France

Somewhere in France

The collected letters of
Lewis Windermere Nott
January – December 1916

HarperPerennial
An imprint of HarperCollins*Publishers*

For my beloved parents, my wife Caroline and my children, Matthew, Amanda, Catriona and Ingrid

HarperPerennial
An imprint of HarperCollins*Publishers*

First published in Australia in 1996
by HarperCollins*Publishers* Pty Limited
ACN 009 913 517
A member of the HarperCollins*Publishers* (Australia) Pty Limited Group

HarperCollins*Publishers*
25 Ryde Road, Pymble, Sydney, NSW 2073, Australia
31 View Road, Glenfield, Auckland 10, New Zealand
77–85 Fulham Palace Road, London W6 8JB, United Kingdom
Hazelton Lanes, 55 Avenue Road, Suite 2900, Toronto, Ontario M5R 3L2
and 1995 Markham Road, Scarborough, Ontario M1B 5M8, Canada
10 East 53rd Street, New York NY 10032, USA

National Library of Australia Cataloguing-in-Publication data:

Nott, Lewis Windermere.
Somewhere in France: the collected letters of Lewis Windermere Nott.

Bibliography.
ISBN 0 7322 5667 4.

1. Nott, Lewis Windermere - Correspondence. 2. Somme, 1st Battle of the, France, 1916 - Personal narratives, Australian. 3. World War, 1914-1918 - Personal narratives. I. Nott, David (David Bruce). II. Title.
940.4272092

Text 11/14 Bembo
Printed in Australia by Griffin Paperbacks, Adelaide on79gsm Bulky Paperback

9 8 7 6 5 4 3 2 1
99 98 97 96

Preface

The letters published in this book are the thoughts of one soldier during his time in France in 1916. These private writings could only be published because the Nott family cared enough to keep and preserve the letters for 80 years. Regrettably, keeping such treasures as diaries, letters, certificates and medals is a task undertaken by few families today. Where these collections do exist in the family home they are constantly at risk from fire, flood, dispersal to disinterested relations or theft.

These constant risks highlight the importance of keeping family treasures in a secure place. Letters such as those written by Lewis Nott to his wife are important because they are Australia's richest source of historical information of a personal nature on the Great War. They enrich not only family history but also the history of our nation.

To ensure the safety of such valuable historical items, families should seriously consider placing their wartime records with an institution like the Australian War Memorial. The Memorial will ensure that such valuables are stored securely and professionally so that they remain available for future generations of the family to read with interest and pleasure.

I congratulate David Nott on compiling ***Somewhere in France*** *and allowing the nation access to the private world of his family who have preserved not only their own heritage but also a small part of Australia's heritage.*

Bill Fogarty
Senior Curator

Australian War Memorial

Contents

Illustration Credits

The illustrated month spreads in *Somewhere in France* feature reproductions and selections from Lewis Nott's original letters, trench maps, and photographs. A portrait of Lewis Nott at the time of his enlistment appears on each spread and additional photographs have been chosen to reflect the content and thoughts of Lewis Nott. The selections from Nott's trench maps highlight the position of his battalion at the time he was writing. All material is from the private collection of the Nott family and is reproduced with their kind permission.

January
The 15th Battalion marching to the front.
Doris at the time of her marriage.

February
An unidentified Royal Scot takes aim.
Doris and Derek *circa* 1915.

March
Lewis and his father, Bundaberg, 1908.
Taking a break, somewhere in France.

April
Lewis with Derek on leave in Glasgow.
Unidentified men from the 15th Battalion.

May
Illustrated postcards sent from the front by Lewis to Doris and Derek.

June
Royal Scots taking a break.
Colonel Archibald Urmston.

July
The lads take a break.
Pipe Major Anderson.

August
Taking a dip.
An unidentified Royal Scot.

September
The 15th Battalion.
Doris and Derek, Edinburgh, 1915.

October
Convalescent tommies, 1917
Doris *circa* 1913.

November
The 15th Battalion's camp
Derek in 1915.

December
The battalion marching to the front.
Doris *circa* 1913.

List of Abbreviations

A	*Adjutant*
ADC	*Aide de Camp*
AMC	*(Australian) Army Medical Corps*
AMLO	*Army Movement Leave Officer*
APM	*Assistant Provost Marshal*
Art.	*Artillery*
ASC	*Army Services Corps*
BEF	*British Expeditionary Force*
Bn.	*Battalion*
CB	*Companion (of the Order) of the Bath*
CIGS	*Chief of the Imperial General Staff*
CO	*Commanding Officer*
Col.	*Colonel*
Com.	*Company*
Coy.	*Company*
CSM	*Company Sergeant Major*
DCM	*Distinguished Conduct Medal*
DSA	*District Supply Adjutant*
DSO	*Distinguished Service Order*
F. Amb	*Field Ambulance*
FOAO	*Forward Observation Artillery Officer*
FRCS	*Fellow Royal College of Surgeons*
GHQ	*General headquarters*
G.O.C.	*General Officer Commanding*
HA	*Heavy Artillery*
HE	*High Explosive*
HLI	*Highland Light Infantry*
HQ	*Headquarters*
Hon.	*Honorary*
KOSB	*King's Own Scottish Borderers*
Kt.	*Knight*
Lt.	*Lieutenant*
MC	*Military Cross*
MD	*Medicnae Doctor (Doctor of Medicine)*
MG	*machine gun*
MID	*Mention in Dispatches*
MO	*Medical Officer*
MM	*Military Medal*
NAAFI	*Navy Army AirForce Institutes*
NF	*National Front*
NCO	*Non Commissioned Officer*
NML	*No Man's Land*
OBE	*Officer of the Order of the British Empire*
OR	*Orderly Room*
Pvt	*Private*
QM	*Quarter Master*
QMG	*Quarter Master General*
RAMC	*Royal Army Medical Corps*
RFA	*Royal Field Artillery*
RFC	*Royal Flying Corps*
R.N.	*Royal Navy*
RTO	*Regimental Transport Officer*
Sgt	*Sergeant the Subaltern*
TF	*Territorial Force*
TM	*Trench Mortar*
VC	*Victoria Cross*
VD	*Volunteer (Officer's) Decoration*

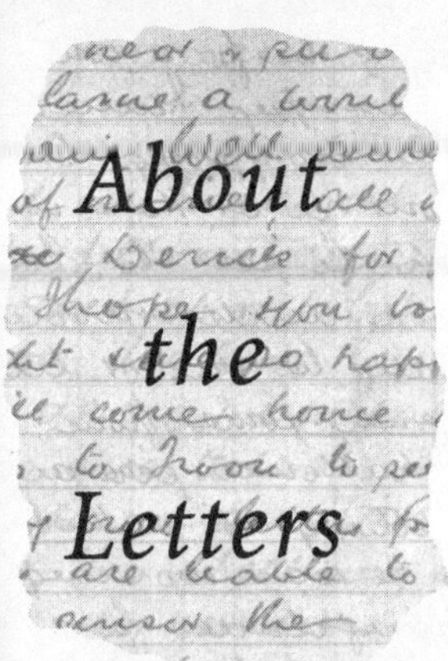

About the Letters

Brethren, how shall it fare with me
When the war is laid aside,
If it be proven that I am he
For whom a world has died?

'The Question', 1916, Rudyard Kipling

The letters of Lewis Windermere Nott (LWN) were written between January and December 1916 to his wife Doris and young son Frederick (Derek/Deckie), who were living with relatives in Glasgow and Troon. There are 132 letters in the collection — the first written on the day the battalion arrived in France and the last shortly before Christmas. All the letters were in his neat but quite difficult hand, and were written in both ink and pencil on signal paper and on paper sent to him by Doris. The scans of various letters that appear throughout this collection have been taken from the originals.

The letters were all dated with only a few exceptions, which were dated by Doris on receipt. Many carried the heading Somewhere in France — hence the title of this collection — and all were signed with love or from 'D' (for Daddy). In this way in the event of his death the letters would serve as an intimate correspondence to his then only son Frederick.

These are letters of the tedium of war, of the fear and the unending trails; of the weariness and the fatigue. They are also an intimate glimpse at a love affair. However, by their very nature there are of course unanswerable questions and inconsistencies in the letters — notes have been added throughout to provide a context for the many people, events and places mentioned (and not mentioned, due to censorship). LWN's punctuation and spelling have been followed exactly, except in instances when extreme circumstances and absent-mindedness have resulted in an obvious mistake which has obscured sense and clarity. In these instances the errors (if possible) have been corrected or supplemented with an author note. The following symbol — has been inserted to mimic LWN's censorship slash.

Sadly, we do not have any of Doris Nott's letters to her husband. Only one letter by Doris, written to her mother-in-law, has survived, and it has been placed at the beginning of LWN's October letters for a glimpse at her style of letter writing.

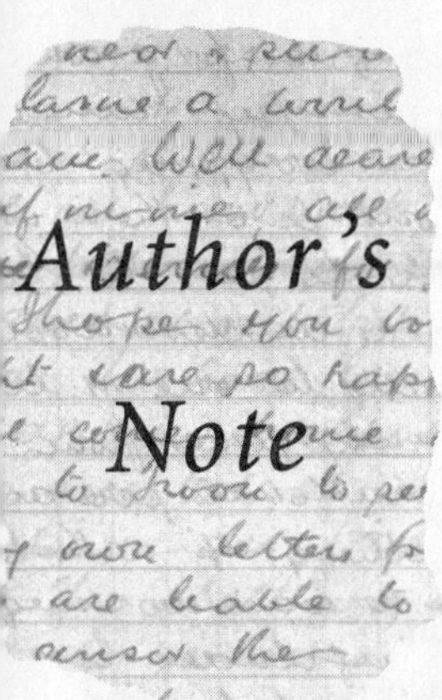

Author's Note

I first heard the story in 1945 at Kioloa, a tiny settlement on a warm and friendly beach of the same name on the far south coast of New South Wales, then uninhabited except for the Moore family: Hum, his two sisters, Postmistress Bernice (known as Bobbie) and Mrs London and her daughter, Joy. The Moores had arrived from England many years before, and had cut out a lifestyle in the beautiful hardwood State forest at Kioloa. Physically, by hand with axe and adze, the little family had carved a track from the main road and built bridges, a homestead and a row of diminutive cottages on a track down to the beach and the Pacific Ocean. We were staying in one of the cottages, having driven along the beach in our 1928 Buick to discover the Moores. Hum, who is the only person I have ever known called Humbert, was of great interest to a 14-year-old boy. I helped him start the meticulously maintained, shiny green- and red-painted single cylinder diesel generator with its gleaming polished brass and copper, whose job was to charge the batteries for the tiny settlement, and marvelled at his 1939 Dodge and listened to his stories about the early days of the timber industry on the south coast and of his narrow escape when the Packard bearing Hum and Bernice was blown up by angry unionists. Bernice (Miss Moore, to me) still carried the scars of the severe facial injuries she sustained.

On that evening my father, comfortably relaxed in one of Hum's huge leather chairs, took us to France and the Somme of July 1916. He talked of the mud, the noise, and the stench of rotting friends and foes. We felt we were there, too. He talked of his friends Lodge and Harrison, of Colonel Urmston, and of his great friend, Colonel Rose. We heard the whizz-bangs, the deafening crack of the German 5.9s, and the mortars. He took us to the trenches, one hour before zero hour, on that dreadful July 1st. His memories overcame him then, and the conversation flew to the present, today's large snapper and my mother's way of cooking it.

To my great regret, that was the only time I heard him talk of the Great War. I treasured those hours at Kioloa. The memories of the horrors, the flying, deadly shell splinters lasted. Our family returned often to Kioloa, but I don't remember any other return to the Great War. I am sure there were no more.

Then, some years after my mother's death in 1970, I discovered among boxes containing her precious things a worn cardboard box, about 15 cm by 8 cm. I was amazed to discover that it contained hundreds of tightly written pages of thin, nearly transparent, faded paper tied with a ribbon. Did I have the right to enter this secret, private world of my parents? With great respect and reverence, I started to read. It soon became clear that here was a complete record of my father's 12 months on the Western Front in 1916, detailed in daily letters to his young wife and son. I could barely read on, but did so, for hour after hour. It was all true, that nearly forgotten evening on the south coast with the Moores. What I had heard was an eyewitness account of the great opening offensive of the Somme. How I regretted not being able to ask all the questions my reading raised.

The letters are written on torn-out pages of field message pads, often on both sides. The paper is ruled into small squares, probably to facilitate the drawing of maps. Some were written in pencil, others in faded home-made ink. I wanted to read and reread them, but first I needed to be able to read them without difficulty. I set about transcribing them all. Some took many hours, requiring oblique light and the use of a powerful magnifying glass, but when done, I found I had a wonderful story of one man's war, a year of horror and death, in the mud of far-off Flanders and Picardy. Here was the day-to-day record, the light moments, the serious episodes and the very bad experiences. This was the agonising of a recently married young man, a doting father separated from his young family for almost a year, a year of horror and death.

A box of old maps which had always exuded a mysterious scent and aura suddenly assumed real significance. I pored over them. Here were all the maps he had brought home and stored away: War Office maps of Lille-Tournai-Thielt, Armentieres and Zilleberke (described as *Secret, 28 NW*), a street map of Ypres, and trench maps of Mametz Wood and La Boisselle. Here were all the places mentioned in the letters, the names hallowed in the history of our country's wars: the Somme, Villers-Bretonneux, Pozieres, Sausage Valley and Albert, and its famous virgin. It was possible to trace on the maps the route marches and to find Jesus Farm and Hallobeau, the farmhouses used from time to time as headquarters. It was easy to find the canal where father and his friends would ride. I relived the war through his eyes and ears and by his words, and in a strange and rather wonderful way, seemed to be in contact with him.

Here was a job to do. Put the letters in context, relate them to the chronology of the war, and annotate them so that I could obtain a full understanding. This was a real chance to study the war at first hand. Major Mason, at the headquarters of the Royal Scots, The Royal Regiment, in Edinburgh Castle, sent me a copy of the activities record of the 15th Battalion written daily by the various commanding officers during the period my father was adjutant of the battalion, from January to December 1916. This enabled me to piece together the movements and the places mentioned but not named in the letters for security reasons. Gradually the story emerged. The project demanded that I read as much as I could about the terrible war.

I had visited the regiment at the barracks at Glencorse, near Edinburgh, in 1960. It was an emotional visit for me, as I was aware of my father's involvement with the regiment but had no details of places or people; that would only come later with reading the letters. Now I had the letters, the maps and the battalion records, supplemented by my reading about the regiment, which gave me a new understanding of the times, of the war, and of my mother and father's life together and apart in Scotland. I became a troglodyte, inhabiting the wonderful newspaper room at the National Library of Australia. I spent many hours reading the newspapers of 1916 — *The Times*, *The Scotsman*, *The Sydney Morning Herald* — on microfilm. Here it was possible to read the papers that my father read, the items he commented on to his bride.

The next step followed automatically. The books and papers published about the Great War are numerous and fascinating. Biographies, autobiographies and formal studies of aspects of the war assisted me in the project. I learned about trench warfare, about tanks, about the Battle of Jutland and the aircraft industry of the time.

And what of my father? Who was this man, so far from his country, separated from his family, in a world war? Lewis ('Lew') Windermere Nott, a third-generation Australian and the fifth son of one of Queensland's sugar pioneers, Frederick Lewis Nott (see Appendix I), was born at Windermere, Bundaberg, Queensland on 12 February 1886. He received his early education at Maryborough Grammar School, Queensland and later studied at the School of Mines in Ballarat, Victoria, where he obtained his degree as a mining engineer with the intention of assisting his brothers set up a gold-mining venture. They met with some rather sharp and unpleasant characters in the mining industry who were not to the young men's liking and the whole idea was dropped. During his university days Lew participated in the Dramatic Society and was a very successful athlete, specialising in track and field, and like his brother Arch, he was a crack shot.

Lew began a degree in Medicine at Sydney University, but following his marriage to Doris Ashbury in July 1913 the newlyweds travelled to the United Kingdom and set up their home in Edinburgh, where Lew intended to complete his degree at the University Medical School and the Royal Infirmary. His mother's family welcomed the opportunity of getting to know their colonial relatives, and the early months in Edinburgh were extremely happy ones. But the spectre of war was looming, and Lew wrote to his brothers in Australia that if war came he would hurry home with the family to enlist — hopefully, by that time, as a fully-fledged doctor.

This plan was not to eventuate and at the outbreak of the Great War he was in his final year with about six months to complete before graduation. Finding that there was no way he could return to Australia, he enlisted as a private in the Lovat Scouts. Lew and his final year medical student friend, Nairn, agreed to conceal their imminent graduation from the university, fearing that such knowledge would have delayed their entry into the army, and they joined together.

Due to his love of and skill with horses, Lew had earlier applied for a transfer to the Royal Horse Artillery and by May 1915 he was commissioned in that famous unit, but later transferred to the 15th Battalion, the Royal Scots, with the help of his relatives, several of whom were in the regiment. He was made adjutant of that unit soon after joining, and acting Commanding Officer for a period in 1916. He was extremely proud of the Royal Scots and remained conscious of the honour of belonging to such a famous unit (see Appendix II).

Lew Nott spent most of 1915 training in England, with the 15th Battalion, known as the 1st City of Edinburgh Battalion, mostly in and around Warminster, on Salisbury Plains. When the battalion went to France in January 1916, Lew and his horse went too.

The letters

la Boisselle

MESSAGES AND SIGNALS.

Words Charge

Sent

At.......m.

To.......

By.......

This message is on a/c of: (P) Service.

(Signature of "Franking Officer.")

Recd.

Date.

From.

By.

19: 1: 16

Day of Month

In reply to Number

January

JANUARY 11TH
Somewhere

My dearest little wife,
At last I've got a minute to spare and although I must not tell you where I am, I can at least tell you some of my experiences. Arrived at the port,[1] we disembarked and some of the men were sorry specimens. I was not a bit sick but was so busy and worried to death. After disembarking we went to a rest camp for one night, four and a half miles up the most awful hills, it was so hot, and all of us with such overloaded packs and overcoats on. However we arrived at the camp[2] and got a great reception from the French people. My pony behaved in a most alarming fashion and would not take things seriously. Anyway arrived in camp the men rested. We went off to try and get some lunch at an *estaminet*. The result was ludicrous, you would have screamed to hear us all trying to order meals and the arguments about the change were terrific.

However we managed somehow and left next morning at 4.30 am for a 23-hour train trip. Train was awfully slow and we were up all night, in fact until last night I had not had one night's rest and had not changed my clothes or boots.

We arrived where we are now[3] yesterday morning and had to march nine miles to billets. RBG[4] met the CO[5] and myself, and we were whisked off to find billets and the CO and I had to do the billeting, what a job, dearie. The people are awfully good but as you can imagine not keen on having soldiers bounced on to them. However the CO, footsore and dead to the world as we had to do everything on foot, and I managed to billet the battalion[6] in farms and in the village. I got on surprisingly well with my French which came at the critical moment in a wonderful way.

We commandeered a big chateau for our HQ and then the CO and I settled down with the MO. Very comfortable indeed. Our horses are close by and today I visited all the billets and found the men settling down and making the best of things. But oh what a job it was getting them on to billets. The men were great; they are splendid fellows so anxious to do the best to help me. We can hear the big guns booming and rumbling away ahead, and don't know how long we will be here. I cannot help remarking on the change in them, they are splendid, created a great impression on everyone.

Richardson is in high feather. I must tell you what he said to me at breakfast. He said that there were some eggs for breakfast but no bacon as the French people did not know what bacon was, so I said that *cochon* was the French for it, but he said, 'I know what pig is, it is *du lard*, the woman told me'.

I had a lonely bed last night, just fell into bed, Anderson[7] and I in the same room, so things are fine, but what a time I've had. I had my first shave yesterday since leaving. Major Rose[8] has been splendid and helped me with my job as well as his own, he speaks French very well. We are progressing most favourably under adverse conditions. It is most thrilling to hear the big guns doing the heavy strafing each day, like distant thunder, day and night.

Well sweetheart mine, here is all my love to both you dear sweet little things. Give all my love to all at No 3 and tell Mrs McOmie[9] I will write sometime, but I don't get many opportunities as I have to do everything and see to everything.

Goodbye dearest and brave little woman, love to you both.

January 13th

Today we find ourselves a wee bit more settled down, the men learning to make themselves comfortable and everyone busy trying to establish friendly relations with the French. Our HQ is rather a palatial residence rejoicing under the cognomen of the 'chateau les Affres', but what that means *il ne sais pas*. Our host is an old pig and speaks a peculiar dialect, half French and half Flemish, always the other half! Madame is more amiable, does her best. There are no children but several maids. The old man is a great liar, at first he said every room was full but we got thirty men from the battalion HQ staff fixed up at last, to the great distress of mine host. He gets most passionately angry and shouts at the top of his voice, and is ever running in with complaints. I expect it is pretty rotten to have a great crowd of soldiers dumped down, still it is the exigencies of the times one must put up with. The company commanders are out at the farm and are doing famously well, the men clean up the yards and stables, mend fences, fetch for Madame and she treats them well. Our French is improving rapidly and we all more or less can get along and get anything we want. I was very modest and shy about my *grammaire* and my pronunciation at first but now by gesticulating, shouting and much hard swearing I can get anything.

Today we had a short six mile route march. The men looked fine, only two off parade with bad feet. The roads are paved with big square stones and very hard on the men and horses, but I hear that one soon becomes accustomed to them. You would scream to see and hear Gee trying on the French. He gets hold of a single noun and repeats it, shouts, grabs the book and then gets tired. My horse is settling down a bit, the great weight is steadying her, for we must go everywhere fully armed and equipped; when we left the rest camp she was the centre of great excitement. The rest of the brigade[10] arrived yesterday and are billeted in and around our own area but we don't see anything of them. I met Platts yesterday. He told me that Major Maxwell's pony died that morning. That is the one he won the prize at the show with.

The big guns are pretty quiet today, usually they commence soon after daylight and continue till noon and then commence the evening hate about 3.30. Aeroplanes are very common, of course, and sail about like big and little seagulls. The land generally is like Lincolnshire — flat and wet with great dykes and canals and good woods. In the summer it must be very pretty. Spring is not far away now; most of the trees are budding and some of the earlier ones are already in leaf. Well dearest little wife and son, I will write to you just as often as I can and you must write too sometimes. I'm so busy you will still only get skimpy letters. Send me some Gold Flakes[11] please Pettie, a pipe and tobacco, the French cigarettes are vile. Gold Flakes are not procurable here.

All love, dear heart, to you both . . .

JANUARY 15TH

Now I can say that at last we are really settling down in billets and work is getting once again into the usual routine, billet inspections, orders and company work. I got your first letter sweetheart and it was just grand to get it. I am so glad you arrived safe and sound in Glasgow and I know just how comfortable they will make you at No 3.

Yesterday John and I went in the mess cart over to the nearest big town to get some supplies. I wanted cigarettes, tobacco, paper and odds and ends, it was a matter of ten kilometres and as the day was a beautiful one we had quite a nice run out and back. Had lunch at a restaurant and got on famously with our French. What a time I had doing the billeting here when we arrived. My French absolutely deserted me but it has since come back splendidly and I am always trying conversations with the people!

The chateau where we have our HQ is a fine big palatial place. We have beds but the owner is really an old French pig. He refused us everything and used to weep copiously and bellow like a bull whenever we demanded a key to look at another room. He said he only had room for five officers but now we have five officers and 33 men in the chateau. We have our own cooks and commandeered half the kitchen, leaving half for Madame, and can she cook an omelette.

The men are all in barns, stables and lofts and the officers live in the farmhouse. The country is very like England but the avenues must be wonderful in the summer time. Spring is just commencing to come in so very soon it ought to be very nice. It is bitterly cold but has been fine since our arrival.

Major Rose, the four officers commanding companies and myself go up to the trenches for instruction on Tuesday. We will be at the trenches for six days, I believe, so if you do not hear from me for some days you will know the reason. It is wonderful here to see the huge convoys of enormous lorries and motor ambulances, miles long. Flying cavalry patrols, French and English, flit in and out of the village all day and lend the picture a very pretty effect. The guns we can hear roaring away but the last two days they have been a great deal quieter. You would be very excited if you knew where we were[12] but I cannot tell. Everyone near military age here in uniform; the men in the shops, the ploughmen, field hands all wear the uniform and are either wounded or on leave. So far we've not seen one eligible Frenchman in mufti. The last people here who moved out just as we came in left the billets very untidy but our men are winning a great name for their conduct and discipline. There have been some aeroplane raids hereabouts and some civilians killed and more are expected. They do relatively little damage, but their contribution may be a big factor in times to come.[13]

Well now dearest wee wife and son of mine a big hug and kiss . . .

January 16th

I was so glad to get your two dear letters and one from dear wee Deckie.[14] I am so glad he is so well and that his appetite is so good. Troon[15] will do you both the world of good and you must rest all you can to get that dear little double chin back. There is nothing very fresh to chronicle here, we are still jogging along and the path is becoming easier each day as we fall into the routine.

Tomorrow four officers go to a place not far distant for further bombing experience. It is a big school of instruction and I expect to go up to the trenches this week as I told you. There must be something more than the usual calm there at present, for the big guns roared and boomed all day yesterday and even continued right up till midnight. The CO, the Sub, Lodge[16] and I played bridge up till midnight listening to the guns. There was some heavy firing again today but not nearly so thunderous as yesterday. Today Anderson, Lodge and I went for a long ride through a big forest, of course the trees are leafless but it was very pleasant. The one good feature here is that I get some time to myself and manage to have some nice rides and the pony is rapidly settling down now and looks so well. Lodge is a great sport, and can you believe, he is over 6 feet 6 inches tall, but a wonderfully calm man.

There are no lights allowed here at all so the men turn in very early as it is dark at 5 pm. We have breakfast at 8.30 am so that one gets a little time to prepare for the trials of the day. I usually go round the billets and inspect once a day, the rest of the day is spent in the orderly room. Everyone is settled down, the billets are comfortable and the rations full so that there is no grumbling amongst the men.

One of my biggest and least happy jobs is the censoring of letters. I do all the HQ letters and it is a wearisome job. Not very nice prying into other people's business.

We had the first church parade today, a fact that curiously interests the French people. My French gradually improves and now I do quite well. The interpreter is attached now and I always speak to him in French for practice. He is a weird little specimen and does not speak English much better than I do French. He speaks with a Yankee slang as he was in Chicago many years ago. The old pig at the chateau continues to be disagreeable but now we don't mind him and use what we want without even consulting the old fool. The men are behaving just splendidly giving no trouble and have worked wonders in cleaning up around the billets etc. The majority of the people are *tres content avec les soldats*.

Today by riding out ten kilometres we had a very decent look at the country which is really a replica of Lincolnshire. The land in and around the vicinity of the billets for many miles' radius is flat and well intersected with canals but the tree growth is very good. Some of the forests are very fine and extensive and the chateaux in most cases are neatly packed in the centre of the wood. Outside about a nine or ten kilometres' radius there are some low hills, which give an expansive view, but they are quite miniature affairs and the whole countryside can be described as flat. I remember reading that the birds sang whilst the gunfire continues, but it is a bit of a flight of fancy. I've seen nothing but magpies and carrion crows, millions of the latter, the disgusting brutes. Well, Pettikin, I am expecting a nice long mail from you tomorrow and possibly some Australian mail.

So goodnight, dearest . . .

JANUARY 18TH

I cannot understand why you had not received any of my letters for I've written about five now, this must be the 6th, they must be going astray, or being kept at the base. I hear that letters are not sent every day but wait a couple of days and then a whole cargo of mail goes across.

Well yesterday we had our first real sight of warfare and it was of the most thrilling kind possible. There have been some air raids lately, not very big ones and not much damage has been done, but the Boche[17] tried something bigger yesterday but with no better result. I don't even think he killed a civilian. The day was fine but cloudy and the clouds were low, an ideal day for aeroplanes. About 8 am the guns near us commenced a violent bombardment, and in less than no time our aeroplanes were skimming and flying everywhere. Things settled down again for a brief period. Shortly after there was another violent outburst and we could see what appeared to be a big German battle plane with about a dozen or even more of our planes flying all around it, any amount of machine guns squibbing[18] off. A little later still, the big guns nearest to us commenced to boom away in rare style, and right up in the air almost like a swallow we could see a Taube[19] with the shrapnel[20] bursting all around it and in a very few seconds out came about a dozen aeroplanes. One went up and up in a bee line for the Taube which turned tail and bolted, hotly pursued by our plane. Other planes cut away into the distance to try to cut off the retreating Taube but I don't know with what luck. It is a glorious sight to see so many planes, and it must be some thrill, up in the air with bursting shrapnel. To us the shrapnel seemed to be bursting all around the Taube but we were a long way off. Still the elevation was right and sometimes the shrapnel puff would obliterate the Taube altogether.

It is raining today, the first wet day we have had since coming over. I see my Gazette is in the paper today, and I'm antedated to December 4th, so that's not bad. On Thursday we are to be visited by a very great soldier,[21] but I cannot of course mention his name. Last night we had an alarm and the battalion turned out in rare style.

It is so nice to hear how wee Deckie is coming along. He must just love the big bath. No bath here of course, but nor are there many baths in England or Scotland. Our friend the chateau host is just the same surly old boor but we just ignore him completely.

Well sweetest and dearest Tuppie, bye for the present . . .

JANUARY 19TH

Dearest little sweetheart and wife,

Just a tiny note as I have not much time today for we have a big inspection tomorrow and I have to go out and reconnoitre the spot. Yesterday it rained all day, not very heavy but a most miserable drizzle. The result is mud like nothing I've ever seen before. The mud was pretty bad at Sutton Veny[22] but it would bog a duck here. Today has been a beautiful day, a rare spring day. We are, on the whole, having the most excellent weather. I have not had a letter from you for an age. I do hope that some will come tomorrow to tell me you are well, and how you and dear wee Derick are getting on. Don't bother at the present moment about sending me any papers as I can always get the English papers here, and they are only a day old when we get them; but what I do want is plenty of letters. Sweetie, I do so long to hear and see you and Deckie about, it is all so lonely and unsatisfying without you.

The big guns have been going at it the last two days. Judging from the sound, the very biggest must be at it. There is at present some religious festival on at the church here, and things are quite lively today, crowds of people, chiefly ladies, in almost every case they are in mourning. One thing that I do not see here is the slacker, everyone is in uniform. There are no French eligibles about other than men on leave or wounded. The Red Cross cars are an awful nuisance. They dash along, great long convoys of them and don't care how they go round corners. Today one nearly settled QM Smith, he was very lucky. We detained the driver, he was less lucky.

Sgt Duthie, my clerk, is off duty ill, some slight indisposition but I hope he is fit tomorrow as it is a big day and many returns[23] are due. Major Stocks came down to dinner with us last night and then played bridge; he was in a very argumentative frame of mind and he and I had a go in, but I had to leave soon after dinner and get on with some work so we did not finish the argument. Brand is out on a farm with his company and is looking very fit, you can tell his sister.

We are all in the good books of the French people here and I believe that even our ungenial host is beginning to unbend a bit, and is realising that his warped judgment was wrong. Yesterday was the first payday of the men in France. They were paid in French money which obviates them changing the money and is in that way money saving, for the French have so many coins in circulation, silver, nickel and copper, that our men have occasionally been done rather badly.

Money matters are very queer here, and one must be on the alert. There are coins and paper money of the Republic, also local municipal money, chiefly paper. The municipal paper money is not much good outside the municipality it was issued in, and the inhabitants love working it off as change, otherwise the system is good and easy to follow. There does not seem to be much doing in the papers on other fronts and except on our own immediate front we rely solely on the papers for our news. Well dearest little treasure of mine, take good care of that precious little self of yours and of our dear wee son.

All my love and thoughts are of, and with you. Goodnight . . .

January 21st

My dearest little sweetheart and wife,
I was so sorry to hear that you had not yet had any of my letters. I cannot understand at all as I've written every other day and most times, each day. The base censor must be keeping them back for some obscure reason.

I expect you will see in *The Times* that Brigadier-General Fitton[24] was wounded by a sniper and died next day from wounds. He was so proud of us all and had such high hopes for the brigade. He will be so badly missed, his untimely end has cast a pall of gloom over everyone. We all try not to think about being killed, and the matter is never discussed, but when the Brigadier goes, we can't help discussing it.

Yesterday we were inspected by General Sir Douglas Haig[25] and by General Joffre.[26] I had a real good look at Joffre; he is a dear looking old chap, so pink and white, with such a kind but strong face. He is wonderfully well preserved, not a wrinkle, his face is like wax, so smooth, his eyes are so fine and twinkly. We were all impressed, he looks altogether resolute and capable. Haig is the real dashing, spare, virile type of soldier that all England loves; beautifully turned out, fine, clear-cut features, with a keen and intensely alive look about him. It was intensely cold and windy, with driving rain squalls, and we all had to wait for such a long time. General Joffre sent a special message to us through General Williams saying how splendid we were, how steady and how soldierly the bearing was, so that everyone was tremendously bucked up and just as he was inspecting us the poor old Brig was dying.

Dearest, this is a short note; all or nearly all are away on special duty and I'm very busy as there may be a new move any day.

All my love to both of my dears . . .

JANUARY 22ND

My own little sweetheart,
I'm so pleased to have your letter today and to learn that at last some of my letters have been arriving. I was going to try to frank a wire today, but now all is well and you will be getting a real swag of letters soon.

All is much the same here, some rain, wind and mud, the whole place is a quagmire. The whole country is so flat and low, one inch of the pave there is nothing but a sea of mud. The pave is very hard on the men marching, but no other roads could have withstood the traffic, the paves themselves show no sign of the heavy traffic. It is fairly quiet, just the occasional big gun going, and nothing at all doing in the air. The aeroplanes do look fine and some just scud past our head, going scouting over the Hun lines.

Don't worry about the cigarettes and tobacco, my dear, I can manage to get it from a big town about ten kilometres away Last night we had a sudden alarm and the whole battalion was underway and on the road in an hour from the call which was excellent considering the way the men are split up in the billets.

I am glad that you are both having such a fine time in Glasgow, and that our lad is so well. Wasn't it sad about the Brigadier, poor old chap, these snipers are very wily birds; however we will very soon, I hope, more than settle accounts.

Major Stocks' horse was sent off to the base vet. hospital owing to a bad kick, and another one of the horses died from pneumonia. Old Stocks is in a great way about Sutie, he was very fond of her, at least he could win arguments with her, which he can't do with me!

I don't know if I told you the Colonel and I had a mascot. We caught a French field rat, that is at least what we can make out it is from the old pig at the house. It is a pretty little thing about half as big as a grey rat, with a pretty little white face and bushy white tail somewhat like our flying squirrels in Australia. These little beggars do no end of damage to houses and gardens and our old host nearly died when he saw it in the cage we made for it in the dining room. He exploded, threatened, wept and carried on in a most unusual way. The Colonel thought to shoot him to put him out of his misery, but we decided to give him a bottle of Champagne instead, he being an ally! He really is an extraordinary old pig.

I got some new riding breeches yesterday from a store in — for 26 francs. You would be so proud of your old Queensland sugar farmer, if you could hear my French. I can change a 20 franc note, buy a bottle of *vin ordinaire* and get the right change. The drinking water is no good here, so we live on *vin ordinaire*, it costs *1.25 pour la bouteille et il est assez pour les soldats, comme ca madame ma cherie, Puisque on dois soujourner quelquetemps dans cette ville, j'ai resolu de me perfectionner dans la langue du pays!!!*[27]

Well dear sweetheart, give all my love to that dear product of our great love and as much to you . . .

JANUARY 24TH

My dear wee woman,
This will tell you of our last move. We got orders at midnight on Saturday [28] to move at 7.40 am. What a bustle, what excitement, anyway I had, as usual, the whole duty of moving the battalion and was up all night. In fact I was in bed when the order came so that I had to get up. We got away to time but Russel's[29] Coy was late and got mixed. However we marched all day, and arrived at last in our present position.[30] I had to go back and look for our transport, which had been cut off by the divisional train. Anderson was called away on brigade duties, and only his sergeant was in charge and of course some officer in the ASC[31] bounced the sergeant and passed through the column cutting the transport off. However the CO and I overtook the ASC and then we did some of the bouncing. I had a great ride galloping about looking for the transport and then after rounding it up I had to go out again and whip up stragglers. We arrived here in tears almost, hearing the guns roaring.

It was a beautiful day, calm, sunny France at her very best. The country is better here, more productive and more hospitable looking, the people more progressive, more kindly tolerant to the soldier, everyone trying to help one and most of the people speak English more or less, but the French hereabouts is really hard to follow. The people are a mixed Flemish and French breed and talk what to me seems a *patois* of some kind. The weather has been extraordinarily kind to us so far.

I expect some of your dear letters today; eighteen bags of mail came in but are not sorted, surely in eighteen bags my little wife will have at least one for her lonely old sweetheart.

I did not have to do the billeting this time, the regular billeting crowd were sent in advance and made arrangements. We soon settled headquarters at a big farmhouse. Anderson and I are in the house billeted with most kindly people, and wonderful to relate I had the luxury of sleeping between sheets, nice clean ones and I was so comfortable I could not sleep at all. We each have a room and are extremely satisfied, the only fly in the ointment is we leave the billets tomorrow to go to the trenches. The Colonel is living at a big farmhouse just down the road from me and is in fine fettle.

We brought our wee mascot away with us, and he is so perky, a rare game little beast. I was hoping we would stay here for about ten days, to let things settle down a bit, and give the men a few days' routine work, but no, it's on the move again, but this time only about three miles to go. Today the Army Corps General[32] inspected us and afterwards expressed great admiration of our physique and soldierly bearing. If you watch the casualty lists you will see where we get our first big move on.

Aeroplanes here like crows all over the place, they look so fine and thrilling. The papers seem to be making a great fuss about a new German type of machine, the Fokker.[33]

We are all wondering how the daily call ups are getting on and who will win the Slingsby case.[34]

Here we are right handy to the fine town of —,[35] formerly in the hands of Monsieur le Boche and we are hoping to get some rare old hot bathes and a clean up. My feet are pretty sore. I had a thick pair of socks on and doing so much rushing about seeing men fixed in billets etc., I raised some blisters but in a day or so they will be alright and where we are going to now one can't rush about.

I am fortunately getting a great hang of the adjutant's job on active service, and things come a great deal easier although I am expected to be here, there and everywhere and to know this and that and every other thing. I am just hoping there may be some Australian mail in the bags as well as your dear letters. A big bunch of mail would buck me tremendously. We get the daily papers only a day old but they cost 25 centimes or twopence halfpenny each. However, there is not a deal to spend money on here. It only cost me 26.25 francs, just a pound for ten days' living expenses, including all wines.

I was awfully pleased to see Sir Geo. Reid[36] had entered the English Parliament. I read his first speech and thought it about one of the best I've read.

Well dearest wife and sweetheart of mine I hope you are not forgetting your old man doing his bit. Give dear little Deckie a big long love and squeeze from daddy. Tell me how you are getting on, you clever little woman. We are all finding it less tiresome than the training and already trying to pass as old soldiers . . .

January 27th

(The Kaiser's birthday!)[37]

I don't know when you will get this or when I'll post it, but here we are at last in the trenches,[38] so after all, at last we are real live soldiers. We marched up from our last place, a matter of twelve miles, through country like Lincolnshire, flat, swampy and very boggy. The roads are only metalled on the top and the mud at the sides is appalling. Any amount of troops about, motor convoys and many aeroplanes. We saw some shrapnelling bouts against Taubes some of which flew over us like lost seagulls. One sees any amount of shelling, and all that sort of thing, but the aerial bouts are the most thrilling. Our part of the line is considered to be relatively quiet and respectable; the fact is due to our great preponderance and superiority of big guns hereabouts. The Hun is very loath to start shelling here for we take it up and return it with compound interest.

We arrived here and were split up, companies being distributed and billeted in and with other units. The General called on the CO at 4 pm but the CO was out so I did the entertaining. Tonight the CO and I are going to dine with the General.

Our battalion HQ is situated about 3000 yards behind the firing line and in a building still occupied by civilians. Three doors from us a large shell landed and blew the side out of a large house. The German trenches are 400 yards away from our line but at one place there is a salient or spur running out towards us and it is only 70 yards away. Everyone here says the Germans are beaten stiff and judging from the way civilians go about their occupation it certainly looks like it. Of course that does not mean that the war is over. Our trench mortar batteries are splendid and Mr Hun has great respect for them.

In our last billet I met a great crowd of Australians. It was also the HQ of an Australian convoy commanded by Captain Jones of Brisbane, a man I knew very well, we were overjoyed to find one another. There were also four Bundaberg men, who I knew well, used to play football in a team I was captain of. Pvt Wicks, one of the men, sent me up a bundle of papers, Brisbane and Bundaberg. One had a social column and I saw that Mother was in Brisbane. Also met Bill Aye, who has just returned to his unit after being wounded. We are now no longer in the 3rd Army, we are in the 1st Army, no less. If you are asked what Army I am in, it is the 34th Division, 3rd Army Corps, 1st Army.

The men have done wonderfully well, so far only three have fallen out, with bad blisters, and everyone is tremendously impressed with our bearing and generally fit look, so that is some consolation to my soul so sadly overloaded trying to keep things efficient, by dint of much worry and hard language. These have been strenuous days, sweetheart, but never once have I forgotten either of you.

We expect to go back to rest billets on February 1st, and will move back about six miles and then I will be able to write you nice long letters and tell you all about where I've been and what I've seen, of course not actual names, but just all about everything.

I saw Captain Greig for a moment and he tells me that Mrs Greig has been to see you. Twenty-six bags of mail in today, I'm hoping. So far I've not seen any exhibition of the Hun's horribleness. Certainly churches are all burned and the villages and towns bear sad evidence of heavy shelling in places and a road 800 yards from the village our HQ is in is unhealthy as it is covered with snipers.

Most of the civilians hereabouts talk a good deal of English, better than our French. The Tommies take everything very complacently and one sees Tommy arm in arm with a French domestique just like peace time.

The steel helmets that our men wear are the queerest looking contraptions imaginable, but I imagine efficient. Not as good as the French one which has some shape to it, ours look like jelly moulds and shake about.

Today is the Kaiser's birthday, we are expecting some exhibition of frightfulness. There was a big machine gun duel at 4 am, 5 am, and 6 am today, but no great heavy or violent strafing as yet but the day is still young. I don't know what kind of excitement is in store for the inhabitants when they try to till the ground, whenever that may be. A transport officer was riding along the canal and his horse trod on a rifle grenade, and was killed straight away, a fine big bay. The officer was not injured, but imagine trying to plough!

All my love . . .

JANUARY 30TH

My dearest wee sweetheart,

By the time this reaches you, you will be in Troon. Well we have been through the mill and came out with flying colours. If you watch the Edinburgh papers you will see all about us, in a word the men were magnificent, not a flinch and there is no doubt the officers did well too.

What a time we had following the day of the Kaiser's birthday — things were quiet enough during the day, just an occasional burst of machine gun and rifle fire. Towards evening things woke up and the rifle and machine gun just spluttered and rattled away with an occasional big gun and shrapnel pumping in at us. The flare shells were always the signal for most violent outbursts on either side. Things progressed until 11 pm when the Hun woke up and gave us a most extraordinary shelling which was at once terrifying and magnificent, the shells just scream like some mad fury overhead. It's an awful screech when they come so low and then a terrific roar and mountains of mud and wood go up a mile high. They pumped over 800 shells into our sector of the trenches, quite the heaviest shelling in months.

Our own guns soon woke up and pounded the gentle Hun to pieces and soon he quietened down. It is the grandest sound in all the world to hear your own big shells screaming over, of course they are much higher and the difference in tone is very noticeable. The Hun sends them low over our heads, howling like a weird animal; ours fly over, chuckling and purring. The shooting on either side was awfully good, sitting against the parapet with an eye on the periscope we used to watch the result on the Hun lines. Things quietened about midnight but woke up again at 3 am, hard as ever, and then died away at daylight but at ten it was just the same all over again.

Our dugout took lots of the great big brutes, some only fifteen yards away; the most appalling sounds and sights, but the men turned not a hair, superb to a degree. The Colonel and I went along the trenches, like snakes, and to every inquiry we got the same answer, 'Everything alright, Sir'. The worst things are what are called 'sausages'. These are hurled from a big sort of trench-mortar and come at us bouncing over and over like a big German sausage. They are easily seen and can be easily dodged if their flight is correctly judged. They go off with a terrific roar and do no end of damage and harm if anyone is about. The 'whizz-bangs' fly over with an eerie scream and then a thunderous burst. It is altogether a very nervy business. One tries to stop ducking every time but it's not easy. You may be walking along a communication trench, suddenly a wild screaming is heard, half like steam escaping and half like wind whistling and sobbing, then you duck, probably it has gone wide away on either side. Shrapnel is very pretty as it bursts into its fleecy clouds with a bright flash but it is very nasty stuff. It was all around us; the escapes were marvellous.

Eckford, the cook of A Coy was at the back of the camp kitchen, cooking and was carrying a dixie of water when the whole thing was blown clean out of his hand. I really don't think I can tell you what he called the Hun. Lt Shields[39] went into his dugout, put his valise and equipment down and had just come up when a shell came clean in through the roof and he lost everything and was hurtled along the trench, but was not injured. Matthews, a man who got six months for desertion and for striking an NCO did a marvellous job, was applauded and I will write him up for a mention.

Sgt Barnes had a dust-up with a 'sausage' and the whole pack was blown off his back. His rifle was twisted up like wire but he was not touched. Of course we too had our casualties, poor chaps, just as game as the best, not a murmur, not a complaint, usually an apology for getting it and then a cigarette. What I like the best is that there is no swank, the men just recognised the seriousness of things and did just what was expected of them.

We move to rest billets[40] on Thursday, I will write then.

All my love to the two of you, and love to Mrs Wallace, Nancy and Bobby . . .

January 31st

My most dearest wee wife and son,

This letter will I hope arrive just about your birthdays[41] and so I want to send my very dearest love to the two dearest little souls in all this muddled world. Just fancy, dearest it is two years since the fateful night when my dear little wife paid the price of love and gave her poor old man such a dear wee little baby son. I'm afraid it has been a pretty irksome two years, but the worst is over. Thank you so much for the fountain pen, it will be so handy, but one has real trouble getting ink. All official documents are allowed to be in indelible ink . . .

The battalion is now on a brief relief, and LWN repeats most of his previous letter as he doubted it had arrived. We know that it did, so I have not repeated the text.

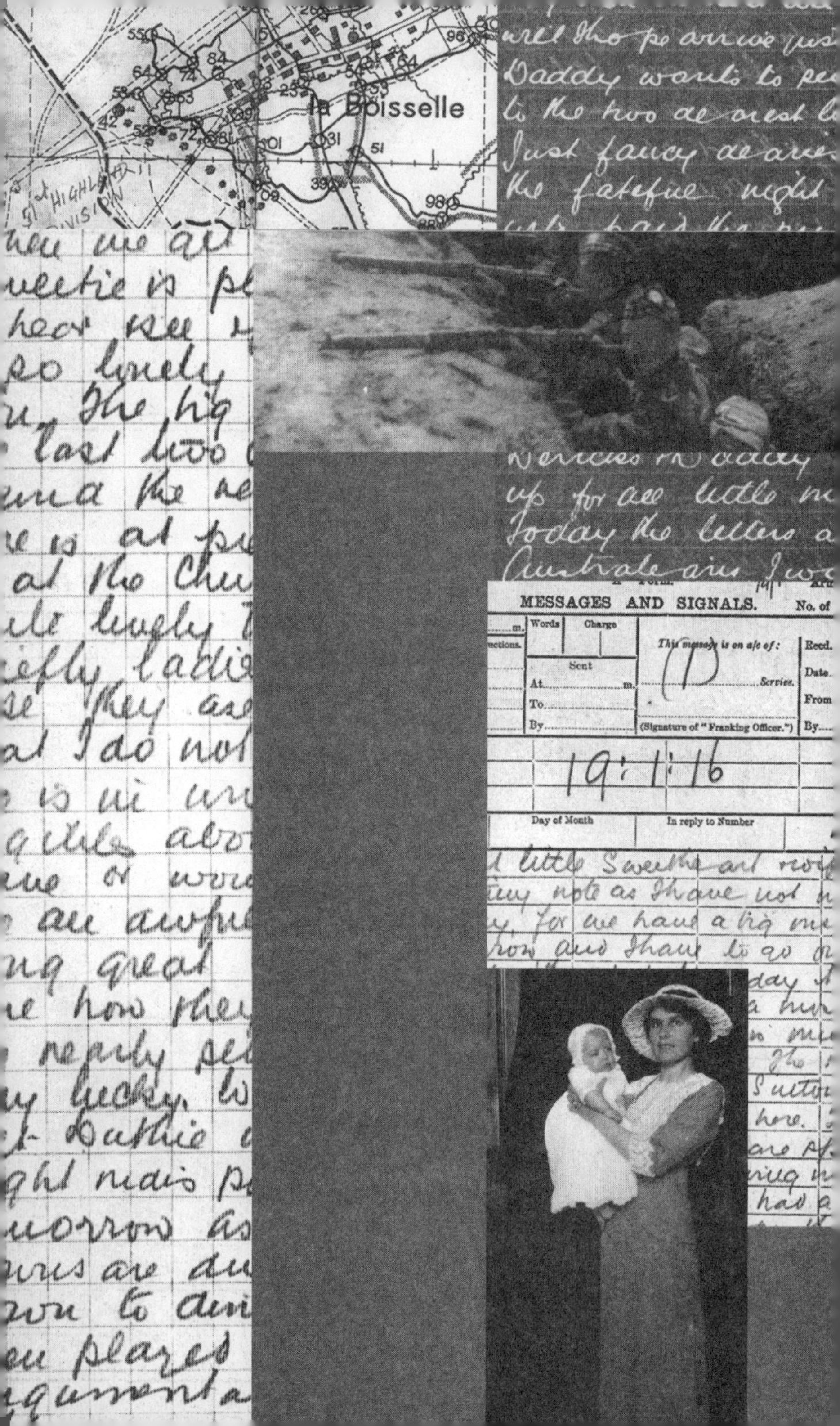
la Boisselle
MESSAGES AND SIGNALS.
No. of
Words
Charge
This message is on a/c of:
Service.
Sent
At
To
By
(Signature of "Franking Officer.")
Recd.
Date.
From
By
19:1:16
Day of Month
In reply to Number

February

February 1st

My dearest wife,

Here we are up to our necks in mud and slaughter. Last night the Hun woke up at ten and by eleven we were under the most intense bombardment. The shells just screamed and whistled overhead with an awful bang, bang crash blowing in the side of trenches. Machine guns and rifles just rattled out, it is most intense and awesome but the men were superb, just like veterans, not one inch did they flinch. They jeered when the Hun shells fell short and they cheered like fury when one of our big fat shells landed in amongst the Hun; they are truly magnificent. Of course we had our casualties but none killed and the wounded were so cheerful and made light of things.

The CO and I were in a dugout together and the big shells screamed overhead and plinked in all around us and by 11.30 pm it was just one inferno. Every time a shell screams overhead, low and threatening, one just crouches and hopes for the best. The nearest shell was only fifty feet away and it blew up a tree, making a tremendous hole. Soon after our own artillery commenced, they give one such an indescribable feeling of thanksgiving and security.

It is dinner time now and the firing is easing off, the Hun is hungry as we are, and we get a few moments of peace. I cannot describe the effect when one hears away in the distance the gun go and then the shell can be heard coming over, high pitched and sighing with a most ominous note. One gets goose pimples and the hair on the back of the neck stands up as we all wait, then a terrific bang. One can't tell whether it is high or low, right or left, and of course ours are all high and the note is different and so welcome. The thing that pleases us the most is the spirit and eagerness of the men Today whilst things were at their worst, the CO and I went along a front fire trench and every man was as keen as mustard — 'everything fine here, Sir', 'No complaints, Sir', 'This is the life, Sir', and comments like that. Dear old things they are, one gets to love their old faces and forget the bad things about them. They have all grown up in the last few days; haven't we all. We get back to our billets today or tomorrow and come back up on the 20th.

The whizz-bang is a funny shell. He comes across with a great fuss and goes off with a tremendous BANG and everyone ducks, but he has long since passed. The big chaps come over with a wizz-er-er, or wobble wobble-bang and then a shower of mud, wood and sandbags and a big sigh of relief — until the next one. Our trenches are heavily sandbagged and between 300 to 70 yards away from the Boche line. I got out of the trenches for a while today and went with the Colonel to ——.[1] I got a shave and a shampoo and felt all the better for it. Several shells landed in the next street with a horse blown to bits but it is really remarkable to see how the people carry on their business here in spite of everything and are living in the same way as they always have.

I don't seem to be afraid, just tense and overstrung, and the biggest emotion is relief when it is clear that that one missed you. We are looking forward to getting back to the rest camp, what experiences we will have to relate. I am so sorry, my dearest, to hear that you are not so well, please see a Dr. I got Deckie's lock, the dear wee son; it is pretty hard to have a wife and son, Pettie and be at this game. It is tough turkey but has to be digested.

Goodnight sweet love.

FEBRUARY 3RD
Somewhere in France

My own dearie,

You will see that this is written with the bonnie pen you sent me, it is such a lovely one and I must take very good care of it. I am afraid my letters will not just now be reaching you with any sort of regularity as we have been having such stirring times and our postal arrangements became more or less dislocated. I've written as often as I could but they were posted under all sorts of conditions, so no doubt they will arrive at all times and dates. I wrote one specially to catch you on your birthday, I imagined you reading it to Deckie.

We are out of the firing line now in rest billets,[2] canvas tents, and oh heavens it's cold. I was never in all my life so cold as I was last night. A terrific wind was blowing, raining too at the time and one could not get warm. We are still within the sounds of the guns and yesterday as we marched away from the firing line there was a most intense bombardment. It's nice to come back for a rest and we will be here some days to refit, reboot and replenish stores.

And so Pettie, after so long a wait, we are at last real soldiers. We've been through the mill, and it was a severe enough test, but we romped home winners. The men were just magnificent. At the very hottest time, and it was hot, they never wavered; never turned a hair. The shelling we had on the 27th and 28th was the hottest ever experienced on the part of the line we are on.[3] Now there's a hint, dearie, to tell where we are, I saw the reference to it in the English papers.

I expect you are wondering if I killed any Germans or how many I saw. Well, I saw some German soldiers, but

I never fired a shot all the time I was in the lines. Of course my work is just to ferret around and see that everyone else is doing his own particular job, the rest of the time I put in dodging and ducking about to try and miss trouble. It was an experience I will never forget. Those big shells are absolutely paralysing when they come close. Of course one ducks or goes flat but by that time it is usually well past. Still one imagines one is doing something in the way of protecting oneself and no doubt it is protecting against 'back blasts' and shrapnel splinters.

The best dugout in the world won't stand up to the high explosive shells. The trenches or rather the parapets themselves are protection enough against the sniper from the front; the worst of it is they get sometimes inside our own lines and on the flanks and then of course one gets it unawares. Now and then one sees a German head bob up over the parapet for about three seconds, and at the same instant about ten of our snipers' rifles ring out.

At night, the men from either side, patrols they are called, go out into No Man's Land and patch up the wire damaged by shrapnel, dig listening posts and generally reconnoitre. The Germans do the same, suddenly up go the star shells and then the machine guns fairly splutter away. The same thing happens in the fog and that is when I saw some Boche at work. Suddenly the mist cleared for an instant, we got one short fleeting view just time enough to swing the machine guns on to them, then all quiet. I think we must have bagged some of them.

It's nice to be out of it for some time. Living like a mole and always waiting and watching, dodging and scheming is very wearying work, one gets at times too excited to sleep and then next day one's life is a burden, but on the whole I must say things are bright and cheery and companionship is close and very friendly and hospitable and the general conduct of the men is exemplary.

I see that the French have had their beloved Paris bombarded again by Zeppelins, the London season will surely soon commence.[4] I am so glad that you and Deckie are not in London. These Zepps carry such huge stuff, it is not so much the actual bomb, it is the resultant fires that do the damage. I am so glad to hear that you are feeling better — makes the whole mess fade into insignificance. Fancy, a month has gone since we landed, a month crowded with incident indeed.

In our new billets we are lying just off the main road leading to —,[5] ¾ mile from —[6] on one side and ½ mile from — on the other so we are in the centre of civilisation, but the military authorities run everything so things are fairly quiet. In the big forests, and there are some fine ones here, one sees where all the best trees have been cut by the Germans who did not have time enough to use them. Of course in the city of —[7] just behind our firing line there was every evidence of the Hun, not a single window intact, not an intact roof, streets torn up with huge shells, and shells falling each day in the streets. Still there is a considerable business done and the civil population is more or less still hanging on.

Well my dear one, I must finish now as I want to go into —[8] to buy some blankets. I am not very much taken with the French women, and except in Havre we have only been in the war area, and I suppose all the better class of people have gone away, leaving the old women to plough the fields. They can be seen 2 or 300 yards from the exploding shells, grim and gloomy and no great temptation for the men. My French is now good, I converse well and nearly always get not only what I want but get the correct change. There are some shops here that are the limit for pictures, everything in the nude! I'm afraid there is some competition amongst us to decorate the walls. Every dugout along the line is filled with these pictures, some are exquisitely coloured but all are very warm indeed. The CO sent a bundle to Mrs W. I'm sure you are too young to have any, but then why, my God you are a divine wee wife.

Goodnight to you both, give my love to all at No. 3 . . .

FEBRUARY 5TH
Somewhere in France

Just a wee note as I am very short-handed in the orderly room. My clerk is away at a course in Rouen, the result is that I am up to my eyes in work, however I got through somehow. I had three clerks sent from the companies, but I had to kick them out as they were useless. At last the rain has stopped. It has been awful, the mud just seething everywhere. We are under canvas. The camp has been here for a long time. The Engineers[9] have done a great job, but it still leaves a lot to be desired. You would be surprised to see what good footpaths inverted Bully tins make. Everything is normal again. We have got over the initial experience of trench life, of death, of noise and fear, and I really believe that the men would jump at the chance to get back to the trenches if they had the chance. It's quickly forgotten, it's like having babies, isn't it, dearie, only the best of it remains. Only a note as the mail call is up.

Best love to you both . . .

FEBRUARY 6TH
Somewhere in France

My own little sweetheart and wife,
I got your letter today telling me that you were not too well. I do so hope dearest heart of mine that today your own and our dear son's birthday that you are feeling a great deal better. Yes, I think you will appreciate Troon after a round of Glasgow gaiety. Troon is an awfully nice place and it ought to suit you and Deckie admirably. I hope so anyway. Deckie ought to revel in the sand; when it gets warmer you must give him some little swims, but be careful, dearie, not to terrify him. One terrified Nott is more than enough just now.

It is still very cold here and the wind just whistles round and through the canvas. Yesterday the afternoon was beautifully fine but icy cold. We saw a wonderfully fine scrap in the air. A beautiful white Taube sailed over us, had a good look then turned north. Immediately the guns started to play on her, the shrapnel bursting all around her in delicate white fleecy clouds. She never shifted or bustled one iota, just ignored it all. One expected every moment to see her come down, but still she sailed on. Then up rose five of ours, three going off towards the German lines to wait for her return, and two going to look for some trouble. There was only one big cloud and into it she sailed. Every now and again, she would edge out one side or the other. The guns would rattle away, and into the cloud again she would hop. Our two planes chased into the cloud, and out would hop the Taube and make for home, with one of our machines above and one below, and rapidly overhauling her.

The artillery opened up again, the shots were wide; the machine guns rattled on, when suddenly one of our chaps stopped, some of our shrapnel bursting right under him. He rocked violently and then commenced to plane down with a big list, landing alright, just 100 yards away. The gallant airman was not injured. What a pity, as we had all hoped for something so sensational, all so close and clear. The Taube continued towards her own lines, when out hopped our other two planes and took up the scrap, but they soon were too far away to see. The planes do look so fine, I think it is a very safe branch of the Service.

We have not been doing much in the way of work here in camp; bombing classes, machine gun classes are the chief things keeping us busy. The rest of the time we put in cleaning and draining the camp. Wherever we go we seem to do an enormous amount of cleaning.

Organisation here is very good. There is no trouble to obtain stores of any kind. One just indents and the next day or so it comes up. The men's clothing is lifted each morning and goes away and an equivalent of clean clothing issued. When the dirty stuff is cleaned someone else gets it. Hot baths capable of dealing with 100 men a day are at —— only three miles away. ——, the big city just near us has been placed out of bounds as it is only half to one mile away and was so handy for little things.

Lodge has been mess president. Our mess consists of the CO, 2nd, Lodge, Anderson, MO and self; but he was such a rotten caterer that we had to get Major Rose to take over; the result is that we are feeding a great deal better. Rose's sister is sending over twice a week a bundle of kippers and they are so fine for breakfast. Can the Hun compete against such spirit? Well, dearest love, my love to both of you. Tell wee D that daddy will soon be rattling down to old Boulogne, across the Channel and home. *I love you all so much, want you badly . . .*

TUESDAY, FEBRUARY 8TH

My dear wee wife,

Nothing of great interest to relate today. The weather has been most atrociously capricious, beautiful fine, cold for a time then torrents of rain, real April weather. The mud is terrific, knee deep in places.

Today we were all gassed. A big shed was erected and two cylinders of chlorine gas were introduced and hissed away most venomously as we walked in. It is surprising how effective the gas helmets are, only one or two men were at all affected and it was in both cases the way the men adjusted the helmets.

The gas in the huts was tremendously strong, far greater than it ever be in a gas attack. Rats that were thrown into the middle of the shelter died almost immediately, so provided the helmets are intact there is, beyond the uncomfortable nature of things, not much in it. We all use two helmets now and the machine gunners, who are not allowed to leave the trenches at all during an attack, have three, the third one being a most complicated one called the Salvies set, provided with oxygen cylinders.

We leave here and go up to the trenches again on the 18th, remaining there till March 6th, so it will be a long spell of hard work the next time, and I hope that things are no warmer than they were last time. Everything, at least all the papers, are pointing towards a final German thrust on our front in about three weeks' time, if not sooner. Well the sooner the better, and I know that there will be many a Hun who won't get back to the Fatherland. I do not think we have a great deal to be afraid of, our people over here are not asleep, let's hope the big brass in London are awake. In fact, I think the Hun is held here, as stiff as can be. He may make a big splash along some portion of the line and capture a few yards of trench but he never holds it and his casualties are always heavy.

Well dearest wee little wife, goodbye for the present, love to you both . . .

FEBRUARY 9TH
Somewhere in France

My dearest little woman,
Today I received the two dear pictures of the two sweet little faces I know so well. Oh Pettie they are so nice, did you take them yourself and you never told me that they were coming. When the box came to me today, I thought at first it was one of those muslin undervests, so, sweetheart, you can just imagine how pleased I was and how surprised. I love the one of dear Deckie lying down or reclining with his old woolly dog. The other one is unfortunately not so good of Derick or yourself, but I cannot tell you how good they are to have. I am the envy of the mess. So many thanks for the birthday wishes,[10] I wonder if you got mine for yours and Derick's. The mails here are really more irregular than was the case in the firing line. There is not much regular routine here — one more or less scrapes along in the rest camps. The weather has been terribly cold here, but today was gloriously fine although icy.

We have been having an extraordinary number of air raids the last few days. Today just after breakfast a beautiful Taube, snowy white, sailed away on our right. It evidently suddenly spotted us for it turned sharply to the left, passed over us, whilst we waited to hear the bomb burst. However it was fired on just over us and it crossed us to the 16th Royal Scots and bombed them but with no result. In a few moments our buzz flies were out and set sail after it and brought it down at — a few miles from here. That is the fifth they have got in the last three days, including two of the celebrated Fokkers, at least that's what the Sgt Major of the Air Squad told us. I know that they got this one today, but I don't really know about the Fokkers.

Today we were visited by our new Brigadier. General Gore by name, rather appropriate, isn't it. He seems very nice, a fine man and by appearances should do very well. He was most impressed by the men. Col. Rose got General Fitton's big old horse and gave Whitesox to the General. We were all sorry to see her go. She was a nice old thing. My mare is dead lame at present. She badly strained her shoulder and I have grave doubts that she will be better for some time in which case she will be returned to the mobile vet. hospital and I will be issued with another one. She is a perfect little devil at times but all the same she is a bonnie wee mare and I am not keen at the prospect of a change.

I forgot to say I got the *Bulletin*[11] and am expecting the Australian mail any day. I noticed in *The Times* today, which is of course two days old, that the Australians are in action again but I could not make out from the paper where they are. In Mesopotamia fighting is very severe and our casualties are very heavy, but there is not going to be any doubt about the result. The papers are making a great fuss about the coming push of the Germans in the west. From all indications we will be there when it comes, and I don't think many of us are worried. I notice that Andy Fisher is over in old General Reid's billet, he ought to do pretty well as he has got more sense now than he had when he went into Parliament.

Well dearie, everyone has just come in, very cold and crying out for hot food. Major Rose has just come back from —— in the mess cart, and has brought something special for dinner. It is a surprise and everyone is trying to guess what it is but I know it's lobster, he promised to bring one home alive.

Dearest wee wife and sweetheart, all my love and thanks for everything, fond love . . .

February 12th

Today I've missed the mail again, the mail motor lorry calls at uncertain hours just now, and of course it does not wait. Sometimes it comes at 8 am, others at 10 am; today it came just as I was getting my returns in, and so I had to miss it Today is my birthday, dearest sweet wee woman, and I only wish I could have spent it with you and dear little Derick. He must be a dear wee son, the nice little son of a dear little wife and mother who is loved so hard by her old soldier man.

Yesterday was a most wretched day, one of the coldest and rottenest days I've spent. At midnight I got an urgent scream from the brigade to say that Kitchener[12] was to inspect the division, and to be ready at 8.45, out at ——,[13] four miles from here. That of course meant my getting dressed and getting out special orders, reveille at 6 am, and it was an awful rush, and to make matters worse we woke to a great rain and snow storm. The sky was as black and evil looking as Satan, and the wind just howled. At 8 am we got another wire to say that Kitchener would see us at 10 am. We got into position at 9.40, with the rain pouring down in buckets, of course we felt anything but smart soldiers. My feet and hands were almost frozen hard, the men were marching and so had at least warm feet. I was on my mare and the cold made her just play up fiendishly, so that I got pretty well drenched. I find that my big leather gauntlet gloves are not of much use in the rain. The water collects on the sleeves and runs down into them so I had to take them off. That Burberry kind of a coat, with the lining which I got at Warminster is perfectly waterproof under normal conditions but the mare bucketing about tore two buttons off, so that I got pretty well drenched.

We waited and waited for K until 1.30 pm and at last he arrived with a big staff. Our whole brigade was drawn up in one field in a hollow square, and the other brigades and artillery of the division were in the neighbouring field, a perfect Godsend for a Zepp. Kitchener passed down the ranks, and was greatly pleased, he said that the 101st and the Tyneside Scottish were the two best physiqued brigades he had seen. He said to General Pulteney, who commands the 3rd Corps, 'Use them with ease, don't rush them, they can do anything and are the men for Germany'. Of course we were very bucked up. I really think that after all the inspections and the reports we must be a crack-looking battalion, brigade and division.[14]

Now I expect you are wondering what Kitchener is like. Well, he has changed a great deal since I saw him in Australia. Of course he is over 66 and one forgets about that so used is one to the photos one sees of him. He is not the clean-cut military type one sees in the pictures. He stoops badly, leaning heavily on a stick and rather drags one leg a bit. I don't mean that he has a limp, he just walks along like a big old man of his age. His face is very red and bloated looking, no doubt much of the redness was due to the cold; but his eyes are bloodshot and puffed out. This, no doubt, is hardly the picture of the man that we all think so much of, who holds the grip of the situation. The voice alone is what one expects, deep, loud and resonant. Of course 66 is a fair age and what work he has put into his 66 years. We got back to camp about 2.30 pm and of course had nothing to eat and then I had to set my office in order and get things straightened out a bit, so that altogether we had a rotten day.

Our camp is just now floating on a sea of mud. Things have been quiet here for a day or two, the wind being in the wrong direction, we could only just hear the big guns booming. The wind and the wet are too much for the aeroplanes. I told you about some Fokkers being brought down just near us, and at the time I did not think it was true but I have since learned that it is quite correct, they did get them. The sky will soon clear and then there will be a great deal of aerial activity, for neither side has had much opportunity of seeing what is going on behind the lines.

The trenches will I am afraid be in a very rotten condition. The German trenches are situated higher than ours, and they drain into our lines, a canal running right down through No Man's Land. That is how their snipers are at an advantage here, they rather overlook us, not to any great extent, but enough to cause trouble.

Spring is getting ready to smile on us and soon the grass seeds etc planted on the sand bags and dugouts will commence to grow and offer us some better natural cover. You were wondering whereabouts in the line we were, dearie. Well sweetheart, it is not a very nice place, it is not noted for its beauty, nor for the spans of life that the inhabitants are blessed with. There is any amount of activity and business is brisk, but I cannot say where it is.

I think I told you in a letter, sweetheart, that when the shelling first commenced in earnest we found Armand in tears[15] — with excitement! This letter will no doubt find that you have gone to Troon. You have not yet told me whether you are going to the Bungalow or to some other house, so I will address this to Glasgow. Fancy half of February already gone, in another seven or eight weeks we will be due our first instalment of leave — seven whole days. That means from the time we leave Boulogne till the time we arrive back in Boulogne. I pray that they give those officers going all the way to Scotland a couple of days extra as it takes so much longer; the people in England get the pull on us. If I go by way of Boulogne, I will call on Sister Murray. And then home like an arrow to the dearest wee loving woman and baby in all the world. Just right home to love and be loved, just as two old sweethearts can love, and help me forget this Hell. I hope and know that you and Derick will be fine in Troon, eat plenty and fatten those dear little thin legs a bit.

All my love and thoughts . . .

(Good night dearest, my own little one, your old man wants you so much, LWN.)

February 13th
Somewhere in France

My dearest wee wife

I'm not feeling over fit today, been getting a bit too much work I think, and not enough sleep. It is so cold here at nights under canvas that one never gets warm. Anderson and I went for a ride this afternoon, right through a big wood and along the bank of a canal. It was very nice and the sun actually managed to be out for a while. It has been dreadfully cold at nights and everything is so wet and muddy. The mud begins to get on one's nerves.

We had a very sensational visit from a Taube yesterday. Just after lunch we spotted him going along very high, the anti-aircraft guns made play at him and he turned up north-east and we lost him. Evidently he came back for suddenly there was a most awful crash, quickly followed by another, and we spotted the Taube again going east for all he was worth with one of our monoplanes[16] following him. They soon were lost to sight, so we don't know how the beggar fared. The bombs did no harm, only blowing large holes in the earth, and one did not go off at all; it buried itself in the mud, and there it can remain. They are much too dangerous to try and dig up, one only has to touch them with an implement, and up they go.

We are really having too many visits from the Taubes — we are in the direct path to ——[17] and that's where the aerial HQ is and these beggars are trying to bomb it and when they are observed they hurl one at us just for luck, as they pass.

We are doing very little work just now other than specialist course and all the men are trying to clear up and drain the camp which is really a swamp of mud. All day yesterday and up till midnight last night the big guns fairly hammered away, someone must have been getting it hard. We sat up and listened to it and I personally thanked my stars that I was not in it. One gets any amount of this sort of thing without wishing or asking for it. We go up into the line for a month in a few days and no doubt we will be in the thick of it.

Comic Cuts, the official French record, will be out tonight and from it we will see who got it. *Comic Cuts* is the name applied to these official war diaries that come out every day. They contain every scrap of information about the enemy and what has been going on in each particular area. They come to each unit, each night. We won't be sorry, in many ways, to get out of this quagmire and we'll go out knowing that we have improved the camp.

My mare has gone so lame and I am going to lose her. She goes to the mobile vet. hospital. I hope that I don't get a crock in her place. She was a bit nervous and flighty and sometimes caused me to badly perjure my soul with bad language, but she was a dandy mare.

I hope that dear wee woman is well and getting fine and plump. I'm so longing for you both, dearest, I know that you would not let me be so cold, would you. I love the pictures of Deckie you sent out, and will return them soon. Haven't Pat and Bill[18] grown? Pat has changed a good deal, it may only be my fancy, I hope so. The cigarettes you sent have not arrived, dearie, I expect they are delayed. The letters sometimes come in a day or so, and sometimes they take weeks.

Well dearest, all my love to you both, from . . .

FEBRUARY 15TH

My own little love,

Here it is still raining away and blowing a hurricane, ever since we came here. We, with the assistance of the Engineers, have been cleaning up, and generally trying to make life more comfortable. We erected a big bath shed, canvas most of it. The Engineers supplied the pump and heating apparatus and we had 12 shower baths fixed up. The bathing was to commence today and we hoped that every man would at least have one bath before going up to the front line again, but last night the wind was too much for the structure and blew it all down. Platts had all his transport animals in an old disused house and it was blown down on the top of all the horses. The men were foolishly at their meals at the time, despite the fact that the house was rocking. No horses were killed, some were injured and two men very badly injured. The weather here was so fine when we first came out but now it is abominable, rain, sleet and snow, with such awful winds. One cannot walk against it.

I had a lovely dream last night, dearie. I was reading some magazines before going to bed and was looking at some pictures in the *Sketch* and I'm afraid I was thinking of you at the time too for I dreamed later that I met you here walking on the road in pink pyjamas and you just did look so pretty. Your hair was hanging down and you said, 'Here I am, Pettie' and I was with you for such a long time and then I awoke. Someone was tapping on my door, it was a messenger to say that some horses had arrived for us. I was so mad, and had to get up and go out and wake Anderson. I'm afraid that I was very angry. It is not very nice to have to get up, and go out in the rain and wind in British Army underpants.

Well, dearie, you just looked so beautiful in pink pyjamas, I think we must get you some. There is just nothing pink or soft here. I have so much to tell you, so much time to make up. Could you come to Edinburgh to meet me, we could have a night at the theatre, there or in Glasgow. I was so thrilled to hear how well Deckie is doing, he will surely be chattering away like a maggie. He will so love playing in the sand. I think, dearest, that most of the trouble is over, as his teeth will soon all be through, certainly by winter's end, then he will have all the summer to build up.

We are getting ready again and will be on the road and up into the line[19] again, very soon. We won't go into the fray such novices this time, for we now look upon ourselves as real soldiers. We have just had an issue of a big cape, khaki waterproof, a splendid thing and we also have had steel helmets handed out, so that we really look more formidable. The helmets are like jelly moulds and are not a bit comfortable, but I expect are very useful, especially against shrapnel and stray bullets. I would not mind coming to this camp in the summer as the canvas would be very comfortable and the situation too is nice or would be in the summer time.

The cigarettes arrived, my dear, and most welcome, all shared out. No papers here yesterday, so we felt a bit lost, it is nice to know each day, all the news and rumours from England and also how things are going at the other fronts. The Balkans are causing a good many casualties I notice, but there is no word of what nature the operations are there or against whom they are being worked. Mesopotamia seems hung up with bad weather, there ought to be any number of troops there for a big push. I do hope the Australians are there and have the opportunity of wiping something off the slate with respect to the odious Abdul.[20]

Yes, I wrote to Mrs Done to thank her for all she had done for my dear little sweetheart and for a big boy. I really think, my dear, we must soon think of a dear little girl, don't you?

We have just got a great rumour here about a huge naval victory, thought to be twelve German and five of our vessels sunk! It is apparently a wild rumour.

Goodnight, my love . . .

FEBRUARY 17TH

My dearest wee one,
Just a few lines today as I am very busy indeed getting ready for a move up, and there is a lot to do, casualties making a great deal of alterations and correspondence. The wind has died down a bit today but yesterday it reached a maximum. It blew tremendously, so hard that most of the hutments carried away, three men were rather badly injured and were removed to hospital. Today it is still blowing very hard, not as hard as yesterday, but as long as it keeps up there is no chance of aeroplanes visiting us, for the present, at any rate. We have beenvery lucky so far with aeroplanes. Taubes have repeatedly hovered over us and dropped bombs, but every one fell wide, the nearest one actually failed to explode, but buried itself in the mud. The 16th too had one into their camp but it was a 'dud'.

Spring is coming in now and we are all welcoming it and everyone is hoping that summer will come in early, but they seem to forget that it means so much added daylight, so much increased chances of being hit. We have rather good fun here dining out at the different messes. We mess as HQ and four companies now, and the different companies ask their HQ officers out. Last night I dined with D Coy and C Coy who run a joint mess. We had quite a good time, any amount of toasts and singing. I had an argument with Stocks, and he bet me five pounds that the war would be over and peace declared by the end of May. Somehow I think that the money is won, but wouldn't it be a great bet to lose, provided that the Hun has had his richly deserved hiding.

Not a great deal in the papers just now except any amount of artillery activity. I know what that means, when you read about artillery duels and artillery activity, it is not the artillery that gets it, it is known out here as artillery retaliation when the merry Hun has slogged us for hours at a time, our artillery slogs him one better, but all the time it is the infantryman who gets it in the neck. But all the same we must credit our artillery where credit is due, they can shoot, it used to cheer us up to the skies to see the Hun lines going up kite high.

I wrote to Pat and Bill yesterday and next mail I will return the photos you sent me. I would have kept them but they would only be spoiled here, besides I have four wee pictures of the faces I love. I expect wee Derick is enjoying himself in Troon, I bet he has a rare old time in the grass in the garden where he ate all the Vaseline.

I'm glad to hear Robert is doing well. How is Nancy, tell her I am a great friend of Father Crottee, the R. C. chaplain — who, by the way, dearie, has the best collection of naughty postcards and French so-called art pictures I've ever seen. I am officially recorded here as a Church of England at present, I expect the reason is that there is no Calathumpian chaplain.

Next time you write, my love, put in a diagram of that game we used to play at the Bungalow and also its name. We sometimes play Ludo at nights for cigarettes and tea tablets, but it's not as good as our game. I tried to introduce the spelling game but everyone voted it too intellectual so it had to be discouraged. Give Mrs Wallace my best regards, also remember me kindly to Mrs Brand, tell her that her brother is doing well. He is to be second in charge of a trench mortar battery, certainly not an enviable job, but don't say so.

Well dearest little lump of love of mine, good night, love . . .

FEBRUARY 18TH
Somewhere in France

My dearest wee and loving wee wife,
Your two lovely letters to hand today, also a letter, some socks and chocolate from Mrs McOmie.

I'm dreadfully busy today, for we move up again tomorrow. The weather is still terribly rough, wind and rain, but last night was a beautiful night — calm, still and full moon. Harrison, Lodge, Stocks and I were playing bridge and were just finished when we heard the humming of aeroplanes, we blew out the lights and made the guard put out the fire, the noise increased and then — crash — bang and up went a terrific roar, then again there it was still and quiet — the engines had been stopped, then another terrific crash and two more, then the anti-aircraft guns got busy and the air was lit up with angry bursts of red and the shrapnel broke the air. I don't know how close they got to the machine. There were evidently two Taubes, or at least judging by the peculiar noise the engines of one was making, we took her to be a Fokker. I never saw either of them, but one could feel their very presence, it is a very queer sensation, they were so directly above us and it was so still. We stood and waited for the crash each time hoping they were not coming nearer. No one was hurt and very little damage was done. It must be very hard to drop bombs in the right spot, for they all go wide, thank goodness. It is due to the great speed the Taubes go, I expect.

Anyhow judging by the wind tonight there is not a great chance of us being disturbed. We look upon the wind as a good pal here for whilst it is blowing hard there is no chance of a gas attack coming off. However the helmets we are provided with are very good and effective, so long as they are undamaged. If one suspects one's helmet, it is condemned without any fuss. To see the whole regiment in helmets is a most weird and unholy sight, something like the old marauders in the days when the king's highwaymen held sway.

The people who are coming into this camp, that is the regiment we are to relieve, have already sent in the party to take over. I fancy they will come in for any amount of attention from the Taubes as this camp is marked down and one of these times it will be strafed.

And so dear heart of mine, it is once more unto the breach and a long breach it be, but there is a very silver lining to the cloud in the shape of a few days' leave, how I wait. I hope that none of those big ugly lumps of shrapnel catch me unawares, very hateful and odious stuff is shrapnel.

I am always delighted to get away from here, there is a certain fascination at the forward area and one can get a bit warmer even if at a greater risk. There is always so much going on, so many men about that one forgets about the mud. It is just mud, mud and seas of mud! I hope it is fine tomorrow, so far our luck when moving has been extraordinarily good.

It was awfully good of Mrs McOmie to send me the socks and the chocolate, and at the first opportunity I must write and thank her. I don't think, dear sweetheart of mine, that there is anything I would like you to send me except perhaps a shaving strop. Richardson forgot to pack mine.

My clothes are rapidly becoming much the worse for the active service conditions. Please don't mind me when you see what a mess I've become. I got dear little Deckie's letter, I'm so proud of you both. By the way, I've found out the game we played at Troon, and have introduced it here, and everyone is so keen on it. It will serve well in the trenches to beguile the weary hours.

I'm in great disfavour just now with the 104 F. Amb.[21] They came down or rather yesterday sent an orderly officer to look around the camp and report on the sanitation. The MO was incensed naturally at them butting in and then when he came to me with a long face about it I soon got fed up and gave the orderly officer something of my mind. These people are a perfect pest, anyway he won't butt in here again for awhile.

Well, dearest girlie of mine, there is really no more news here only I send all my fondest love, and just long and long for the day and the night too when we will be together again. I want to hear dear wee Deckie gurgling and burbling and watch him loving his pretty little mother, my own little wife.

I don't know when I'll get the next opportunity to write as on the move the facilities are not good and then the day being occupied with the move gives me so much extra work at night. However once settled down in the trenches I will have more time effecting reliefs, reorganising in the trenches which is really rough on the adjutant. It is really not fair to have the responsibility of having discipline and also all the correspondence, especially in the trenches, where returns are hard to get in, where everything is making some difference to our establishment either in personnel, ammunition or stores; however someone has to do it and I expect I'll get through alright.

Goodnight my love, hold Deckie tight and tell him his soldier daddy loves him and his dear mother.

Love . . .

FEBRUARY 22ND
The trenches

Sweetest dearest,

I'm afraid that this letter will have found you waiting for a letter. We've moved up and taken over and are now on our own.[22]

What a busy time it has been, last time we were here we were only in four days attached to other units. Now we are alone and all the detail had to be done by us, what a job it is, to be sure. The poor adjutant is supposed to be a perfect encyclopaedia.

Well, we arrived at night but the Taubes followed us, circled and hovered over us most of the way up. Our brigade got blocked by an artillery convoy, the roads were narrow and carts got bogged. One cart and six mules capsized into a ditch. We had a terrible time, cursing and swearing like maniacs at drivers and animals. Taubes circled over us and the anti-aircraft guns fairly rained stuff up at them, but they just sailed serenely on, quite unmindful and not caring a bit. At one time there were 27 planes up in the air at one time, ours and hostile ones, we were below and of course expected to get the benefit of the resultant scrap. One shell flew over the top of Russel's head and buried itself in the earth just fifteen yards from Russel's Coy. They dug it up afterwards. Two aerial torpedoes landed very near Brough and the Q. Master. What a scream they came down with, worse than big shells, then fell in a ploughed field and went off with a tremendous bang, no damage was done. The shrapnel is so pretty up in the sky when it is cloudless, there is a flash and then a big white cloud like a washed fleece hangs on the air, in a moment it is joined by several others and very soon there is a pretty picture. The planes are wonderfully brave and bold and just wheel round and deliberately sail through the smoke clouds. It must be intensely annoying to the gunners. Of course when our own planes get across they get it and do just the same. From what I've seen I reckon the air service the safest branch in the whole business. We are in the same trenches we were in before and they are a little better than they were; some decent cleaning up has been attempted. I expect the outgoing unit was so pleased to get out that they did not mind the cleaning up.

It is snowing so hard today and so cold, my hands and feet are like ice, so you cannot expect a nice letter today. Most of the shelling today is on our part, our fellows are just chucking their weight about. Some of our guns sneak up just behind one and of course we don't know and then off they bang and the concussion and noise nearly lifts one out of the dugout.

The machine guns had a great old go last night, almost the whole night they ripped and roared, till one could not hear one's own voice. It is just extraordinary the way they blatter away. One commences and then away they go on either side, and then it dies down just as suddenly as it commenced. The bullets hum and zip, zip into the sandbags and overhead. The Huns seem to be shelling some towns a good long way behind us for their shells are passing over and very high and from the row they make I think pretty big ones.

Well, we are out of the mud more or less, but it is just as cold and one cannot move about like we could under canvas, but at least there is something going on all the time here.

Last night when the transport was bringing up our rations, one of the big carts went into a ditch and we had nothing till 11 pm; however at 11 pm it turned up and about 12 midnight we were eating a rattling grilled kipper and very fine it was. I have to send in reports to brigade HQ at 3 am and it is not very comfortable when one gets wakened at 2 am to have to consolidate Coy reports and wire it through to the brigade. As long as the snow lasts we won't get any trouble from the aeroplanes, it's too risky, the planes won't come down low enough to risk observation.

As soon as I get warm, sweetheart, I will try and send you a nice long letter. I was trying to get warm up till 2 am and then had to get out for two hours and have not got warmed up yet. There is only one part of me that is properly warmed, dearest, and that is my heart, it's kept so warm by the very true love it has for the dearest and sweetest little mate of mine. Oh! a big gun just frightened the life out of me, I thought it was a Hun shell in on me, these big ones of ours seem to go off just near one's seat and they shake the earth like a volcano. After every shot we wait for the next, it does not come and one forgets about it and then off she goes with such an unholy blast that everyone jumps.

I must be off to work, all my fondest love to you both . . .

FEBRUARY 23RD
In the trenches

My little wife and sweetheart,
So cold dearest, dreadfully cold, snow and nothing but cold and snow with a raging wind, not even mud. How can we last this cold, and so hard to cope without sleep, cold, cold and tired. The shelling has been quieter today but tonight the sky is clear and the moon out; a cold friendless moon, and oh dear how cold. The machine guns are running riot and sound very angry. My hands are like ice and my eyes like boiled gooseberries. I was about all night, phone messages, urgent reports etc. I am on duty from 12 to 5 am every morning with reports and returns. Then when I could get a rest the big guns commenced and one cannot sleep much for the noise.

I got your dear letter and parcel. The socks are lovely, I've not worn them yet but will as soon as I get the chance. It is really too cold dearest wee soul of mine to write, my hands won't go, one cannot keep warm. I will write you a nice long loving letter first chance, if I get some good sleep I'll be up to it. I am feeling perfectly fit otherwise but so cold. Goodnight dear little woman, bless your dear little heart.

All my love to my two little dears, my love is all for you and I do want and need yours and you . . .

February 27th

My own dear sweet wife,

My letters just now are very irregular and I'm afraid it can't be helped. The Germans are keeping us tremendously busy and my work is heavy, just at present. Things are going along alright. It is still cold and the ground is still all snow covered. The German snipers are very busy little bees in every sense, one cannot move, but a bullet clouts the sandbags. If we just come outside a dugout and the light just shows through a chink, ping-ping the bullet raps out. Then the machine guns sweep our dugouts and HQ; the effect is sickening at first, but I think I'm used to it now, it is bad to become used to such horror. One gives an involuntary duck when the parapet is clouted, if the bullet comes close it sounds just like a stockwhip in the ear.

The shelling is going on all the time, but on Thursday night it was very heavy. Yesterday the Huns sent across any amount of whizz-bangs, ten landed in our HQ. One rattled into the bottom of the Colonel's dugout but did not burst. One landed on the top of the dugout occupied by the orderly room runners and went off with an appalling crash. Some of the shrapnel and fragments from it going slap into the OR. All the sandbags were gone but none of the runners were hurt, pretty shocked, and all rushed out without waiting to finish their lunch. I was lying on my bed at the time trying to get a bit of rest, with my feet inside a sandbag, in an effort to keep the bed clean and my feet warm, listening to the shells coming closer and closer, and wondering if one was coming my way, perhaps through my door, which opens towards the line. The runners' dugout is ten yards from mine. I bounded up and didn't take long to get rid of that sandbag.

Those whizz-bangs make a great fuss, they scream out and then a terrifying crash but they don't really do as much damage as one would expect. Also on Thursday there was a gas alarm, someone sent an SOS down the line. Immediately our helmets were on and all the gongs and bells going. Our guns started within one minute and gave them hell for fifteen minutes, pouring in big and little. The next morning the Hun lines looked most bedraggled, with a much blotted out appearance. Then the very next night we got another gas alarm from the left of the line. We stood ready, but no gas, we did not need to call the guns up again. Since then there has been almost continuous rifle and MG fire. Did you ever see a picture in one of the magazines, or *Punch* I believe it was, showing the effect of a bursting tyre on a subaltern from the front? I can assure you it is just what would happen to me if I heard a motor tyre burst.

Last night I went down to see a casualty and was returning with the MO when a MG rattled on the parapet just at our heads; down we went into the mud, flat as brick bats. As soon as we got up, when along came a screaming whizz-bang, low and venomous, down we went again and lay there for about ten more minutes as a sniper was plinking into the parapet at our heads. It is weird and fascinating but very nerve-wracking and makes one very irritable and hard to get on with. The mud is awful here and we are just covered in it. When we come out of this I will need a complete new outfit. My British warmer is caked with clay.

We are to be relieved on March 10th, so we still have got twelve days to endure. We go back to a rest camp for eight days and then come up again. The weather has been very unfavourable for aircraft work for some days, but last night a gentle German Dove flew overhead and dropped some mighty weighty bombs. It passed over us and dropped its stuff on our next-door neighbours, and judging by the crash, must have been big ones. They are rotten things at night, all is serene, and then the most mighty crash.

I've not seen anything of Captain Greig for a long time. The staff keep a long way back and do not take more risks than possible and I don't blame them either.

Your letter and the Australian mail to hand, a decent bunch too. What lovely kiddies Jean and Colin are. Jean is like Arch and Hilda, but Colin is the counterpart of Arch.[23] Pleased to see Cis did so well. Really, dearest one of mine, I think that the Ashbury/Aspinall[24] people must have some brains after all, what do you think? Surfing makes my mouth water, here we haven't had a stitch off for eight days, only two shaves and one decent face wash. Spring is beginning to show up a bit, perhaps when it is full spring, this mud will be gone.

The Germans are on high ground for most of our line, which gives the cursed snipers such an advantage, they fire more or less down into our trenches. They are only slightly more troublesome than the rats, appalling, great big fat slimy chaps that peer and poke about, their little beady eyes shining in the dim light. They come out and run all over one and eat holes in everything.

Now my dearest love, my great and only comfort, here is my thoughts about you both, that you are happy and comfortable. Soon I hope, I will be with you both again.

A squeeze and kiss to you both . . .

la Boisselle

MESSAGES AND SIGNALS.

No. of

Words	Charge	This message is on a/c of:	Recd.
Sent		(D) Service.	Date.
At......m.			From.
To.			By.
By.		(Signature of "Franking Officer.")	

19 : 1 : 16

Day of Month | In reply to Number

March

March 2nd

My dearest wee darling wife and sweetie,

It seems ages since I last had the pleasure of chatting to my own wee woman but ye gods what a time we've been having, I think we are now fully entitled to call ourselves soldiers. We have been in the trenches and under fire twice during the night of February 21st; however most of the time is passed, possibly the worst is over and we go back to rest for eight days. I don't know if we are going back to the canvas home we were in before but I don't expect we will. I rather expect we go back about three miles to what are known as fatigue billets, for whilst there we are called upon to supply all working parties on the roads etc. However, though under shellfire all the time, one is safe from bullets and there is not the continual necessity of groping along trenches knee deep with slime whilst snipers bang and bang away at every corner.

The sniping business is a very trying and nerve straining business and the Hun sniper is a bold and cunning blackguard. I had the most miraculous escape — I was going into my wee hovel to try and snatch a few hours' sleep, the dugout was not well situated, the tiny door facing the Huns. I got halfway in when I found the doorway blocked up with a chair that had fallen down, so I just struck a match, and as I bent down onto my hands and knees to do so, the match had just lit, when ping, ping, ping three vicious bullets zipped into the sandbags just over my shoulder. Had I been standing or only just stooping I would have got both. You can bet I did not strike any more matches. Anyway about half an hour later I got a great spraying from the machine guns. They rattled and ripped on to the dugout all the rest of the night, but unless one goes out the bullets only waste themselves in the sandbags. From dusk until daylight these snipers are very trying, one only has to move and ping. One doesn't even have to move at all, they just fire all night at recognised spots where they know men must pass, and one has to just grope along on hands and knees at certain spots which we call 'unhealthy spots'.

The cold snap is over, and we now have glorious days, fair and fine as could be, but, oh it was cold, everything was frozen stiff and stark and there was not nearly enough fuel. The trenches were slippery and we fell everywhere. Then came the thaw and mud, heavens what mud, seas and seas of it. The dugouts leaked and our mess dugout had three inches of water on the floor.

The past two days the aeroplanes and artillery have been tremendously busy, on both sides. How they manage to avoid all the shrapnel that they do beats me. You can see the flash up in the sky and then the white fleece hangs in the air, sometimes the planes just sail through it. It is really most remarkable. The Mad Major, an artillery observer, flies over the Hun lines at about 80 to 100 feet and they just paste him but never get him. The Huns never go less than 4000 to 6000 feet. It must madden them to see the Mad Major just flying over, I cannot understand how he misses it all; he has been doing it now for eight months.

The shelling the last two days has been wonderfully accurate, the Huns landing some big stuff over, terrifying stuff; these 'coal boxes', or Jack Johnsons, are so called from their size and the black clouds of dust and smoke they raise. If one lands near one there is little or no chance as they make a fifty foot crater. Fortunately, they must be very expensive as they don't use many. Our own artillery is ripping at one salient spot where the opposing trenches are only seventy yards apart and yet from a range of 3000 yards our artillery knocked the German front line to smithereens. One of our trench mortar batteries had a rare shot. They of course fight in the trenches and are very effective using a sixty pound shell. Well, a dugout was spotted over the way and we put the TM battery on to it. The first shot fell on the German parapet and blew out about twelve yards of it, the next hit wallop on the top of the dugout and up it went, sandbags, boards, rifles etc. and didn't we cheer. It was a ripping shot and we know it hurt for immediately the Hun retaliated with twenty-seven whizz-bangs into our HQ but did no harm.

The men are seasoned now and settled down and are wonderfully good. The night before last we got a wire to announce a big French success at Verdun, I hope that it is correct and that they have recaptured all they lost. At present we are waiting further news and hoping someone will send a paper.

I got the razor strop alright dearest, it is very nice and did not arrive a minute too soon, as I have been so busy that I have not been able to shave for a week. The lot of the adjutant is very busy, and the work is never done, as I am always on duty, which is good in a way as one has no time to get jumpy or nervy.

Major Stocks and I have had a great row, both the 2nd and the CO gave him a rare telling off and so did I. He tries to make my job as difficult as possible.

I have a nice new horse so Anderson tells me, only up to the present I've not seen or been on it, and am looking forward to trying him out. How is my pretty wee boy, give him such a love and kiss from his daddy. Can hardly wait till I see you, but I'm such a mess, my clothes are mud, slime, and you won't recognise me.

Now my dearest heart, I must close, dearest, all my love.

MARCH 4TH

It is so cold again, snowing for the last eighteen hours and not enough frost to freeze it, and the sun waned and a very high wind so things are not too pleasant. After our last very cold snap I was beginning to hope that a change for the better had come over the weather, but at present it is very bad. The mud is terrific, thigh deep and very tiring to walk in. My feet are just like ice slabs and are so cold now that I hardly feel them. Last night my old dugout leaked all over the place, and I had to shift about from one corner to another.

Tomorrow we are changing over to a new sector of the trench, still in the same area, and just immediately to our own left as it is at present situated. The trenches are better and some of the HQ dugouts are, I believe, made of reinforced concrete so they should at least be waterproof, which is something to hope for. About the 11th we go back for eight days into working billets so I hope when we are there that the weather is nice and fine so that we can get a bit of decent sunshine and warmth. All the officers are being pretty hardly worked just now. Three of our officers, Brough,[1] Shields[2] and Devine,[3] are in the hospital which means extra work for their fellow officers. Poor old Shields, I don't think we will be seeing him again out here. He was an awfully nice boy and we all miss him, however it is the luck or bad luck of the game.

Things are not exceptionally lively just now on either side. There have been one or two very heavy artillery duels, terrific roars and blinding flashes. Our own guns just pour in the metal. I don't think there is any shortage of ammunition just now. Anyway, I am glad that I am not to pay for what is passing overhead. When the Hun commences, he picks out a spot and does the job very thoroughly, fairly flattening it. Our HQ came in each day for about thirty rounds of whizz-bangs, wretched, vicious, venomous affairs. One soon loses respect for them and that is what does the damage. I have seen men hearing them coming over, jump on the parapet to see where it is going to land, the result is the shrapnel gets them and the wily snipers too. Sniper is a wretched fellow and makes life a bore. It is so tiring to continually move about stooping and groping about the wet and muddy trenches, and not to do so means a sudden exit. The snipers know our trenches by air photos; they post themselves after dark and sight on to some spot they know will be used and fire round after round all day and all night at it. If one wants to pass, one waits till the next shot rings out and then darts across before the next is off.

Today the 'city of many tears'[4] is getting a great drubbing. The gentle Hun is sending over a great many 5.9 shells, high explosives. They are falling well into the city and we cannot see what the result is. I only hope that the hairdresser does not become panicky and leave the place as I want to have a hair cut as I am beginning to look like a cinema artist.

The situation at Verdun[5] is interesting us immensely but we cannot get any decent news of the result. We had a wire that was sent by the French Premier to us and we cheered most lustily. Since then nothing further has come through. I think the French ought to be able to hold them there for they will have the tactical advantage from the position of the ground. Anyway, someone is going to have immense casualties. I expect the Salonika picnic party will wake up soon and get a move on. There ought to be a very big force there now and Salonika defences should be perfect.

The rats are very bad here, great big fat slick chaps, such merry little beady eyes and so friendly, just perhaps a bit too friendly and curious.

Well, dearest sweetheart, how are you and our dear wee son? Give him such a big hug for his daddy and tell him to give his mummy one for his daddy too. I am afraid that when his daddy comes home he will love his mummy all to pieces. I do wish I could just hop into Troon tonight about 10 pm and sneak upstairs without waking you. I would see first of all our dear wee son lying so snug and pretty in his wee bed. Just make the door and then, on looking across the room, I would see the sweet little face I would love to kiss, the dear little woman I do so love. Then she would wake up and give her old man a loving welcome and they would all be so happy and warm.

The Australian mail has just arrived and your two dear letters, the others are very nice but yours are just the best. I do love them. I do wish I could be with you to hear Deckie and all his little sentences. He must be a dear little chap, so he ought to be with such nice parents.

And now, my dear, goodnight . . .

March 8th

My dearest wee Pettie,

If you cannot read this don't blame me, for I just had the most appalling fright. The Hun has been shelling our battalion headquarters all day long, but until a few minutes back he had only been using whizz-bang and shrapnel, however I was lying down in my dugout having a rest when I heard a Jack Johnson scream through the air. Then there was the most appalling roar and thump. It was about 100 yards on the right of my dugout but I got up as I expected some more over. The next minute one came screeching down and then there was such a bang. I heard windows bang and a hot blast swept across my face for a moment. I did not know what had happened.[6] I looked at my dugout and it was alright. Major Rose's dugout is next to mine and just about ten yards from his dugout there was a hole ten feet by eight feet. I came into the mess dugout and had just got inside when another came down quite within 100 feet of the mess. Where one is half asleep these things just about convulse one for the moment.

It is beautifully fine and clear today, not a cloud in the sky, but the whole country is white with snow. We have had very bad weather, the trenches are just one sea of slush and slime, something shocking. One goes thigh deep in this stuff. The result of the snow is very trying, the added weight breaks the parapets down when the thaw comes and everything is just swimming and flooded. The dugouts have as much as four inches of water on the floor. However it is Wednesday today; on Friday night we are due to be relieved and go back to billets where we remain for any necessary fatigues and then back after four days to some billets about ten miles away for eight days' rest. One wants a rest after a tour in the trenches like we have had. It is very trying and very weary to be closed in by sandbags for so long. One gets sick of dodging and worrying about bullets too and the continual broken sleep tells. I have not had my clothes off since February 21st. We are not allowed to undress at all for in the case of a gas alarm one only has 45 seconds to put the helmets on and no time for clothes.

I am afraid, dear wee mate of mine, that I have not had much opportunity of writing as often as I would like. My job is a big one and never seems to end. I am on duty from 12 midnight to 5 every morning writing up reports etc, beside that I am expected to be on duty at any time. Then it is so cold at times that I really cannot do anything, but put my feet into two sandbags and fall into bed. If we start a fire the wretched Hun promptly drops shells on us, whilst an aeroplane sits up above us to tell the gunners how he is getting on. So we just sit up and let our feet get on as best they can. The Taubes are out very strong today and do look so pretty away up in the blue, they are so much more graceful than our planes. The continual wind, bad weather and snowy weather has kept the planes quiet but as it appears to be fining up a bit better now they will come again like swallows. Brand rejoins us tomorrow for the first time in the trenches, so far he has not been under fire but I expect he will do alright. He and his merry men do not come out on Friday. At present we are about sixty men and three officers short, however a draft has arrived and soon we will be up to strength again.

And now my own wee sweetheart all my love. I do so long to see you again. It won't be long now.

Goodnight . . .

March 9th
In the trenches

My dearest and pretty wee woman,

My pen has run dry today and so I must just fall back on pencil. Tomorrow we come out and go into the reserve billets for four days and then go back for eight. So far we don't know where we go back to, but it will be about seven miles back I expect. The trenches are in an awful state. The thaw has set in with a vengeance and the mud and slush is thigh deep and horrible, our dugouts have about six inches of water in them. However the men have worked like Trojans and only for their perseverance, the trenches would have been uninhabitable.

The Hun gave us a rare pasting yesterday with shells big and little. In the morning our guns ranged up on the Hun barbed wire and front line and sent yards of it sky high, he retaliated on our headquarters and all along the line, keeping his shots wonderfully well. He has us down flat in the mud and kept our stretcher bearers very busy. However I know he got it too for our artillery fairly planted it into him. The snipers are a bit quiet just now for we got on to a few of theirs and could see two drop. One was in a tree and he just tumbled out. One of our patrols out last night ran into a German party and a scrap. Three of our men were wounded but we managed to get them all in. We are expecting a reinforcement draft on Saturday and some new officers. Just at present we are very short and greatly handicapped.

Russel has an awful cold, can hardly speak. How is Mrs R? Must be about time she was expecting her trouble.

The first thing I am going to do when I get out of the trenches on Tuesday, or rather from the reserve, is to go for a real good hot bath. I have not had my clothes off since I came up on the 21st. I am wearing one of your little singlet affairs and so far have not met any wee friends. Up to the present I have only heard of one or two cases of men meeting them.

Today seventeen of our aeroplanes passed over the German lines, bound on a raiding expedition somewhere. They were heavily shelled but as far as we could watch they were alright. A minute or two ago there were some tremendous reports but whether it was distant shelling or bombs I cannot say. The Huns planted some very big stuff in on us yesterday. One landed right beside my dugout but not in it. The report was sickening. CO was talking to Captain Todd and three sergeants when a shell fell ten feet away and burst, the CO and Todd were knocked flat into the mud but not hurt, whilst all the sergeants and three men besides were wounded, two of them dreadfully. One man had his right trouser leg blown right off and his leg scorched with the explosion. Each had a miraculous escape. The piece of shell that missed him was as big as two hands. He is an awfully game wee chap and is great company.

Well my dear, I won't be sorry to get out of the trenches for a spell. I will be able then to write to you some nice long letters.

Love . . .

March 12th

We are out of the trenches and back in billets just a mile[7] from the firing line. It is such a relief to be able to walk about upright and to miss the continual and nerve-straining ping ping of the sniper. We are not, of course, out of range here and this morning Major Bruce's company (D Company) was shelled in the billets. They are only 400 yards away from us. We heard the shells go over and went out to see where they were bursting. One went through the kitchen of the farm but did not do anybody any damage, but materially added to the ventilation scheme of the culinary department. Bruce was in bed with a heavy attack of 'flu and had to skedaddle out in a hurry; however only six came over and then he crept back to his flea bag. Most of us have 'flu or colds as the weather and the water in the trenches was just awful. I never had anything like it. We were wet to the thighs the whole time, the mud is just awful, horrible slimy and evil-smelling stuff.

The Hun pasted us rather badly at times. I am afraid he wanted us to imagine he was going to attack and so save us the trouble of running to Verdun to help the French. A city of many tears that was lying just behind us got an awful pasting one day, Thursday I think it was. We counted eighty big explosions which were shells from a naval gun, however I don't know what actual damage was done, but tomorrow I will see as I am going in to have a bath and my hair cut. The farm we are in just now is a big one, the inhabitants have flown or were ejected. There are 180 men at it besides us, so that it is not as quiet as it may be. The men are all on the top floor, we are underneath, and as they rise at 6.30 am we don't get any sleep after that hour for the noise overhead is like a blessed convoy of mules passing over a bridge.

Anderson's groom shot another soldier dead on Friday, accidentally, with Anderson's revolver. The poor lad is terrified, he is very young and the man he killed was his best mate. He was cleaning Anderson's revolver when it went off.

Our first reinforcing draft arrived yesterday They arrived looking so nice and clean. The men gave them a great reception and took them in hand like old soldiers do. We do fancy ourselves now a bit. You don't realise just how dirty and ragged our men are until you see them besides the men of the draft. It is the same all over here, it cannot be helped and so long as the rifles and equipment are kept clean, that is the main thing.

Padre Black came into lunch with me today. He and I are great pals, he came up into the trenches one night and brought me some chocolates and papers, we all like him tremendously. Tell Nancy I thank her for her letter and will write her soon. Just fancy us out for eight days We move back the day after tomorrow and can hardly realise what eight days' comparative rest means. It will do the whole regiment good as our casualties were heavy in the sense that men who were sharing responsibilities got potted and that means a great deal of extra work as in the trenches until one is sure one cannot delegate responsibilities. Eight days will give us a chance to reorganise and put everything in order. Richardson is awfully seedy, a very heavy attack of influenza. I wanted the MO to send him to hospital but he refused to go to hospital, fancy refusing a soft and, at any rate, a clean bed and preferring to sleep in a dugout with four inches of slush and wet blankets.

Tomorrow I will have the first try at my new mare. I have seen her and had Dickson, my groom, bring her down. She is no beauty and is dreadfully quiet, not the capricious prancing little thing my other one was. I have not seen Brand since he went away to the trench mortar school but I had a report from the commandant of the school; he speaks most favourably of Brand and his gun team. I especially selected the team for Brand and he has a ripping twelve men. He is in the trenches now, I believe, with his trench mortar. The trench mortars are the things to wake things up with. They hurl a sixty pound bomb and do terrific work.

Well, dearest little woman, it was so nice to hear you were going out and having a good time. Fancy you winning the prize and also knitting me some more socks. I think you are a really dear little wife and I think I must love you a lot, don't you? I am glad to know that you are trying to fatten up your tiny wee legs. I know two ladies that want fattening up too, I wonder do you know who I mean. Two ladies I am very fond of. I will send back the photos to you as soon as I get them, at present they are with my spare gear in the transport lines. It is a good thing I said not to take these into the trenches for they just all would have been ruined.

Aren't the Russians doing fine in Mesopotamia, I think that Baghdad will go this coming week, not so much to the British as to the Russians. The Turk has a very strong position and has got us in a strong pocket at Kut. It is a wait and see game there for us, but it will turn out alright. I think the abominable Abdul will soon put on his considering cap and wonder if the game is worth it all. Bulgaria would soon follow his lead and then our friends the gentle Hun will feel some pressure. The French and English can hold him here alright. He may break through here and there with sheer weight of numbers but he cannot go forward but what a price. The carnage at Verdun has been terrific. The worst yet including even Mons and the Marne.

Well now sweetheart I must close for I am sure I have told you all the news.

All my fondest love. Goodnight . . .

March 16th
In rest billets

My dearest,

I expect you are wondering what has become of me and why I have not been sending you some nice long letters, but the fact is I have been laid up, had just a terrible time with an abscess in the ear.[8] I felt it coming on the day before we came out of the trenches, a continual throb, throb in my right ear. I thought it was only due to the continual row of the guns but in the afternoon before we came out of the firing line it got worse, not any great pain, just the continued pulsation. The first night out I was a bit better but the next day it commenced to pain dreadfully and at night it nearly had me distracted. The MO was attending me and he and the Colonel wanted me to go into hospital and Major Rose too, but I did not go, refusing flatly, for if one goes to a field hospital with sickness, one is then sent to a field rest station and there all chance of leave is stopped for the rest of the field convalescence. Hospital is supposed to pick one up again, anyway on the night of the 13th the abscess was the limit and I decided to go to hospital but I took a sleeping draught and went to sleep at about 4 am and the abscess burst whilst I was asleep. The thing was much better and I stayed in bed all day and the relief was tremendous, so I again refused to go and aren't I glad now for it would mean being on the bottom of the list due for leave, and as it is now, Pettie, I will be one of the first. I am still very deaf in the right ear and cannot use the phone.

What excitement there was at the last billet. The weather was superb, not a cloud in the sky, and aeroplanes were all over us and dropped any amount of bombs, all wide, thank goodness. I was in bed and used to hear just the muffled roar, some of our guns took up a position near our billet and commenced to shell the Hun. He put up some observation balloons and soon spotted our billets and our guns and the big shells commenced to drop in around us. The regiment that was relieving us had nothing to look forward to and the very billet that Major Stocks' company vacated was blown just to smithereens. The recovering regiment was a new one, just up for restructure and I felt desperately sorry for them but I am glad to get out of it.

My horse was ill, some colic or something, and so the CO insisted on me taking his and would hear of nothing else. So off I trotted on Troon who played up very badly when the shells burst. I got home here and Major Rose and the MO, who had come with the advance party, insisted on me going to bed at once and I was glad to do so as I felt clear washed out. It is a long time since I felt so done. Anyway I had a bed with sheets, had the same room as I had when I came here the first time. I slept like a log, not a single ruffle in the bed and next morning felt as fit as a fiddle.

The weather is glorious just now, not a cloud in the sky, spring has really come at last. However, I have thought that so often now that I must be more guarded. The hedges and the trees are all budding and the farmers and their families are all sowing wheat, so at last spring must really be on hand, but whilst in the trenches there was not much evidence of it. I never felt so cold or saw so much snow, muck and slush. I am here for eight days and we are all trying to make the most of our rest. No hard work for the mess, just short route marches and clearing up. I have had breakfast in bed two mornings. Of course we are liable to be shelled any time but there are no batteries near us so the chances are that we will be only concerned with aeroplanes. I have seen hundreds here the last two days, mostly ours of course, and one of ours came down in the field opposite last night. It had been over the Hun lines and had a piece of the propeller knocked off and was gliding down into a ploughed field but when the wheels hit the clayey soil they bogged and the plane stood on its head. Neither the pilot nor the observer were hurt and both had dinner with us. This morning a new propeller was fitted and away they flew. Today the planes are everywhere, some away up just like insects in size, others flying low and droning away in great style. Five Taubes flew over us at a great height and up our fellows climbed and we could hear the machine guns rattling away, but they soon disappeared from view. However we are quite used to these things now and don't work up much excitement over an air fight.

We had a long and hard time in the trenches. The Hun kept on pasting us to try and impress us that he still had a big punch left and he certainly sent over some mighty big shells and once or twice caught our men with shrapnel, but he always got it back. Once or twice he commenced to cheer with great gusto, no doubt some lie about Verdun set him off. We sandbagged and obstructed the river that flows from him to us and must have made his trenches in a pretty rotten condition as we could see him pumping water over the parapets. Time after time at night he sent out working parties to dig and clear the obstruction but our machine guns caught them. We also breached his parapet for about forty feet opposite a communications trench and we could see the Huns trying to crawl along the trench to repair it. Then our snipers got on to them. It is all very exciting but it is time to get a good old rest and I do hope the weather keeps fine and gives us a chance to have some exercise in comfort.

The French are doing alright at Verdun and seem to be more than holding the Hun up, whilst he must be spending thousands of men. Even if the Hun took Verdun now, the game would be ours for he has certainly sent more men over the 'great divide' than ever Verdun is worth to anyone. Abdul the Turk is getting a bit fed up too, I think that Baghdad must go in the next few days then Trebizond after which I am afraid that Abdul won't find the war such a glorious business. Anyway, not such a profitable one as he imagines. The Salonika people seem to be sitting mighty tight. We call it the Salonika picnic but I expect they are waiting for a little opportunity and for a big force and it is well known by most of us, if not the generals, that some of our enterprises have been spoilt by using too few men. I hope that the smellful Bulgar gets it firm and hard very soon. Roumania will hop in once the scale is thoroughly turned. There are a good many Australians at Verdun. The whole of the siege battery that I met in London are there, so they will have plenty of excitement. I hope there is no shortage of ammunition and I don't expect there is.

I hope you are having a fair spell of decent weather at Troon. How is dear Derick's cold, the dear wee chap? Give him a kiss from his daddy. I would love just to hop across unannounced and see you both. I so dearly hope there will be no stoppage of leave. At present all leave is stopped but that is I expect all due to the Verdun business. Major Bruce is away to hospital suffering from pleurisy and exposure in the trenches so at present Gee is commanding his company. He had a tremendously close call at the trenches. He was in his dugout and heard a whizz-bang coming over and thought the next one would come pretty close. He got up to go out and it did come, very close and went into the dugout, clean through the roof. Gee was at the door and got blown into the trench without being hurt.

And now, my dearest wee bundle, I must close. I would like you to get me three or four khaki collars dear, you can get them at Troon, get me three size 16½ and two size 17 for the ones I have shrunk up to nothing. I got a pair of socks and a chocolate, they are a lovely pair and I am using them today. I am getting used to thick socks now; of course, I don't get much walking to do. They are not very easy on my feet when there is much marching.

My dearest love . . .

March 20th

My own wee woman,

Your dear letters arrived, also the pictures of Deckie and yourself. I just love the one of your dear wee son standing with his hands behind his back. He is a dear wee man, isn't he. The one of you and he where he is hanging over your shoulders I tore up, it was terrible. He has his face all puckered up.

We have been tremendously busy the last few days doing up our kits, repairing, refitting and on top of all that we were reinoculated so we all felt a bit wretched. We have a wire from the brigade last night about leave. Two officers were allowed to go, leaving on 22nd from Boulogne and so we had to draw lots and Captain Lawrence won one place and Major Rose the other. So the lucky beggars go off on Wednesday. The Colonel wanted to send me in view of my bad ear, which is still as deaf as a post, but it was decided to ballot for the places. It is not yet certain if Major Rose will go as he is to go on the Divisional staff for a sixteen-day course. If he goes on the course straight away it means he won't be able to go on leave and then I would stand a chance. I never hoped for anything so much, I did so want to come over to you and our wee boy. Never mind, the time will soon be up and then it will come around by rotation. I am feeling a bit used up with the inoculation, dearest, all stiff and headachy so will close now.

With all my love . . .

March 22nd

Well, I thought we were going to have a nice full rest until Friday but last night we got an urgent wire to go down and arrange to take over at once a new sector of the front line,[9] and of course we all swore tremendously, more especially since everyone was inoculated and feeling very seedy; however we just had to crawl away down and arrange things. It is a new section of the trenches that is new to us and six miles from where we were in last and a very unhealthy spot to be but it is prettier country, not quite so flat as the other place, but unfortunately as usual we are at the bottom of the hill and the Hun is at the top. The village which is contiguous to the trenches, and which gives the line here its name,[10] is shelled to smithereens; there is not a single intact roof, the streets are just littered with red tiles and bricks and huge holes where the big shells have landed. Every bit of wall is loopholed and the village itself, perhaps one should say a town for at one time it had 7000 inhabitants, was the scene of some of the most desperate of all the fighting and has been alternately in our hands and the Hun's time and time again. There is a big boarding school and convent, the scene of some terrible outrages by the Huns. The incident was the subject of an inquiry long ago. In the lines there are hundreds of buried little white crosses just dotted about everywhere and some English, some French and some German. There are some lovely orchards, or at least they were once but now of course are untended. The trees are blossoming finally, so soon there will be some apple pies and stomach aches. This is the worst example I have seen so far of the frightfulness of the Hun — nothing stands, every yard or so has had a shell and not a civilian is to be seen. It is still shelled lustily and every time a shell lands amongst the tiles and bricks a huge red crowd of dust goes up and hangs in the air.

Major Rose and Captain Lawrence left last night on seven days' leave, lucky devils. Don't I only wish that I was puffing away across the Channel in the old *Henrietta*, that's the boat we came over in. I know one dear wee sweetheart and two other precious ladies who I would kiss and love just so hard and one dear wee son who would have very long games with his dad, but my time will come and it won't be long. The only trouble is seven days is very short. Lawrence got a wire just as he was going off to say that his brother-in-law (Patterson) had been killed somewhere here.

To all mine, my love . . .

MARCH 25TH
In the trenches

Sweetest and best,

This leaves me just snowed up again, goodness me what luck we are having with the weather, it always seems to snow now when we are in the trenches. The trenches here are the worst condition of any I have yet seen, some places the water is so deep that we cannot use the trench at all and one has to get out over the parapet and chance it. The snow has made matters far worse. Our headquarters are in an old dilapidated farmhouse,[11] and there is no roof at all, it was once a two-storey place and must have been a decent place but it has changed hands and had so many gruellings that nothing but the basement remains. I have what was once the pantry as a room and the snow melting has just deluged the place. The snow his time was a very heavy fall and has not nearly all melted so that we are in for a worse time yet. However the sun is out today and that compensates for a great deal and one soon forgets about discomforts. It is a very unhealthy spot and the MO is kept remarkably busy.

Well dearest sweetheart, I must close, there is a chance to get this off, my love . . .

Later

My sweetheart,

I had to finish up very abruptly last night just when I was getting settled down to a nice long letter. General Williams[12] and staff arrived at our humble abode and stayed on and on, I am just in time to finish off and catch the mail. I think

I had just got to telling you all about the big fall of snow and how uncomfortable things were. Well the discomfort has increased. The trenches are canals, pure and simple. You can't walk along the communication trenches at all, one just has to get out and cross the orchard and it is very mighty unpleasant and of course the casualties are mounting up too steadily. We were coming up to the HQ the other evening, the CO was leading our gallant little headquarters' party. The MO and I were at the rear whipping up the stragglers when the bullets rattled on the road at our feet. We were using a road instead of the trenches just immediately in front of us and just in front of us were two stretcher bearers and suddenly an awful sickening thud and one of the stretcher bearers collapsed with a gasp, shot through the shoulder and chest. At the same moment, Heath my runner from A Company, staggered and grunted and he went down, shot through the arm. The MO got one through his equipment. It was all too serious and uncomfortable to be exciting and it was terribly cold and dark. The CO wasn't sure of the road and the little party kept halting. At last we got in and the CO didn't even know that two men were wounded. It just shows how fine the men are, not a whimper, not a bit of complaint.

Today we got a terribly hard drubbing. Sir George McCrae[13] and Robertson[14] the adjutant of the 16th, came up to arrange about the relief for we are to go back to brigade working billets in a day or two. Sir George had only just arrived when a big 5.9 landed on a farm on our right. We put on a game smile and pretended we were used to it when there was the gurgle, gurgle, SSSSSSH — quiet, and then a roar. A 5.9 landed within fifty yards so we went into the CO's dugout and into the orderly room. Beech and I were in the orderly room with the regulars and servants who called in Sir George. The CO and the MO were in the CO's dugout when the Hun just pasted us with HE, whizz-bang and shrapnel. A huge old pear tree, right at our kitchen, was just blown up, three went through the old thatch roof, one just hit the chimney and knocked the corner off and then we heard a scream, whizz, errr, upp, gurgle, thump and roar. One got the orderly room dugout and blew out the end but it burst against the reinforced concrete. Had it come through, every one of us would have gone, and the CO too, as the dugouts face one another. The next one was a dud, that is that it did not burst, the next one wounded four men and the next one was a dud and three hit an out-building and settled it. The old house here got such a shaking that it will leak worse than ever. It was a hot time for a while, we got about sixty over altogether and the shooting was splendid. All the time an Aviatik was above watching the fun. Our artillery phoned up to know if we wanted them to shoot back but we said no we did not want the Boche to know he had annoyed us so much, and if he thinks he wiped us out he may leave us alone tomorrow. Anyway, there will be some sandbagging to do tonight.

Well dearest, wee wife I was so glad to have your letter enclosing the Australian mail. Nothing doing yet about leave, I expect once our three months is up there will be something definite doing. I am so disappointed when I could not get there to see you before but if I had gone then I would be just getting ready to come back now which would be very depressing. I have still got everything to look forward to.

Goodnight my dearest . . .

MARCH 28TH

Here we are back in fighting billets. We were relieved last night by ——[15] and are now in support just eleven yards behind the trenches in a village,[16] or at least on the outskirts of a village that has been battered out of recognition. We have our headquarters in what must have been once a very nice house, brick with a red tile roof and nice garden and grounds but the top storey is gone and big gaping shell holes are to be seen all over. All over the walls and sides. The top part is well burned out too. There are some great big 'crump' holes all around and likely to be some fresh ones in the next day or so as there is a battery in the field next to us and it will get sought after as soon as it opens on the Hun. Great excitement here, we blew a big mine and our troops rushed to the crater and then dashed on to the other side and gave the artful Hun perfect hell. The artillery was tremendous, it commenced at 4 am with a most terrific roar, that was the mine, then the rifle fire and machine guns just ripped and sobbed and spluttered and then the big guns just roared and boomed. The whole sky was lit up with the continual flashes. It was a cheery sound, especially as we knew what was going on and who was getting the hiding. We were not in the scrap itself but were admiring spectators. The whole affair went bang with great snap and we got a bag of prisoners.

We are out now for a few days and go back into the same sector. A very unhealthy spot it is to get into. The communication trenches are still completely flooded so that we are still exposed to the machine gun fire just to go from trench to trench. It is very tiring and trying to hear the guns swinging on to one and then hear the bullets cutting into the mud and sandbags and then hear someone gasp and fall, I know I felt just like bolting for it. The man right next to me got such a clout, the thud of the bullet was sickening and he was tremendously game, and talked to me about his new wife; he lasted only a few minutes, dying in my arms. At the same moment another got it and the stretcher bearer who came up to speak to the doctor and myself had one pass clean through his pack.

Well dearest, there is nothing further at the moment. I am just in time to catch the mail and I will send you a nice long letter tomorrow. I am enclosing a copy of a letter[17] that was found on a prisoner. My word, Pettie, I think I will desert and join the German army and see the privileges described in the letter. Nothing further about leave just now but it ought to commence soon. I dearly hope that I will see you all soon and I am sure that there is someone up above who thinks of lovers and my wish for leave must come true.

Bless you my dearest . . .

"Committee for the increase of the Population. Notice No. 13875.

Sir,

On account of all the able bodied men having been called to the Colours, it remains the duty of all those left behind, for the sake of the Fatherland, to interest themselves in the happiness of the married women and maidens by doubling or even trebling the number of births.

Your name has been given us as a capable man, and you are herewith requested to take on this office of honour and to do your duty in right German style. It must here be pointed out that your wife or fiancee will not be able to claim a divorce; it is in fact hoped that the women will bear this discomfort heroically for the sake of the war.

You willbe given the district of........... Should you not feel capable of coping with the situation, you will be given three days in which to name someone in your place.

On the other hand, if you are prepared to take on a second district as well, you will become a =Deckoffizier" and receive a pension.

An exhibition of women and maidens as well as a collection of photographs is to be found at our office. You are requested to bring this letter with you.

Your good work should commence immediately and it is in your interests to submit to us a full report of results after 9 months.

W.L.O.TWISS, Major,
General Staff.

1st Army.
22.3.16.

la Boisselle

until tho po arrive just
Daddy wants to see
to the two dearest l
Just fancy dearest
the fateful night

up for all little n
Today the letters a
Australia are I w

MESSAGES AND SIGNALS.

No. of

Words | Charge

This message is on a/c of:

(P)

Service.

(Signature of "Franking Officer.")

Recd.

Date

From

By

Sent

At m.

To

By

19: 1: 16

Day of Month

In reply to Number

little Sweetie are not
any note as I have not
y. For we have a big m
row and I have to go

last two
is at
at the Chu
I do not
is in
all awful
how the
reply
lucky
Duthie
night
morrow
guns are
down to
we played

April

My dearest wee sweetheart,

It was so good to get your nice long letter last night, just as we were going back into the trenches.[1] We are now in again, after being only out three days instead of the usual five. There is a good deal of reorganisation going on just now, and the ordinary method of relief has been a bit upset. In fact, there are many big changes on the way and the rumour is that we move down south[2] in a few days to take up a new line, and that an Australian division is to relieve us almost immediately.[3] The general rumour is, of course, generally wrong; but I saw some Australians here the other day myself, and an officer told me that he had passed the Australian infantry division on the road about seven miles out.

The weather has moderated a bit and we have enjoyed the warmer spell. Things are a bit lively just now, next-door to us. There was a mine blown and we rushed the craters. The Hun has been intensely angered at the success of the venture and has shelled us a great deal since.

I hear that they are torpedoing vessels in the Channel again, well I fancy I would risk it. So far no further word of leave. Major Rose and Captain Lawrence come back tomorrow, so I expect that today they are a bit miserable. I reckon I ought to be back home to you and Deckie within a month. I can hardly wait for a time with you, it has been a long, long and hard three months. I have done a great deal of hard work and feel pretty used up at times. The continual strain and the presence and dodging of death tells a hard tale and soon wears a man out. Three months is about enough of it at a time. Major Bruce broke down under it and so did Shields and Devine. Bruce is still in hospital at Nice, Shields and Devine are in England in hospital. I really think that the continual never-ending sea of mud has a great deal to do with it. An officer's responsibilities here take the ginger out of one. It is easy to be brave and stand up to machine gun fire when one has slept well and is feeling fit, but when the strain is on, the same feeling is not there and one inclines to nice fat sandbags and big parapets. Still, everything considered, everyone is in magnificent heart and doing wonderfully good work. It is funny how men whom we thought were to be so good have gone to pieces, Bennett went all to pieces, shellfire broke him up completely. Anderson is splendid under fire, on the whole though our men are just superb, what they put up with in the way of work, water and mud is astounding but things are improving now. In a month the mud will be heated.

Stocks and I still have our great rows and the culmination of one the other day he resigned but withdrew it next day when the Colonel told him he was going to recommend his resignation, a funny wee chap.

Well dearest wee wife of mine, soon I hope to be with you to love you and hold you just as I used to and to see my own dear wee son and his dear wee mother.

Goodbye dearest.

APRIL 2ND

My own dear sweetheart,

Today is a beautiful day, not a cloud in the sky and just a nice nip in the air, the guns are fairly ripping it in and aeroplanes are very busy. Yesterday one of the batteries just 800 yards from us got an awful hammering. The Hun sent in 140 big 5.9 crumps and our poor old guns did get it hot. An ammunition depot was set on fire from the blazes and the explosions we could see from here, and we could see the men rushing about trying to get things in order. The Hun evidently noticed it for he commenced to pile shrapnel on; today, however he is getting it back as our guns have just rattled on incessantly since daylight and must have sent over a power of stuff. Two Australian commanding officers called on us today and are looking around our trenches. They are to relieve us whilst we go down further. We will be here for a few days yet. It was great to meet and have a long chat with them. One knows a host of people I knew in Victoria.[4] I wish we were going to stay on here so I could see more of them. I don't know the date of our move yet, but I expect it will be soon, down to some spot where there will be a push. It is funny the way units are pushed about here, all we seem to be doing is lots of work repairing trenches and putting things in order for other people, just now we have these trenches in such fine condition. When we took over they were rotten and unlivable.

Well dearest, this must be a very brief note as I am still very busy explaining the system of reliefs here. I have just managed a moment to get this off.

With much love . . .

April 3rd

My dearest,

Nothing very great to chronicle here. We are still in the trenches and the weather has improved considerably and some of the trenches are becoming dry. The Huns have been very active here lately. I think there must have been a relief in their lines the other night as now they are a great deal more active all day and night. I expect you noticed in the paper that Anderson[5] had been shot through the head and had gone to the Great Divide. I mean the Anderson who used to bath at the Bungalow, a very decent fellow he was and a good soldier too. Russel[6] got welted in the head, a wonderful escape that you will have seen in the paper too. Russel was splendid. He sent for me as he was on the trolley and asked me to do several things for him. His coolness and bravery tremendously impressed the men. I thought there was a good deal in him beneath all his manners. Will you write to Mrs Russel and tell her how game he was and what a good impression it made on all the men. Major Rose is back in charge and the CO is away on leave. I believe I will really be away one of these days.

The Taubes are very busy today, one was above, wheeling about and prying into our business all the morning. He was really searching for some guns of ours that are near here. Anyway we expected to be shelled any time today, a prying Taube usually means business.

We heard today that there had been a Zepp raid in England and at last a Zepp has run into a shell and come down. I expect it is true but all the same what my experience in anti-aircraft gun teaches is that it was a lucky shot. Of course a Zepp is a big target and the men have something like a fair mark but as far as aeroplanes go they are a washout. When they open fire on the Taubes everyone here commences to laugh and joke. We were watching, or rather listening, to the German eight inch guns, perfect nightmares, shelling a battery the other day. We were sitting in the trenches with our backs to the German lines whilst the big coal boxes shuffled across when all of a sudden there were two huge roars in the Hun lines. Two of the Hun coal boxes fell short into their own lines. The men almost had hysterics and one wag said 'Good Lord, they will send that gunner into the anti-aircraft corps'. That is about the correct feeling here about the anti-aircraft guns. I expect you read about the nice little push here following a mine burst. The men are still holding it and ought to be able to do so now. The papers we notice are making a great mouthful out of it.

The men are all splendid and the pleasant spell of good weather is making new men of them all. There have been no more Australians calling on us, I wish there were. Well dearest sweetheart, soon I hope that your old man will have seven days' leave to come home and look after you both, as you both deserve. I think our dear Deckie has a lovely little mother, she is only a little handful and has such tiny legs but still she is a sweet wee thing.

All my love . . .

April 8th

Dearest,

I am afraid that you will find my letters pretty irregular just now but dearest wife it is not quite my fault. We came out of the trenches last night and will be out for about three weeks, so far as I can make out. We are being relieved in this area by the Australians and on the tenth we move west for three weeks' intense training, whatever that means. All our spare gear, extra blankets, equipment has been withdrawn so it looks as if we are to join in a push somewhere. The whole countryside is overrun with colonials. They are everywhere and it is a treat to see them about. I have met such a great crowd, most of whom I know quite well, also had a letter from Paddy Jekyll. We have been tremendously busy, for the past week we have had Australian officers[7] attached to us for instruction and had to show them everything connected with the trench business.

There have been no end of board of survey on old clothing and one court martial. One of my police sergeants belted two gendarmes, the result of which was a court martial. I, of course, was prosecutor and there were a great crowd of witnesses. The French witness had to be interpreted and then the English evidence had to be interpreted back to them so the whole business was delayed and very wearisome. Anyway, the sergeant was acquitted. The Australians are a husky lot and should do well over here, but at present the cold has them all doubled up. I don't know what they would have done here when it was snowing. We are moving well back into the country and where we are going for the next three weeks we won't even be able to hear a gun. The trouble is, it is a five-day march from here and the men's feet, after being in gumboots so long, will not be in a condition for much hard marching on the pave. I don't know what part of the line we go to after the rest but I expect it will be down south to the new sector taken over by us from the French.

I see that the Zepps have been visiting England and Scotland and generally shaking things up. Poor old Edinburgh will be very excited and insulted to be so rudely aroused from her slumbers. I believe the Infirmary was nearly blown down and Watson's school was badly damaged. I am so glad you are in Troon, dearest, I think it is quite enough for me to be out here, don't you?

So dear wee Deckie is getting nice and brown, the dear thing. What a man he will be when his poor old daddy sees him again. I do wish they would bustle up and get some leave through, though I expect that if leave was granted now I could not get away till after the move. I am just counting the days till I get back to see you, but really I will be in such a disreputable state that you won't know me. It will just be too good for words sweetheart to see you and Derick scampering about.

I must close and get this off quickly, fondest love . . .

APRIL 12TH

My dearest wee darling,

We have been on the move now for three days and are 40 miles from the trenches[8] we left Sunday. We are taking over a new sector of trenches. The weather is awfully cold, wet and windy. The last three nights we have been in different billets, it means a great deal of billeting work and returns. We are to go on till Friday and reach our destination then. We are about fed up with it. I will write properly first opportunity.

All my love, my sweetheart . . .

APRIL 16TH

At last we have reached our temporary destination[9] and I have a chance to send my warmest love and innermost thoughts to my dearest love.

We have been on the trek with a vengeance, and are now a long way back from the firing line, so far that we can't even hear a gun going, it does all seem so strange to be out of the sound of guns and not to hear the horrible fascinating scream of the shells passing overhead.

After so long a spell in the trenches, so long in gumboots, the men were not in a very good state to march for we were only doing twelve miles a day billeting each night at a village on the way.[10] In most cases we were only lucky getting good billets. One place we stayed at a brewery and I had nice white sheets, so cool and clean and another night I was at the *mairie*. The *maire* corresponds to our town clerk and he was a most hospitable host and could not do enough for us. In the room I had a most magnificent view over a valley and it was so pretty to see all the fruit trees in blossom. The next night brought us to last night and to here. This is only a pokey wee village, not a patch on the last place we were in, it is a very old, thirteenth century place, out of date as it could possibly be. The feature of the place is an old Norman tower on the church. It is really a very historical place, the famous Marlborough having used it at the time of his invasion, still it is a rotten old place. I am living at a monastery, it is not really a monastery but it is at present used to house some monks who fled from the area now occupied by the Hun. They are dear, bald-headed old things who walk about all day in flowing robes, no hat and a prayer book. None of them speak English so we jabber away in our pidgin French to them. They have an awfully nice garden and gave us quite a lot of fresh vegetables and radishes. They also have a great big apiary and a lot of rabbits in hutches. Just now it is Lent and they are getting ready for some big fast, so they don't care about dining with us. They are very keen on the Scots soldier and do anything they can for us. I have a nice big double bed with scented pillows and scented sheets, so lovely and comfortable after the stuffy waterlogged and rat-infested dugouts. There is only just one thing needed to make life worth living, dear wee wife, and that is my own sweet wife.

The country here is so pretty, plenty of nice hills, not too high. The woods are all breaking out, the hedges are so pretty and the fruit trees are everywhere in flower, one cannot realise it all after the fearful slaughter and the long days and nights of strain and strafe that used to fill up our time so recently.

I don't know how long we are to be here, not long though, it is just to brush up a bit and is a good idea. The men would all return as fit as fiddles. The continual pigging in the mud and filthy slime makes the men slovenly and untidy and they get careless so that a fortnight here will just set everyone up, especially if we could only get some decent weather. March was terribly cold and freezing, made a million times worse as all our spare baggage was collected for return to the base and we are now in nothing more than we stand, so that we are ready to move wherever we are called and of course we are liable to shift tonight or at any other moment. The next move is quite uncertain but we will not go back to the area we left so I suppose it means down south where we are so the papers say extending the line. It will certainly be more interesting there, as the country cannot possibly be as flat and as muddy as that we have just left.

The mails, of course, on the march were interrupted and we had no facilities for posting letters and none for even writing them. You know what the adjutant's life is under peace conditions. Well, dearest, I hope you are being a good woman and saving up as much love for your old sweetheart. I am just longing for the day when he can pop in and stay for just a few days with them both. What a cruel thing to be unable to see one's first born growing but at the moment all leave for the Army is cancelled, but my dearest I will be the first to fly to you.

With all my love . . .

April 18th

Dearest tiny, wee thin legs,
Here we are sweetheart, still at the same spot and all of us recovering from cholera inoculation.

Today I had a court martial case, one of our company sergeant-majors was being tried for drunkenness. He was convicted but up to the present I do not know what will happen to him, the sentence not yet having been promulgated. It is not a nice job to have to pull a man down from warrant rank but at the same time drunkenness on active service cannot slip by unnoticed. The regimental sergeant-major, Burchell, is still indisposed following his inoculations, he had a pretty bad time but is on the mend again now.

Well my dearest there is nothing further yet in the way of leave. Captain Greig was sent off on leave but was recalled after three days. I met him yesterday afternoon and he was terribly fed up about it. He had been dreadfully ill crossing the Channel and he reckoned that the time was too short to be worthwhile all the travelling. However, my dear, I think I will risk it when my turn comes and travel across the whole continent just for a stay with my wife and dear wee son. I am afraid Deckie won't know his daddy and I am afraid that his mummy too will be very shy. I do so want you both so much and am just longing for the day when I will get away from this mess.

In the meantime, all leave is stopped, I don't know exactly why but I expect there is to be a push somewhere, and if the Hun knows we are getting ready for a push he will push first, like he did at Verdun. Verdun seems to be settling down more or less now to the usual type of trench warfare. It was a big effort and must have cost the Hun thousands of men, millions of shells and any amount of lost prestige, but it was a close thing, the French made no bones about it this time. They stuck it out wonderfully well.

Poor old Townshend seems to be hanging out well at ——[11] but I fancy he is in a pretty tight grip and I really don't think he can hang out much longer and the opposition to the relief force is tremendously strong. He is a brother-in-law of Mrs D. Shand of North Sydney with whom I used to act. Another point of interest just now is Trebizond[12] which ought to succumb in a short time. The Russians are reported to be sixteen miles away. If they can reduce that distance by half they can commence shelling the city with their moderately sized guns, I don't think the nature of the country there will permit them using the big ones. The Salonika picnic party goes on merrily, much to the dissatisfaction of Greece. I expect they are waiting for a general and all-round offensive.

It is raining like old boots today, dearest wee one, just the loveliest day for a snuggle up and a nice long old chat upstairs. It is so nice to hear such good news of Deckie. He must be growing into a dear wee thing now, how I will love seeing him. I did get three collars dearie, three linen ones in an envelope. Thank you so much, the others had shrunk to nothing and you could imagine their colour.

Love . . .

April's letters cease here, as LWN went on leave, back to Scotland, at a moment's notice. In his absence, the battalion moved to Albert, where it commenced the work-up for the Great Offensive of 1 July.

A considerable amount of anti-gas training is noted in the battalion's records, along with practice in removing wire and making 'strong points'.

On 4 May the battalion marched to St Omer, entrained to Longau, marched to Rainville. LWN rejoined the battalion on 6 May.

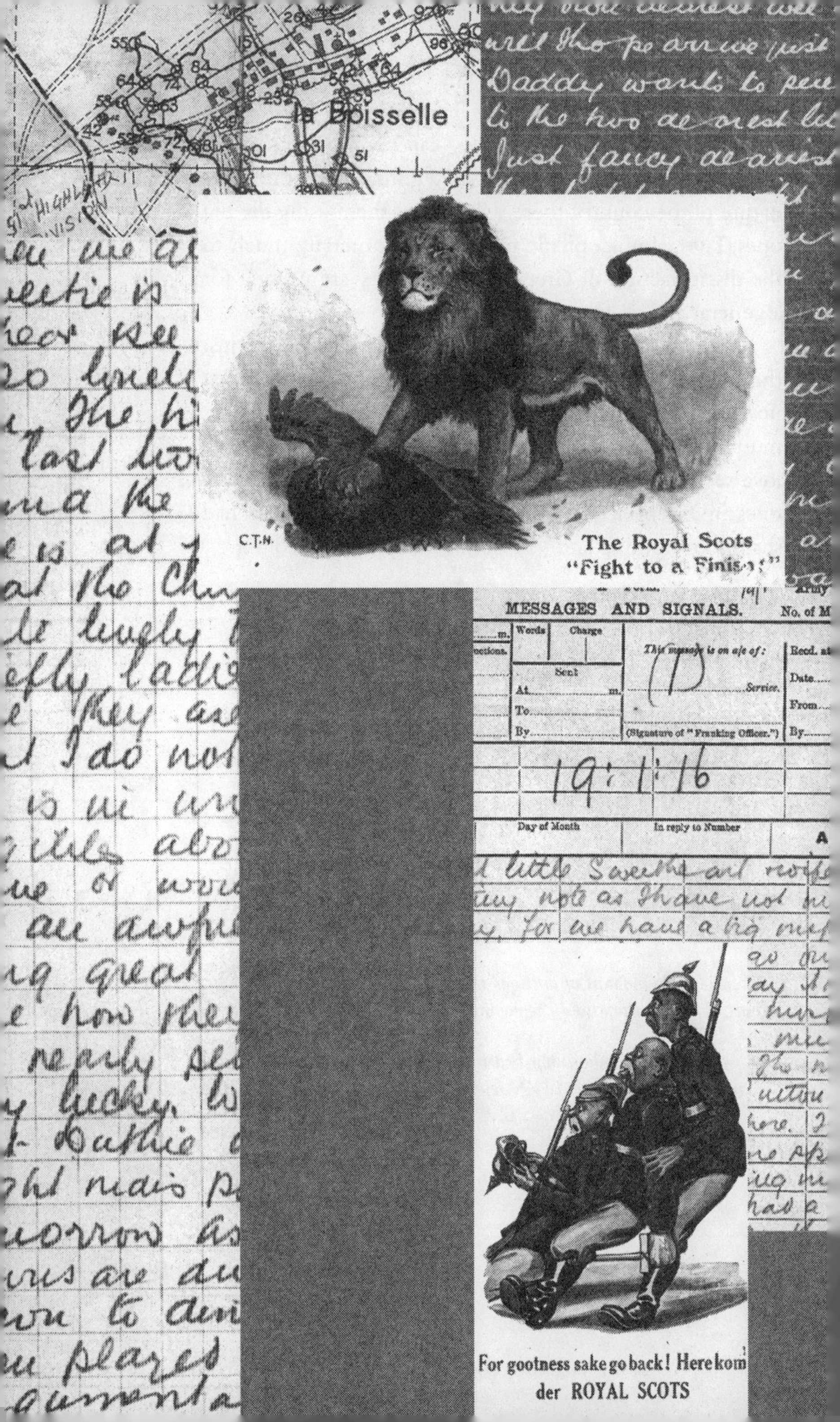

la Boisselle
C.T.N.
The Royal Scots
MESSAGES AND SIGNALS.
19 : 1 : 16
For gootness sake go back! Herekom
der ROYAL SCOTS

May

May 6th
Somewhere in France

At last after a very trying trip I have caught up with the regiment. The boat did not leave Folkestone until 12 mid-day and we arrived in France at about 2.30. I went along to the AMLO who said that the division was on the move and I had to move to a new rail head. So along we went to see the RTO who said that we had to go back to the place we left and that the train left at 6 pm! I just happened to meet Colonel Watson of the Australians and we went and had some tea at the Officer's Club. At 3.30 we went to the train again. Prior to that the AMLO told us again that we were on the move. The RTO visited us getting on the train and at 6.05 we were unceremoniously pulled out of the train and told that our destination was changed and we were to report at 7 pm and go south. We were on the station until 9 pm and finally got away at 3 am, with another change of trains at 6 am. The train was supposed to take us on but at 9 am we were still in the station.

At last we were bustled on to a train and whilst sitting in our train, a special came in with our own men on. Gee and I both wanted to join it and be with our own people but no, we were sent on to a rail head twenty miles further on where the men and the rest of the officers were supposed to be going. We got to the rail head at 10.30 am and of course no one knew what to do with us. Fortunately, we met an officer who used to be with us at Ripon, who had charge of some Hun prisoners. We had lunch with him and played some gramophone music until at 3 pm a motor lorry was obtained and at 6 pm we found our own dear regiment. Oh was I tired.

Well here we are, sweetheart, once more in sound of the guns and from all accounts and judging from the big guns and the number of aeroplanes about, it is more than a lively centre. The country here is so pretty, very like the south of England, beautiful hills and dales but spring is at its full height. The roads have wonderful avenues of fruit trees all of which are in full bloom and it is so pretty. The crops are so advanced, wheat and oats are in ear already, and the clover paddocks look so fine and smell so sweet. It is the prettiest piece of country I have yet seen and just swarming with pheasants, and troops. Oh my sweetheart I do miss you and our little son so much, it is so lonely and hard to come back and commence it all again. I just hate it all and feel so dissatisfied. The billets we are in are so mean, hopelessly squalid and very busy but it must be expected here as so many troops, French and English, have been using them.

Everyone was delighted to see me or at least pretended to be but I'd sooner have the warm welcome of the dearest wee woman in the world than the best welcome a whole regiment could give me, and how are you feeling, dearest? I hope you and the dear wee son of ours are well. I do so miss hearing him calling his daddy. I do love you both so much and I am just so happy and so proud of the both of you.

I got a letter from Graham[1] and from Lill on my arrival here. Not a great deal of news. Graham said everything is doing well, splendidly in fact. He has been through the officer's instructional course and passed his second lieutenant's examination so if he is called up he is alright. I think that is a very sensible thing as I am sure that compulsion will come in Australia. Lill's letter was written just before going to Woolwich. She is very keen on the Woolwich[2] people, likes them so much. I am so glad, it will be so nice when we go back, won't it dearest? Major Rose is on the Brigade staff since Major Taylor transferred so he and Captain Greig are both on the staff just now but so far Major Rose's job is only temporary. It yet remains to be seen if he will be retained on the brigade staff. Lodge is in all probability going to the Royal Engineers for attachment on special duties and 'Blanco' White[3] is also in for something special. As soon as Lodge goes, I go up for my Captaincy, so that won't be so bad, will it? Nothing further now my dearest. Give my little boy a big kiss from his daddy and tell him I will be home soon.

Love

MAY 10TH
Somewhere in France

Dearest wee wife,

Here we are more or less settled down for a few days until our turn comes to go up to the front line. Of course I cannot tell you where we are but it promises to be a very deal nicer than the other part of the line we were in. The country is exceedingly pretty and hilly, spring is very well advanced and the little village we are in is quite picturesque. It is at the bottom of a valley or rather surrounded by hills and has a great many pretty trees all in and around the village but it is very full of 'sojer fellows'. I've not had a ride around yet but I hope to get one tomorrow and see something of the surrounding parts. The Colonel and I are the only ones living in the farm but of course the others mess here.

There is a big pigeon loft and tomorrow we are having a pigeon pie for dinner.

It is a great place for aeroplanes, far more than there were on the other front. I see by the English papers that some Zepps have had it in the neck. Isn't it splendid? I would love to see one brought down. I got two letters from you sweetheart and they were so nice and I hope to get one tomorrow. Mine will have been a bit erratic as we had no chance on the move to either write or post letters. I am so glad you got another house. I do feel so homesick when you tell me about what you and Deckie are doing. I just do wish leave would hurry up and come around again. I had a long letter from Lill, it was almost an obituary notice really. It contained the names of over a dozen friends of mine killed, also told me that Jack, Alan, Bill and Oswald Nott were on the way to the front and that Gordon Alford is on his way with Ray Norris both as lieutenants, all cousins so the family is not doing so badly.

I got back and found a pile of correspondence and work to be got through. Duthie my sergeant clerk is away on leave so I have got everything to do myself but Stocker tries to help all he can, a splendid wee chap. His wife lives in Troon. Anderson, Major Stocks and Pagan[4] are all on leave, Stocks is due back tomorrow. Lodge goes on Sunday so in no time my turn will be around. How is your poor old back keeping, dearest? I hope it is better. Goodbye for the present.

All my fondest love and thoughts to the dear wee team I left behind in Troon. Give my love to Nancy . . .

[Undated]
Early May

We arrived in billets last night and are expecting further orders now. I have been on the move ever since we got back to France and have not had a single chance to send you a few lines. I managed to send a postcard but don't know if you got it. Have you heard anything further about Albert Baker since the Boche had a shot at his lady?[5] We are all so pleased to see she is still hanging about. This is a very pretty part of the country but very hot and the guns are blattering away.

All my love, dearest . . .

May 12th

Dearest,

I got another lovely letter from you today and in it you were wondering why I could not send you a postcard from Boulogne, well dearest I could not for you forget that we can only send correspondence when it bears the censor's stamps, which of course was with the regiment and that was why I could not send you a line. Well, things are very quiet and peaceful here and we all agree that we could put up with a great deal of this sort of life but if everyone wanted to do the same, the war would never come to an end, or perhaps may never have commenced.

Today we have all been through a gas chamber, a huge pit covered in on all sides. The idea is to give the men confidence in the use of the anti-gas helmet which is really most efficient. This part of the line is very often gassed and shelled daily with gas shells. The weather is very good still and we are all getting as brown as we used to be at Troon. Today Hole[107] and I are going for a ride after tea to have a look at the country round about. There is really nothing to tell you about, no news trickles through here except of a kind we cannot disclose.

Isn't Deckie a funny wee character? Wouldn't Deckie get a surprise if I could just pop in and see you both? I really think that this time he really would remember his daddy. Please give me the full address of your new house and send me out some copies of the snaps you took. I will certainly return them as it is not safe to keep them here.

All my love my dearest . . .

SUNDAY, MAY 14TH

My dearest,
Things are quiet and normal here about, and the regiment is more or less rusticating and benefiting from the spell but the idea of a long rest here has been dispelled for tomorrow we go up to the trenches. Of course if I could tell you where we were and where we are going it would materially increase the interest but of course we are not allowed to do so. It seems rather a queer idea all this censoring but it is really necessary for the rotten old Hun gets more than a fair share of information as it is, without men and officers thoughtlessly babbling about this place and that place. The trenches[7] are, we believe, very good and nice and dry so that will be something to be thankful for but it is a very hot spot and in some cases the trenches are only fifteen yards apart, a second Gallipoli. Trench mortars

and rifle grenades are the chief means of displaying hatred to one another and very loud and nasty they are too. The chaplain got back from leave today, I mean Black[8] of course, came along after service and had lunch with me. He was very homesick and was not very bright or entertaining.

It is really sickening to come back to it all after leave. I know how I felt and the worst of it all is that other people will continually tell you what they intend doing on their leave. My dear old sweetheart, just what would I give to pop in and surprise you and dear wee Derick as I did before. Would it just be heaven to just hop right along and see the two wee treasures that belong to me.

It will be very strange for a while going back into action but I really think that the time flies much quicker in the trenches and then before we know where we are leave will be around again. I will be more careful in choosing the dates for leave next time and I think next time I will wire you so that you can come down and meet me in London. It is not very nice arriving in London and have no one to meet one, especially as everyone else has someone waiting on the station.

I've not yet managed to have a ride around to see what things are like — only once have been on my horse except of course on the march up. The country is very pretty indeed, so nice and rolling.

Well my dearest I must go off and do some nasty old billeting returns, not very romantic but very necessary for the French people's point of view. No more now, my darling.

All my love . . .

May 15th

Somewhere in France

Here we are just getting ready to go up and take a new sector of trenches. An advance party[9] goes tonight and I go up tomorrow.

Oh Pettikin, today I got your letter and the Australian mail. I could not understand why you had not got a single letter from me, by now you should have had quite three or four. For the first few days after landing I had no chance to write as we were moving all the time but since then I have sent you a lot of letters, my dear, and I was beginning to wonder what had become of them. No doubt by now they will be commencing to arrive regularly. Your second dearest letter enclosed the packet of Australian mail which came as a relief to me. I am so glad that by now you will be in the new place and having a nice old rest; just be as lazy as you can. I do wish I could just pop home again for about seven days my darling, I do so want you both very much. However, dearest, the time will soon pass and one of these fine days I'll come back to you just like I did. Probably about July 10th I ought to be due for leave again if all goes well.

The area we are going into is a very hot one, the trenches are in places only fifteen yards apart. It is also a 'gassy' area so we must all be at the alert and paste the very life out of brother Hun as soon as he speaks out of his turn. Everyone seems keen about going in again and it speaks well of us, doesn't it, to be put in so hot a corner. There is one compensation for the troops in the trenches only fifteen yards apart and that is that there will be little front line shelling the trenches being so near; but the trench mortars will make up the deficiency.

It was so nice to hear all the news from Australia. They seem to be having a rattling good time with so many soldier boys, I'm afraid that Vera will be popping off one of these days. Aunty Nan's house must look very nice, Lill told me that the rooms were very very nice and very large. Strange that Nick has not got his commission yet. He would be snapped up over here soon enough. It rained all day here yesterday and the wee village was nearly swamped.

Well dearest wee soul here is all my love and best wishes to you both. Sarah asked me if you were still in Troon, I rather think that Mrs U must be wondering. Now Petty for my sake, you must be nice and friendly with her. Get Mabel to call on her and it makes things so much nicer for Major Rose who is back with us again.

All my love my dear . . .

May 17th

My dearest,
Stirring times these, last night we had the heaviest bombardment I have ever heard, it was not at us but was on our left about a mile away, we watched the gun flashes and the angry bursts of the shells. It was terrific. I don't know yet what it all was about. Someone did get it and we breathed a sigh of relief when it eased off and did not spread to us. Today we ought to hear the reason, probably a raid was on. Raiding is a great hobby here, the lines are so close and the huge mine craters lend themselves to it, one has to be very canny here as the trenches overlook one another and one can easily go up the wrong trench and get into the Boche line by mistake. There is not a great deal of rifle fire here, nearly all the fighting is mining,[10] hand

grenades and rifle grenades backed up with trench mortars and canisters. Canisters are really the limit, possibly the worst thing we have had to face. They are nothing more than oil drums filled with high explosive and metal fragments, a long handle at one end which fits into the stem of a mortar and is fired with a charge, and the huge thing comes hurtling out and has a most appalling effect. Most of the casualties from these things are due to 'shell shock' — that is the force of concussion, the noise, the fear and the stress. There are some authentic cases of men being blown right over the parapet and into No Man's Land.

The trenches and dugouts are good, some of the dugouts have 25 steps leading down to them, deep underground and they certainly need to be. Our headquarters are very ramshackle old affairs and need a great deal of repairing but they will be knocked into shape. Owing to the recent rain, the trenches are lamentably boggy but are clearing up. Our men are very busy here and our planes quite outnumber the Hun here and they are a great deal pluckier, just sail about and keep about all day and the last day or two they have been very fortunate in good weather. Night flying is a great stunt here with planes groaning and droning all night long, very eerie indeed as you don't know whether it is a pal or a Hun who is going to drop some pellets. One good thing here about the trenches is one does ten days in or thereabouts and 25 days behind or something like that. So dearie I will have a chance to write regularly when I come out.

Last night was a glorious night, not a vestige of a cloud and the moon was perfect, an ideal lover's night, just the night for you and I, dear heart of mine for even though we have such a fine big son we are still true lovers. I am sure my letters must be coming more regularly now, Petty. It is very hard to write on the move, the field post offices do not get established for some days and it is usually the case of marching by day and just billeting by night and then on the move again so that one doesn't get the chance of sending anything. I did not see any books suitable for Deckie when I arrived, all were too advanced.

Well, my very dearest, there isn't really much to tell you about. I folded up my nice new uniform and am back into the dirty old one. The breeches and linen shirt arrived and it was very welcome, the warm weather is coming on now and lice are becoming very cheeky. They are not like the snake who prefers always to crawl on his own stomach. You will see in *The Times* and the *Daily Mail* a glowing account of a fight in the desert off Suez, the Australian Light Horse were in it. Major Bruce's brother was killed but was recommended for the VC. He died like a hero, a truly game fellow. Well, sweetheart, goodbye for the present.

All my love and thoughts to you both . . .

MAY 19TH

My dearest,

Just a tiny wee note as I am very busy and even now I may not catch the mail. Things are just the same and there is nothing of detail. I hope you are resting and things are fairly quiet. I expect you are letting Deckie have a regular fling in the sands, dear wee man. It is very hot today, very fine and blue and our own aeroplanes are tremendously busy, fussing and flying everywhere.

Well dearest, my love . . .

May 22nd

My dearest,

Not a great deal of news this time as doing a great deal of work in the office and between companies I have been nowhere and I have done nothing. I was hoping for a letter yesterday and today but none came but am sure one will come tomorrow and maybe two will come the next.

The dust is nearly as bad now as the mud used to be and today is very warm and dull; it may bring up a change. I do hope so. Mails just now are very irregular and I feel will become more irregular so do not worry if you don't hear from me, I will be quite okay rest assured. If Deckie was here now he would be just delighted with a cage full of rabbits, such pretty ones all white on the body, grey ears, nose and feet and a tiny grey tail. There is an old man and an old hag living in the house I am moving in, both are in their dotage I am sure and even dirtier than we can ever get.

There are such a lot of aeroplanes here I can see eight out of the window from where I am now sitting, they are all monoplanes and look so graceful as they volplane overhead on their way to the hangars.

I am going to try and get some letters off to Australia today but just as I always get settled down and feeling in a corresponding mood someone comes along to distract me. Major Bruce comes back from leave today. He is the last away and as there are about six subalterns to go yet, I hardly think I will be over until the end of July; however that is not a very big time and no doubt the time will soon fly.

The Russians are still battering away, we are overjoyed at the result, they are truly wonderful the way they can so quickly recuperate and then look at the hoards of them. I am afraid the Prussian pigs are beginning to get very uneasy.

What do you think of that contemptible little spot Greece, anyway she is being treated like a spoilt child now and soon will no doubt by pressure swing around to a more reasonable frame of mind. The French are doing alright, and so are we. Everything is bright and cheery and makes one feel very sanguine.

The Huns are amusing themselves today shelling one of our observation captive balloons that is up at the back of the village. They are sending out timed, air-bursting high explosives and we are all wondering if the observers have got their wind up and how long they are going to stick out without moving. That is the beauty of all the other branches of the service, when things get too hot they decamp and locate more peaceful scenes, whereas we sit it out and trust luck. Some of the new officers saw live shells bursting today for the first time and were wildly excited and a bit scary over it, no doubt in a month they will have seen and heard all the artillery they ever want to see or hear. Personally, I would be perfectly contented if I never saw or heard anything more violent than a Christmas bonbon, however the more and louder we hear it the sooner it will be over.

I was censoring letters about an hour ago and one of the men, a signaller, was writing to his cousin who had just come out here after his honeymoon, and there was also a postcard to the lovelorn bride and I must only say the letter was very amusing. The postcards were French and showed a series of little square pictures on a card exhibiting all the stages that one reads of as originating on, and being made use of on honeymoons! Well my dear I am just longing to get back and see you both. I know just how much you would like to have me.

All my love . . .

[Same Day]

My dearest sweetheart,

I have just received some more mail from Australia and your own letter. Also the snapshots which are uniformly good. The one with Deckie and I seems to be good of me but Deckie is blowing at my pipe and his dear wee mouth is pouting a little. I am glad the house seems to be turning out satisfactorily.

This is a very warm corner; no end of violent strafing but little or no rifle fire. The rifle grenades are still very nasty and very thick. The previous division to ours evidently took things lying down, we are bashing back for all we are worth and giving more than we are getting. The artillery support here is fine, the heaviest stuff that has ever been believed. We seem to have good fire superiority over the Hun.

Today I saw the first Taube I have ever seen brought down. It was a beautiful hot day and he was cruising above us and our anti-aircraft guns were batting all around him when he suddenly spun around, turned over and came wallop down. What a sight. No more now, my dearest, mail will be irregular for the next five or six days.

Goodnight, my dear, love . . .

May 23rd

My dearest,

Here I am sitting on the steps at the stairway that leads eighteen feet underground to our mess. This an awfully hot spot, such shelling, such a hail of trench mortars and grenades and canisters. I thought that I had seen some shelling before but here it goes on day and night. It is awful, the guns here are all bigger and the din of the whole thing is terrible. The trenches are good and some of our dugouts are 25 feet underground. The canisters are awful things, huge oil drums full of high explosives, when they go off the concussion is frightful. It makes one feel sick. We go out of here in five days and won't we be glad for a spell out. The continual and awful bombardment gets on one's nerves and one has always to be ready for gas. However they are getting back with more than interest and old Fritz gets plenty to think about. I'll be able to write you some nice long letters in a few days, my darling wife.

All my love to you both . . .

MAY 25TH

My dearest wee sweetheart,

Here we are still sticking it out and indeed sticking it out with a vengeance. It commenced to rain yesterday and continued for most of the night with the unhappy result that part of the trench flooded and things are really very uncomfortable but then it is not very cold now and things are not really too bad. This is a mighty warm spot and the Hun keeps us on the continual edge but we have been calling up the artillery and giving him some fiendish retaliation. He heaves over these abominable oil cans — really magnified minenwerfers. They are nothing more nor less than oil cans or oil drums filled with high explosive and they are most devastating in effect. Because our artillery support here is the best we have ever had, any quantity of big stuff, yesterday we gave the unspeakable

Hun hell. Our men are splendid, everyone in top form and working like Trojans. However we will welcome the relief when it comes as the nervous strain and the continual effect of the big concussions of the oil cans gets into one and makes one so irritable and makes one feel sick. The wind has been in the suitable quarter for gas attacks and that too is very worrisome and keeps one sleeping with one eye open. I hope you are getting my letters alright now.

Major Rose, the CO and I are all living in one small dugout. The mess was shelled and was blown in and a couple of big crumps fell each night in the air over our own dugout which caused all the trench and sandbags to fall in, so we decided to come into the bigger dugout. It is very deep and ought to be pretty safe. Well, my dearest, I sent back the photos you sent me and I put a tiny wee message on both just to remind you how much dear little Derick and I love you. I hope you are resting just as much as possible and fattening up those tiny wee thin legs.

Goodnight my dear . . .

May 26th

My own dearest wee wife,

Here I am sitting on the top of a big grass embankment watching our big guns dealing out the best quality of stuff to those Huns. From here the German lines are plainly visible, and we can watch the result of the bombardment and note its effect. Last night the whole sky was just one continual sheet of flame, now brighter for a moment as the guns' fire ebbed and flowed. Our big guns have been superb and we have watched the gunners at work, they are so keen and so nippy.

We moved at a couple of hours' notice to our present place of abode which is a bivouac camp. That is the men are living under blankets thrown over a little frame and the officers are living in red and brown (dirt-coloured) tents. Personally, it is far better than houses for the big guns send all the tiles on the roofs scattering everywhere. We move back into the line tomorrow morning at 5 am and we are bound to be very busy, so that there will not be many facilities for writing letters but please don't worry or forget your old husband if there should be some days' delay in letters, particularly as there is nothing very new to tell you apart from this day-to-day routine of terror and horror.

Give Deckie a big kiss and tell him to hold and kiss his mummy for his daddy and tell him to be a good and loving boy and not to worry his tiny wee sweetheart mother. We have been so happy together dearie and if the Boche lands a shell on top of me please remember our great and good times together. The best thing I have ever done is the marrying of my own dear wee wife.

Goodbye for the time, your loving . . .

MAY 28TH

My own wee woman,

We came out of the line yesterday for what we thought was to be about ten days' spell but it is only a joke, we go back into the line on Wednesday. Anyway it is really a treat to be out even for a few days, the sleep that one misses in the trenches is what tells. The area we are in is a tremendously hot one, the amount of stuff that the Hun hurled at us was astounding, the minenwerfers are really awesome stuff. However we did not stick it out for nothing. We really gave him more than he bargained for and he was very loath to start a strafe and when he did commence it, it was always us who said when it was to finish. He fairly got belted sometimes and he won't forget the few days opposite us.

We are in billets, very good ones considering we are so far forward. There are some magnificent chateaux here.[11] Some of the gardens are beautiful, just like botanical gardens only there are no inhabitants. Almost every inhabitant has been cleared out and some took precious little clearing, for in this house the blinds are still up, the furniture is all here, the clothes are all left in the wardrobes and drawers, boots are still in the boot boxes, ladies' hats and some bundles of unmade up costumes are on a shelf in my roof; every other house is the same, just looks as if the inhabitants bolted last night, poor beggars. I'm afraid some of them will find something missing but on the whole things are wonderfully well looked after.

Yes, that was poor dear old Paddy Jekyll who was killed, what a splendid fellow he was. I am sure I never met a nicer fellow. Captain MacDonald and Captain Yule who were killed at the same time were with us at Troon and only recently joined up with the 13th Royal Scots. We have sent old Pagan away as an instructor at the school for a while. He will be away for a couple of months so will be out of harm's way for some time and by the time he returns to us he will be just about due for another leave.

I only wish my leave would hurry up and come around again. I am very keen to get back to the dearest wee folk of mine who love their old daddy so much. Don't think those two dear wee ladies will get any fatter. I am afraid they don't get enough cuddling up these days, that's what is the matter with them. I am so sorry to hear your poor wee back isn't too well again, dearest. I am thinking of you. I am very tired today, I've not had any sleep to speak of for the past six days.

Your tired old sweetheart . . .

MAY 30TH
In billets

Here it is raining again like old boots but never mind we are not in the smelly old trenches and it is ideal weather for a long lay-in, in the morning. We are just about 1400 yards behind the firing line and living in a very big house, a house that the occupants left pretty quickly as all the clothes, linen, dresses, hats, crockery and furniture is still in their places. Big mirrors and chests of drawers full of ladies' clothes. All the houses are very much in the same state, it all looks so sad and desolate.

There is one really most magnificent place here built on the top of a high and very steep cutting, with huge caves and grottoes and the most lovely swimming bath in the centre of the garden. The garden is exquisite, the roses and poppies are just rare but the whole place is overgrown and there is no one living there. Two or three big shells have gone through the roof and the people just bolted, leaving things as they were. The conservatories are still wonderful.

The Colonel[12] is off on leave tonight — rather a forced leave and I hardly think we will see him back in the battalion. He has been all nerves and jumps and used to imagine every shell that burst and every one that screamed overhead either from our own guns or from the enemy was going to land on his dugout. He had Major Rose and I just about rattled in the trenches, it's quite bad enough there when things are pretty hot without someone trying to get one's wind up. Major Rose will, I think, be made the CO and I hope so, he is so cool and calm and more reasonable.

The Colonel was a splendid soldier, very game and he knew his job, but he was very trying. He is going to Troon so no doubt you will see him in a day or two and he will give you all the news there is. We go back into the trenches on Wednesday for another spell and so must just stick it out. I hope the rain has cleared off by then as the mud in the trenches does smell so horrible. There are many Frenchmen buried in the parapets and some are very near the surface and in the hot sun it is not very nice.

Today we actually had a gooseberry pie made from gooseberries we collected in the garden here. This is a very rich district in fruits and in a very short while all the various fruits will be ripening. Pears, apples are getting big and plump. I went into one or two empty houses today and at last we came on one in which there was a lovely bath. A big old tiled one and we (Bunkey) had a rare old tub and got rid of most of the beasties. Thank you so much for the new soaps, they are so nice and make one feel clean and free from the beasties. Hope you had a good time with Mrs Greig in Glasgow. I expect you bought some nice new clothes and hope you will get a nice photograph taken of yourself. The Troon photographer takes nice ones, I believe, so you must get some taken and send me and also send some out to Australia. The poor Australians seem to be getting any amount of casualties in the sector they are in, one or two I know have been killed.

Well sweetheart, I have got a naughty French book that Lawrence lent me so now that it is raining I am going to get into bed and read it if I can and then I will go off to sleep.

My dearest little family, I love you all . . .

MAY 31ST

Just a few lines in time to catch the mail as we go back into the trenches today.[13] The time seems to fly when one comes out but it hangs very heavily in the line. I don't know when we come out, I expect it will be the usual five days in and then I think we are really due a good spell out, we will have done six days in the trenches longer than anyone else in the brigade.

It's a very anxious bit of the line here. The trenches are so close and so much heavy stuff is sent flying about and then there is the continual mining going on.

The Colonel left yesterday, the whole thing is more or less wrapped in mystery. He never applied for leave, got a ticket sent to him saying to start next morning. He has been terribly worried and nervous about this portion of the line and for the whole time we were in I don't think there was anyone who worked so hard, he was on the go the whole time.

I rather think that he is a bit too old and worries too much. Major Rose is now in command and will no doubt be given full command as I don't think they will bring the CO back. I rather think he will find another letter to that effect when he reaches home.

Major Rose and I get on famously and do far more work with less trouble. The CO was so nervy and did worry us all so much. Do you remember that man we met in the Trocadero, Lieutenant Robertson of the Camerons, he was in the Scouts[14] with me. I saw that his name was amongst the killed in yesterday's *Times*.

I got the list of grads, also the notice about Kathleen McMurray. Who is the Doris Ashbury referred to, Petty? I seem to know the name, I wonder if it is a relative of the wee woman of the same name who gave up that name to be the best wee wife in the world. Perhaps you can tell me.

It is not nice to think about going back to the trenches tonight. It would not have been so bad if we had not made up our minds to a long spell out; however it is all in the game and the time will pass. The Boche shelled us here in billets, not very badly, sent over twelve shrapnel bursts. There was a football match on in the town square at the time and it did not take the players and crowd long to disappear. Of course the ubiquitous Taube was above waving directions to his guns. Our artillery here is splendid, we have far heavier stuff behind us here than we ever had before and when we call for retaliation the guns do send it over to the gentle Hun.

Well, my dearest, if you see the Colonel he can tell you all the news about us. I see that Mrs U has not been too well. The other day in *The Times* I noticed a birth notice to Mr and Mrs John Atlee-Hunt so I sent a postcard of congratulations. They live in Devonshire. I had a fine letter from Atlee-Hunt thanking me and telling me all the family news. I would like you to send the letter on to Lill, as she is very interested. They asked you, wee Derick and me to visit them in Devon, they live in a place called Crediton, the older people live in Southampton. It would suit us both fine to have a leave away in the south of England, sounds so far from here. I'll write to them to see if they could find a nice place for you and Deckie to wait for me. Write to me and tell me what you think of the plan.

All my love, a rather hurried note . . .

la Boisselle

51 HIGHLAND DIVISION

MESSAGES AND SIGNALS.

Words	Charge	This message is on a/c of:	Recd.
Sent At ... m.		... Service.	Date...
To...			From...
By...		(Signature of "Franking Officer.")	By...

19.1.16

Day of Month | In reply to Number

June

FRIDAY, JUNE 2ND
In the trenches

Dearest wee wife,

Things are comparatively quiet at the moment, Major Rose is down at the front line with the General,[1] I had a good night's sleep and so I thought it just best to take the opportunity for sending you a few lines. The weather has improved tremendously, the trenches have dried up nicely and only for the aggressiveness of our friend across the way, life would just now be reasonably comfortable.

Yesterday I was just absolutely dull, dead-dog weary. The Hun commenced to hate us at 3 am and never let up all day, but about 8 pm he quietened down, and we were thinking he was about as fed up as we were but just at 10.15 pm he rocked in the stuff to us, 5.9s, whizz-bangs and shrapnel came over, it lasted for about twenty minutes. I never had it like it before, we phoned thro' for heavy retaliation and our own gunners just socked it home, and soon quietened the Boche.[2] You would have thought that no mortal being could have passed through it and come out alive. Again and again the shells hit our dugout, all the candles were blown out as fast as we could light them down in the dugout, and still our casualties were surprisingly light. It is now 11 am and things are quiet and peaceful, an occasional gun and some trench mortars and an odd oil can coming over, but I expect that the volcano will erupt again later today.

We come out again on Sunday and move back for a well-earned rest indeed. The knowledge that this sector is subjected to gas attacks and the continual thought of mining gets on one's nerves a bit, and sleep, when it does come, is so deep from exhaustion that one feels all the good in the world from it. Last night I got on to the floor in the dugout at 12 midnight and never knew a thing till 8.30 am; it was just grand.

I had a letter from Sgt Major Burchell, who wrote to say he was out of hospital but had been declared medically unfit for further active service, he was so cut up about it. He is to get a special job at the base and no one deserves a good soft job better than Burchell, a splendid old chap he was, did a great deal for us and was invaluable as a guide, philosopher and friend to me.

Perhaps you may have seen the Colonel by now and got all the news about us. I don't know what the strength of his sudden leave means, and so far I don't know if he is coming back. I know he was given leaves which he did not apply for. I wish that some of the powers that be would suddenly fancy that I was in need of ten days' leave and send me a ticket. Do you know that the CO went to brigade HQ and protested that he was in no need of leave, that he did not want to go a bit. If I get the chance I know there will be no second questions or doubts. I am pleased to hear that you soon go to Kilmalcolm,[3] it will be a nice change for you both. I will imagine and dream of you there.

A big black and white German dog came across into our lines last night. It was captured by Capt. Gee who sent it down to me. I think he must have been a regimental pet, and not a patrol dog as he is so quiet and friendly to be a well-trained and useful dog. I don't know what we will do with him.

Dearest wee lump of love and gladness of mine, goodbye for the moment, look after yourselves, all four of you, love

PS. *Those are very interesting pictures in the* Sketch, dated *May 24th, not the* Penny Edition, *the* Illustrated Sketch.

JUNE 5TH
In billets

That you are getting another letter from me, sweetheart of mine, is more by good luck than good management. I'm beginning to think, dearest, that the fates that control our destinies have agreed amongst themselves that you and I have not yet had enough life and love to grow tired of each other and they have spared me.

We came out of the trenches yesterday morning and returned here to our billets and now will be here for eight days.[4] We had a perfectly fiendish time, the worst we have had by a thousand times. All the while the Hun had been battering us but each night at a different time he would swing on to us and just blather away with every kind of contraption but it only used to last for ten minutes and as soon as our guns cracked out he would draw in his horns and cry 'enough', but on the morning of the 30th he commenced at 3 am and started to register the range with big guns over all the salient points, such as HQ, communication trenches, signal station etc. etc. Once he got the range he knocked off firing. At 3 pm the same day he woke up again and plastered us for ten minutes with everything he had, then left us, but he did a fair bit of damage, yards and yards of trenches blown in, men buried deep under the debris. Major Bruce's Coy was hit really badly. At 11.30 pm he again walloped us with shrapnel, oil cans and machine guns and then, after our artillery shook him up he subsided till twelve minutes to 1 am, commencing with salvo after salvo of heavy stuff. I have never heard anything like it, oil cans, trench mortars and gas shells, for an hour, it was hell let loose. Miserable. We got a direct hit on our dugout, 5.9 and gas. It was a dark night and within two minutes every telephone wire was cut, except those running back so that we were cut off from all company communication. The shelling was just terrific,[5] one could not get in touch with our own guns for some time, there was a terrific how do you do on our left and right — we knew that there was an attack coming — there was a tornado of crashes, HQ was reduced to smoking, deadly rubble, almost every trench was ironed out, and nothing could get through. I was outside watching for attacks, supplementary signals and the gas alarm. The Hun guns lifted on to our supports, that is over our heads, the object being to stop reinforcements, then the gas and tear shells came across. The shrapnel was awful, you would imagine that no one could live outside when suddenly a messenger rushed in, in a state of collapse. He had no goggles on and the tear shells had blinded him. What a noble fellow, name of Carswell from Major Bruce. The report he carried said that Bruce was having a bad time but he had the situation in hand, and the men were magnificent. I could get no news from Lawrence, so called for a volunteer runner and Hunter stepped up; off he went. He could not go in the trenches as they were filled in, so he went 'cross country' and got Lawrence and brought back a message for Bruce which was reassuring.

The men were grand, they were just wonderful; by the time our guns were busy, the artillery wire was repaired and I got through to them and they started and just gave the Hun perfect hell. We watched the shells bursting in his lines, hundreds of them, then on our right, up went the signal to attack, rockets. They soared up into the sky. In a second everyone was about, everyone groping to his place, sick with gas and then the rapid rifle and machine gun fire rattled, like nothing on earth and we knew the Hun was hit. The artillery was superb, the shrapnel just screamed into the Hun; the firing suddenly took a funny sound on our right. I got called to the phone, had to crawl along to it, over wounded men and they told me the Hun was in our trenches on the right, that is into the next battalion line; he did not get into ours.

Oh it was so grand, the men were superb, and ready for anything. The Colonel of the artillery phoned me to say a counter-attack was being launched to shift the Hun and asked me if we were alright and if he could swing in and assist in our right. I asked him to keep three guns going on our front, firing shrapnel to keep their machine guns and rifles down as we were being so badly treated as we had no cover in many places. He was pleased and away went the stuff on to the Hun, the counter was successful and in about twenty minutes I was phoned and told that all the Huns were out and that we had some prisoners and that none of our men were captured. Wasn't it grand, if only you could have seen our men, they were superb, not a bit 'windy' just ready for anything. By 4 am everything was quiet and we commenced to dig out men and bits of men. Considering all, we had few casualties but lost some fine men. Our artillery fired 10 000 rounds in less than two hours. The gunners were like galley slaves, stripped to the waist with gas helmets, and certainly looked a little weird.

Now that it is all over it is grand to have been through, the men could never be harder tested. The General was just delighted and so complimentary that I almost cried when he thanked us for our rattling part in the stunt. I am so thankful no Hun got into our trenches. All our officers were splendid, Major Rose was in command. He and I of course had an anxious time especially when the wires went. Major Rose is a splendid commander, so cool and calm. Do write and congratulate Mrs R. He also thanked me for my support and my share of the stunt which was chiefly crawling to the telephone wire and phoning the Brigade and collecting information.[6] It was a glorious experience and worth a lot of trench discomfort to share in it. We are now relieved and after tomorrow are to commence a ten days' intensive training and will then possibly move to a new billeting area.

Today we are all resting and going to a cinema show tonight; such is a soldier's life. Would it not have been awful to have failed, but no, we triumphed. We won out hands down, but was I tired. It is a very hot corner here, and no doubt we will get a repeat dose soon, and I'm sure our gallant boys will come out again on top.

I stood at the head of a trench when we were relieved[7] and watched our chaps come out after four days of it, four days of practically continuous action, four days during which the wind was favourable to gas, when no man dare shut an eye. The men were dirty, unshaven, hollow eyed and hungry looking but all had that fine inexpressible look of men who have won. Gas shells are awful things, the eyes just gush with tears in a second, one cannot see but the goggles are good.

I was standing with Brand for a time; he was not in action, one of his guns got an oil can on the top and was wiped out and he couldn't get down to the other one so great was the curtain of Hun shrapnel. A Hun shell burst on the parapet right above our heads, what a crash and an avalanche of clay and slate. Our dugout stood up alright and as well it did as we crammed it full. It got some awful crumps on the top and one or two more would have come through. The holes were big enough to put a cart in.

Well things in general seem to have been lively, the naval scrap[8] was a big thing. Of course it was one squadron of ours up against the High Sea Fleet and when all facts are known we won't have come off so badly.

All along the line things are active. Verdun is rattling away again, I think more than ever now that is a death struggle of the Hun. He realises that the blockade is something and that our men are almost ready to give him the lot.

And now so much for the soldier's life, but what about a soldier's wife, dearest wee love of mine, even in the most awful part of the scrap I could see your own dear face and hear your soft voice, and Deckie's wee prattle. How much I needed to be with you, to feel love and warmth in this loveless cold inhuman part of the world.

I must set about the business of the battalion, so much to be done, so much equipment gone, casualties to be attended to, to be straightened out, mothers and sweethearts to be written to; a sad task.

All my love dearest sweetheart mother of our son . . .

JUNE 8TH
Billets

Comparative calm and quiet again reigns supreme, and we are doing some intensive training. General Williams is a veritable glutton for work, at least he sees that we keep at it, however it is just as well, the men get slack in the trenches and apart from that one wants a great deal of continual hard work to keep fit and stick out the trench spell.

It is so funny the way we settle down here. One day in the trenches, getting knocked about, then some military funerals, some vague regrets and we forget. Isn't it lucky we can forget so readily. It's raining again here, it commenced yesterday where we were on manoeuvres and as we were moving through wheat and barley up to our chins you can guess how uncomfortable it is. I got wet and overheated with the result that I broke out in a rare crop of hives, most uncomfortable things they are.

I expect everyone is aghast at the end of Lord K[9] and his staff, it was a fitting end to a big life and just like Roberts, he died in harness. There is no doubt that some spy knew about his movements.

Things are merry on all the fronts just now. The Russians are on the move again and are more than making their presence felt in amongst the Austrian circles. It ought to relieve the Italian front a bit, for the Italians were getting in a bad way. Things on the whole are not bad, I mean the war outlook. The Hun is showing a certain amount of activity, but I fancy that Verdun is taking the sting out of him. His recent push at Ypres, against the Canadians was a local matter and the Canadians have the situation in hand, I fancy he is a good deal hungrier than a while back.

The naval battle seems to have been about a draw, perhaps the honours slightly on our side. We all feel that the Hun's object was to sneak through but he is back in the old hole patching up a pretty sore head. Of course his hurts cannot yet be gauged.

The parcel came today with the socks and the three *Bulletins*, it is a long time since I had a *Bully*,[10] and they are very much appreciated by all although the dear old Scotties have a modicum of difficulty with the Aussie humour.

Well, my dearest there is not a lot of news, thank heaven. Captain Greig is on leave again, I hear his father is dying. Leave has been cut again, what a pest, but we believe that a big push is on the books. Leave is supposed to be once every three months, but most of our junior officers have been out here for five or six months. The delay in leave puts us all back.

I am glad that you are having Dr Hogg to see Deckie. I hope that you also consulted him about yourself. You are too young and full of life to be feeling tired and listless, Pettie mine. Make sure that you take all the right foods and get yourself sprightly, with those two dear wee fat ladies. You will both have a great old time in Kilmalcolm. Well, dearest I'm off to take a hot bath, at least I'm going to get into a tub, or rather a modified cask.

Goodnight my lover . . .

JUNE 12TH
In training billets

My dearest wee woman,
I expect you will be thinking that I have forgotten all about you and Deckie, but you know sweetie, that isn't possible, I'm afraid I think too much and too often about you both.

We have been working tremendously hard, talk about a rest. I would, and I know all the men would sooner be in the trenches than doing all the work we have been doing the last eight days! The country here is very hilly and is really ideal for training, but every single day we have been at it with the whole brigade. The training area[11] is six miles out, and we march there and back. Breakfast is at 5.30 am, leave here at 7 am, march the six miles then train over miles and miles of countryside all day, then march back to billets, then I start my day's work in the office. The weather has been vile too, rain, rain, rain and everything is inches deep in mud.

We go up into the front line on Thursday or Friday, not certain, but what is certain is that as soon as we get there we will commence to grizzle. We must be allowed to grizzle as it is our one prerogative and though we grizzle like fury at the time, we like talking about it afterwards.

Well, what do you think about the Russians now, the old steamroller seems to have got a bit of a roll up and is ironing out things on the Eastern front. The Austrians seem to have been quite surprised and unable to do anything. A funny old French town crier went thro' this village last night playing a kettle drum and making a public announcement. He looked so funny, like an old Toreador who had had the worst of a tussle with a bull.

Poor old Kitchener has gone, right enough, it is sad isn't it, that he should end his day by being drowned. It really won't affect our plans or military operations. I hardly think he has been taking a leading part in these matters for a considerable time now; however he would have been very valuable in the peace discussions for he was a greater statesman than an actual soldier. Sir William Robertson[12] is the man at the wheel just now, and for some time past.

The Russians will ease the weight on the Italian front, at the same time many troops from here will be recalled by the Hun for provided the Russians have all the munitions they require, it is going to take a tremendous army of the Hun to hold him back. I think that brother Russki is in deadly earnest this time and that Luneberg and Warsaw will soon fall. Now is the time for Roumania to hop in, if she wants to. Things look brighter now than ever before for an early peace. There are of course too many Huns left; if the Kaiser had a chance for peace, he would jump at it.

Won't it be a dream when peace does come, when we can all come home for good, what a time, time for some real life together, let's take a wee small secret place, somewhere near Edinburgh. Then Deckie will be learning his ABC and saying all sorts of things, some to embarrass his dear sweet mother. I think that first we must have a holiday together. A houseboat on the Ouse at Huntingdon would be charming, and a world away from this place. If peace comes in the autumn, the tints are breathtaking. Deckie and I could go fishing, and you could sit on the bank, and read in the sun. Is this a dream or could this madness ever stop?

Tonight I am going to a cinema show. I've been once or twice, and it was not bad. The pictures are shown in an old barn that has been shelled to pieces; there is just one house a night and we all must wait till it gets dark. The men are naturally very keen on it.

Major Rose rode over to see the HLI[13] people the other day before yesterday and he saw Jim Overstone, who is groom to the Colonel over there. Overstone asked after me. They have had extraordinarily few casualties, but the poor Colonel was hit by a falling tile from a rooftop dislodged by a chook!

Yesterday we were paraded by the General[14] and thanked and congratulated for our conduct in the recent action. Everyone is tremendously bucked with us and we have come in for no end of praise, it is all very nice after so much hard work. Believe me, Pettie, I get more than my share of hard work.

Dearest old woman, here is all my love for you both. Deckie must be growing into a real man now. I'm glad you have seen Dr Hogg, and I hope that the tonic puts you on top again.

And now, dear, delightful little woman, all love . . .

JUNE 14TH

My dearest wee wife,
We are about to move up into fighting billets tonight and on into the line[15] tomorrow, to the right of where we were before, on the next frontage, where the gentle Boche got into the line. It has been raining cats and dogs for the last four days so that the trenches will be awful. We are to be in for eight days, that is four in the line and four in support, and will then come back to these so-called rests. There has not been much resting done the last few days as we have been doing most intensive training; all the same, it does everyone good and gets one fit for a long spell in the trenches which tends to makes one soft, fat and lazy. The worst thing in the whole business is the lack of sleep.

There are great rumours reaching us here, from peace negotiations to a big naval battle and of course the Russian push. The Russians seem to be in deadly earnest, and should have taken Czernowitz[16] by the time this letter reaches you. Lucky letter, oh that I could be this letter.

Last night there was a terrible bombardment, on the front, to the east of us. We sat up and listened to it. Some poor devils were really getting it, don't know who they were, we have not heard who got it and who did not.

All the roads are avenued with beautiful apple trees and our hungry eyes are watching as the apples fatten and ripen. I heard the first nightingalc in my life yesterday, he was singing in an apple tree just above our tents and was great though not as good as I thought he would be.

Dearest, I must close now, my love and thoughts with you as always, bless you both . . .

JUNE 16TH

My own dearest wee sweet wife,
Here we are back in the line and fortunately things are a bit quiet just at the moment. There is a good deal of shelling going on but it is going well back and high over our heads so that we can only hear it gurgling and chuckling as it passes overhead; now and again an oil can or a big sausage mortar shell bursts in our front, frightful things they are.

For the past few weeks I have been busier than I have ever been since I came out. Whilst we were in the billets at the back or reserve area we were doing intensive training, out all day long on all kinds of stunts so that I never got a minute to get near the office work, which always just piles up whenever things are exceptionally busy. The war will never finish whilst brigade and divisions have an unlimited supply of paper and ink!!

We moved into a huge chateau situated exquisitely in a magnificent wood. The place must have been an ideal one before this mess, certainly the biggest one we have seen yet, but sadly battered to pieces. It is all of stone and at one time had a beautiful slate roof, none left now. All the walls show remains of the paper which had made the rooms so gracious.

Now it is only a pile of stone and skeleton rooms, with all kinds of cellars and dugouts underneath. In the centre of the wood is a cemetery, a soldiers' cemetery, set in such a gentle wood, so sad. Running up to the main entrance is, or was, a wonderful avenue of what had been huge trees, probably at least 100 years old. The shell fire has cut off every tree just above the ground. We only stayed that night with all the ghosts, one could imagine the cheery French family, enjoying life, not imagining their fate. We were not sorry to get away and back into the trenches.

Many of our trenches are better, and some of the dugouts are steel-lined, but not so much earth on top as before. I must say that I do like to have a good thickness of chalk over my head, the last one was at least fifteen feet down. However this one has a nice table and a floor that keeps the horrible rats down a bit.

Since the last rain it has been very cold, which is hard on the men as they have no blankets at all, but they don't seem to mind. I am trying to get a lot of blankets we found in a chateau, should make a bit of a help to the wonderful chaps.

Everything is so pretty here, nature is doing her best to make up for what humanity is doing. The beautiful red poppies and blue cornflowers are running riot. Here and there we come upon a heap of bricks and burnt up iron and huge banks of peonies, the only indication of a one time house and garden.

We hear of the Russian steamroller; I imagine that it is on everyone's lips at home. By all accounts the advance was more like the spurts and stops of a Sydney tram than a steamroller. I was so sorry to see in the Casualty lists that Cathcart's[17] son paid the supreme sacrifice. I am so sorry for the old man, I will drop him a line. He was with the RFA, a very fine fellow.

Well my dear wee Pettikins, how are the two young ladies and dear Derick? How I long for you both, each in a different way, it seems as if leave will never come. We are hearing lots of rumours of a huge offensive, perhaps by the month's end, I am afraid of what may be the result. If things ever settle down there will be plenty of leave going. But at the moment there is so much activity on all fronts and sectors, everyone is watching and holding their breaths. The Australians seem to be having no end of raids on the Hun. It is so interesting to us to read the news of these raids as we were in the sector there for ten weeks and all know every inch of the ground.

The daylight saving scheme has been introduced here, and now we all get up an hour earlier. It doesn't really affect us at all except for meals as in the trenches we always are on duty one hour before dawn whatever the time is. Dawn is our zero hour, and the rising hour is zero minus sixty as it is technically called.

I got the parcel you sent, dearest wee wife of mine, the one with the socks, the chocolate and the cotton singlet, thank you so much, my dear. I like the cotton singlets well, as they keep off the horrid lice, they are nice and clean and refreshing always to put on. The make is just fine, like everything you do, don't worry.

Give my dear son a hug and tell him his daddy is winning the war, and he loves to hear how he is looking after his mother.

I must hurry to get some sleep while it is quiet, just all my love . . .

JUNE 17TH

My own dear sweetheart,

Mails have been very mixed up but today I received your letter and the parcel, I am so lucky. Sweeties and a fruit cake, which was too rich and sweet for me. I imagine it's something to do with our diet in the trenches — it used to be my favourite. Thank you all the same, it's so nice to have things from your own lover.

The snaps are so good, I love to see you both again. I am so glad you got a game of tennis. Yes, dearie, we did have a raid the other night, no warning, but we held the Hun alright and can do so again. The regiment was splendid and I don't think that it will be possible to have a worse bombardment.

Things have been very quiet so far in the front line this time, but it is a nasty piece of the line and anything is liable to spring up at a moment's notice. The lines are so close, in one section we are just eighteen yards from the Hun. We can hear them talking, particularly in the quiet hours near dawn; I imagine they listen to us. The ground is also tactically very difficult.

I am enclosing a letter from Rene, you will see she is keen to have some snaps of you and Deckie. Give our darling wee son so much love from his daddy, and tell him to give his mummy a big kiss and hug. This is just a little note, my dearest, to tell you how brave you both are.

Goodbye for the present, all my love . . .

[Undated]
In fighting billets

Here we are, dear heart, out of the line again and appreciating very much the change.[18] We are in a village just behind the line and it is quite a pretty place, but just crammed, jammed with khaki. We got out last night at midnight, and I found all the Australian mail waiting for me, such a lovely mail it was and best of all a nice long letter from you. I can't tell you how your letters help me in this time, and to hear all about Deckie. I'm so glad that you are getting some tennis. So you are off to Kilmalcolm on the 28th, indeed a most momentous day, isn't it or won't it be? The sands at Troon are ideal for him to stretch his little legs.

We are so busy here, something is up; no doubt, we will hear sometime soon. Work never stops, new stuff piling up all the time. All the casualties make a great deal of correspondence, and routine work. Today we got six new officers, I'm so glad, as it eases off the duties of the subs a bit. For six months now they have been hard at it without leave. No raids for some days, but ten Hun planes came out at us one day, immediately our own men went at them, not a moment's hesitation and the Hun just bolted, one of their machines came down. Nothing else but a collection of TMs and oil cans; one gets so used to such things they are hardly noticed.

Wasn't that a nice long letter from Vera, she seems to be very keen on Jack Hoskings. I only hope that he comes through alright. By the time he reaches the front the Hun will be on the run, and squealing like the pig he is.

We are all tremendously fit and keen as mustard. The Russians are still letting them know what sort of ammunition they have, there cannot be many Austrians left. I don't think the Austrians are too keen on things just now. Wait till one of these days when we get a smack at the Prussian pigs opposite us, then there will be some excitement.

Tell Nancy that one of my best pals here, Father Crottee, has gone from the brigade, his place taken by a new priest. The old man had a bad heart and has gone back behind the forward area.

Yes, dearest sweet wife, I too will be glad when all is over and we have settled the vexed questions out here, to return to my own dear little family. Then I think that we all will have such a loving time together. You have been just the dearest and bravest little woman, such a loving and true wife, and if I come through all this safely, there is to be so much love and joy in store for us, so much of the real happiness and won't it just be too good for words to get back to everyone in Australia, it is so much to look forward to. I am not going to get a lot of time to write to Australia, till next mail.

Everyone got a great surprise to see Sir Geo. McCrae's[19] name in the 'mentioned' list and no one can understand. Two COs in each brigade seem to have been 'mentioned' but I don't know under what heading. The 16th Royal Scots have not done as many turns in the trenches as we have, and they have never yet had the strafing that we got the night of the raid. Major Tyler of the 101st Brigade staff also got a mention, but why I can't imagine. He was a perfect nuisance on the staff, it would be interesting to find out how they arrange the mentions. Sir Geo. of course raised his own battalion at the beginning and that no doubt has something to do with it. Of course the mentions are dated April 30th, and up to that time all the trench warfare had been in the other sector, where, compared with here, everything was quiet and safe. This is a real hot corner, and is known as the 'Glory Hole'.[20] Anyway the mention has put Sir Geo. in fine fettle, I'm sure he would do anything for me. I congratulated him yesterday in the trenches, he was tremendously bucked about it, thanked me most profusely and insisted on me having a drink and a sandwich.

The third anniversary of our wedding is quietly coming around again. It is just three months to the day since I came home on leave and found you asleep. I would not give up those three years for anything. The only thing that may interfere is a big lump of shrapnel and even that, sweetie, would not stop me loving you. I do so long for you both and at times it makes me so very sad, but I know that you, in your own way, are glad that I am over here fighting and I know that Derick, bye and bye, will be so proud and so glad too that his 'Daddy was a soldier too and not afraid to die'. It would have been just awful to have stayed at home as a slacker and to be dragged into it by the scruff of the neck. Thank heavens, I never had the inclination to do that.

All my long and loving thoughts for you both who are so dear and always so near to me. Goodbye, dear little woman and bless your dear warm heart. I do not think I will get much time to write over the next few days, something is up, watch *The Times*, and say a prayer for us all. I have just been telling the lads that it is no sin to be afraid, I wish I could believe it.

All my love forever, till the end of time . . .

This was the last letter written before the Great Offensive of 1 July. Battalions up and down the line, from Verdun to south of Albert, were totally preoccupied with preparations for the Great Offensive.[21]

la Boisselle

MESSAGES AND SIGNALS. No. of

Words | Charge

This message is on a/c of:

Service.

(Signature of "Franking Officer.")

Sent At m. To By

Recd. Date. From By

19:1:16

Day of Month | In reply to Number

July

July 5th

Well sweetheart,

What to say and how to begin. I am sure I don't know. First I am alright, never got a scratch, but oh so close so many times. It was all so magnificent, so awful, so sad and ghastly. The bombardment was terrific, just one continual roar, roar, roar. Not a moment's cessation, the greatest bombardment ever carried out by the British in any war and we sat underneath it for seven days, such long, long sleepless days, such horribly anxious nights and so much work to be done.

Of course we knew for six weeks before, that the attack was coming off and ye gods how the men worked. The trenches they dug, the overhead ladders they made and put up, the thousands and thousands of trench mortar shells we carried up to the lines at night, the aerial torpedoes, the bombs and the millions of rounds of ammunition and the gas cylinders. The men almost were worked to death but they were so cheerful, everyone's idea being to do his utmost for the big push.

Then the day for the bombardment to commence arrived. We were holding the line at the time and our guns just roared, not only our HA but every sort and size. The ground just trembled the whole time and the noise was just deafening and awful. We fairly smothered the Hun, his trenches were just ironed out, shells streamed over in the thousands all day and all night. At night the whole sky was crimson with flashes. The first two days the German guns replied with everything they had and poured stuff into us but we were too strong, had far too much weight, we just smothered them with everything.[1] Then it commenced to rain and rain and rain and the trenches became awful, blown-in here and there. They soon became a bog, then we went out for two nights' rest and came in on the 29th of June and took up our battle positions in the jumping off trenches as we were to lead the attack. We found the trench drying up but in places very bad. It was very cold. We were not allowed to bring any blankets or Army great coats, just battle kit. The bombardment was just incessant and three of four times a day would reach a maximum. We gave them gas and smoke and got them fair rattled and their trenches were a sight. Then on the night of the 30th everything was ready and everyone in his place.

At 7.30 am on the 1st of July after a hurricane bombardment we had 'up and over' and into the thick of it. Oh the agony of the long night wait and the slow long grey minutes when the dawn crept in. No one slept. It was a beautiful morning but we were all too excited, strained and frightened to really appreciate it. There was a fine mist, but it did little to filter the sun, rising behind the German lines. The Virgin could just be seen, above the mist.

The guns at 6.25 am just poured out shrapnel and high explosives and the barb wire entanglements and parapets just flew like chaff. The Boche have taken a terrible hiding. At a couple of minutes to zero, zero being 7.30 am, two mines went up just on our left and then over into No Man's Land went the first line. Oh! it was cruel but magnificent. The German[2] rifle and machine gun and shrapnel just screamed, it was terrible how anything could live in it.

At zero the guns lifted on to the Hun's second line and like magic our men in the first line were on their feet and like arrows went for the first line and into the second, third and fourth followed. In eighteen minutes exactly we had passed over to the fourth line which was 2000 yards from the place we commenced and it was our objective — that is, it was just as far as we were expected to go.[3]

Once there we were to dig in and stay and had visions of relief on the 2nd of July. As we passed from line to line the Hun threw down his arms and said 'Pardon Kamerad' but as soon as we crossed he would turn his machine guns on us. The regiment on our left was late and did not get on too well so that our own left caught it. I can't go into details as to casualties, you will soon hear about it all. You will see it in the papers. It was all so grand, so tragic and so sad.

We had to hang on and fight like devils till the night of the third when we were relieved at midnight. We took many prisoners and the German casualties were very high, dead Germans everywhere. It is so hard to know what to tell about it and what not to tell. At present everything is so confused and I am so tired and knocked up from it all, but no doubt a few days' rest and it will set me up.

We are now in a canvas camp behind the line and last night watched the guns and listened to the roar as the battle progresses. I had no end of marvellous escapes, the nearest one being a 4.5 shell which came into the dugout, killed one signaller and wounded another. Three seconds before I was using the phone at which the signaller was killed. The back blast of the shell blew me right across the dugout and I think broke my hand. We are anxiously waiting to hear news of the push and are all hoping for papers, because they will no doubt have more details than we can get. General Pulteney, who commands the Fourth Army, paraded us today and thanked us all for our great deeds.

The men were really wonderful. They went over that parapet under the most murderous fire, it was quite mystical and weird to see men all moving along in line under such fire just as on a parade and then suddenly one more and then three together and so on just sink down never to rise again. The wounded were wonderful, not a whimper, not a moan, so patient and long-suffering, lying out in the sun for hours and hours. The Hun snipers sniped the wounded every time they started to try to crawl back to our line, this is quite a fact, we actually caught one doing it and he paid the penalty of his crime. The Hun trenches were splendidly made, very deep and splendid dugouts full of curios and the men got everything of interest they could collect, even a cat-o'-nine tails.

Well, dearest heart, it is all too sad and tragic to dwell on. I don't know our movements, possibly a rest and then at it again. At present I am dreadfully overworked and short handed. The casualty return is making no end of work and I have to try and trace every officer and man for the sake of his relatives. The men scattered and got mixed up so much and went in so many ambulances that it is chaos. Otherwise I am alright, just longing and longing to be with my own dear family so much.

It was all so hard and hopeless at times and when we had no sleep and no meals to speak of, so many wounded, so many things to do, I was so glad to know you and dear Deckie were safe and happy. I never expected to see either of you again. Just love the dear wee boy of our dear little mother. I would so love to see the dear little chap with his hair cut. Take some snaps quickly and send them over as we may be in action again very soon. Your letters I got when I came out. It was just lovely to have them and hear something about you both. Write and tell them about the battle at home and please keep all the papers that you can about the affair and then when I come home I can tell you all about it.

Major Rose is away, he has been given command of the 25th Northumberland Fusiliers (Tyneside Irish) so he won't be with us anymore. Keep all the casualty returns, dearest, and also any photos of any of our officers and men in the Edinburgh papers. I will just write as often as I can. It is my only line of sanity.

All my love,

JULY 7TH

Sweetheart of mine,

I am not going to tell you anything about the war, we are still resting in a canvas camp just behind the lines and the most intense fighting is going on. We move up tomorrow with the remnants of our regiment and go into support in one of the German trenches we occupied about a mile from where the battle is still raging. We've seen no papers and have little or no news as to what is going on. I have been recommended for the Military Cross, but I don't expect I will get it. My God, I did nothing, except what was my job, still the recommendation has gone in.

We are all so tired and worn out; the fighting was terrific, our men were more than men, how they could do it? The whole thing is a horrible nightmare, nothing could have prepared us for July 1st. You will see all the casualties in the papers, my darling. Will you keep all the papers for me? My love for you will save me from all this death. I am relatively unscathed, but may not be so lucky next time. Remember my love and tell our boy his daddy did his job.

Soon we will be relieved and then no doubt there will be some leave. Some men continue to straggle back to us, some dreadfully wounded, but not daring to move till darkness hides them from the Hun snipers. Some men got mixed up with other regiments, and were fighting all over the place, some lost for good in the trenches. Major Rose is back and is now the permanent CO of the battalion, and we are trying to reorganise a bit, for the next killing. I am sorry in a way to see the end of the last CO but he could be extraordinarily difficult at times. I was so sorry to see Geof Brand was killed, I must write to his people.

Our poor old regiment! The draft of fresh men has arrived, one sergeant, one corporal and about 35 men, keen but no experience. The battalion can never be the same. It's all so sad, but we did so well. We just flew to our objective, our assault on the four German lines was grand, the Hun will never forget the Royal Scots. We were up against the Bavarians.

The CO left for England yesterday. He was so broken up at the parting but he is too old and is just done to a turn. I have never seen anyone look so ill as he did.

I am alright, sweetheart of mine, only confused and tired. The bombardment seems to have dulled and deafened me. I only want to be with you and dear Derick. Can I ever hold you again, and I imagine that you have been so worried, by the news and not getting any mail, but, dearest, it will be a while till the mail gets any better. I am just dead to the world and done up.

The fighting was so savage, so absolutely all consuming, nothing else in the universe but to kill or be killed. We wiped them out, the men were up and over with bayonets, superb. For three days, 72 fearful hours it went on. We could not move our dead or wounded, who just lay around, in full view, calling for water; there was none. The Hun is a devil, waiting to see the men move, trying to escape, then shoot them. When cornered they cry out for mercy like babies. My sweet, there is no mercy here.

Everything I think is going alright, it is only a matter of time before he gives out. His defences were extraordinarily strong but we had the great honour to lead the attack, Sir D. Haig personally congratulated Rose and us all.

Dearest, remember that the few years we have had together have completely justified my life. If there is to be no more, then I go knowing of our love.

All my thoughts to you both . . .

JULY 9TH

Pettikins wee sweetheart,
A letter from you today, the first for some days. I was glad to have it and the dear wee 'Forget me Not'.

Well here we are, Pettie, resting in a kind of way, but everyone is confined to camp and we are ready to move forward now at half an hour's notice. I hope we have not got to push again; the men are really only just getting fit again after the awful time we had and they did so well, no regiment did so well, as you will see in the papers. We were the only unit that actually got right into the Hun with bayonet, a wild and bloodcurdling mêlée it was. The Hun did not stick it out long and then bolted and our men pinned him from the back. Man for man we just mopped them up, they could not stand up to us, but their machine guns were terrible, just ripped us about. They were so cunning and resourceful with machine guns and everyone seems to know how to use one.

One must not look too soon for a big crushing and brilliant victory, the Hun position here is tremendously strong. His trenches received the most awful shelling and were blown in for yards and yards, huge gaps, men were buried underneath it, passing along their trenches one met every here and there, hands and feet sticking out. Dozens and dozens met their death this way. Some parts of the line went more easily than others, but ours was the very hottest place. We hammered and hammered for three days. Three days and two nights we fought like devils, awful, the men were so tired that they just fell asleep standing up, we could not keep them awake. There were no stretcher bearers that could come across No Man's Land and the dead and the dying lay in the trenches all around us.

In my own dugout, the signal station for advanced battle HQ, I had poor old Lawrence, badly smashed, what a hero the way he stuck it out. He was shot first of all through the ankle and was hobbling to the dressing station when he was blown into a dugout, which collapsed and buried him. White and I extricated him and then a bomb in his pocket exploded; he will lose his legs, shot to ribbons. Gee was awfully smashed too, about the legs and body, he will never be right again, poor game chap. He went away with a joke on his lips after lying for 48 hours in No Man's Land in the blazing sun, without water.

Douglas had 48 hours in NML, both hands and one leg gone, had plenty of water, but could not open his canteen. I saw him leading his platoon with great gallantry, just as he was hit. Major Bruce was killed at the German front line trench, Brough and Reid at the same place in NML and Brand, Dougal and Grant killed at the German third line trench. Brand was a splendid boy, such a game fellow, he was shot through the neck and died instantly. He was in my dugout till 1 am on the morning of the attack. We talked about our lives, about you and the war, and when we shook hands and said goodbye to go to our respective stations he was so keen and so confident; two hours later he was dead. Today I have been writing to all their relatives, a very sad and horrible occupation but one can so easily write about them all. They were so gallant and game and all died just glorious deaths.

Major Stocks and Hole are both missing and were both wounded. When last I heard of Stocks he had been wounded twice, and was lying in a trench, from which the Hun drove us with a savage and overwhelming counter-attack. We came again at them and won it back but poor Stocks and Hole were gone. Lieutenant McArthur was shot through the groin, but kept going all day. Pinkerton and Brown were caught on the German wire, were riddled with bullets, Brown had 17 bullet wounds. The brutes shot every wounded man who moved or stirred.

Robson did wonderfully well, splendid and an absolutely untiring example to everyone, he fought like a mad man. Richardson, one of my orderly runners, carried some messages for me under murderous fire, at one stage there were three machine guns trying to get him. My other runner, Simmonds, was hit in the throat and McHardie, the CO's runner, you remember him, he used to drive the car, was buried for some hours and now is unable to talk.

We were up against the Bavarians and the Prussians, great hulking big coarse brutes up to everything that was cunning and dirty, but they surrendered at once when they saw the bayonets and grovelled at one's feet offering watches etc. I saw one of our wee men named Quinn marching four huge brutes down a trench, each one twice his size, he was just a bantam! Bunkey Black ran into a German officer and they both got such a surprise they just stared at each other. Bunkey grabbed at his revolver and the Hun fell at his feet, howling for mercy.

Robson[4] led a bombing party and captured the hospital. It was about forty feet underground, had electric light, and there were cots, beds and an underground dispensary and four huge rooms, all boarded up. Their whole trenches are splendid, deep and comfortable and they must save a lot of men by being so deep. The machine gun emplacements are all reinforced concrete and steel girders and only the heaviest shells could touch them. The men got crowds of curios from hats, helmets, cat-o'-nine tails, books, clean clothes, tinned sausages, soda water etc. In the hospital that Robson captured there were twenty stretcher bearers and a doctor. The doctor was sent down to dress the German wounded and so we made some use of him.

All the prisoners were marched down and locked up in a huge wire compound and a brutal and coarse-looking lot they were, strong and heavy in build. Robson made the German doctor dress our wounded in the trench and he was quite gentle with them, but when he was dressing the German wounded, one poor fellow who was badly hit sat up and groaned and the doctor hit him in the face with the back of his hand. Chaplain Black saw it and was furious. Black has been a tower of strength, carrying stretchers and doing anything that was needed.

I don't know what the future holds, we are trying to rebuild and re-equip, and are ready to move up at half an hour's notice. We sleep in full kit ready to move, and I have not had a change or my boots off for thirteen days, as all our kit is at a base depot. We are still suffering all the effects of the terrible weeks' bombardment before the attack, it makes us all slow and dull. We had some fine 12 and 15 inch guns, and when the shells would come over on their way to the Hun, they skimmed overhead like an express train entering a tunnel, followed by an awe-inspiring explosion.

My dearest wee wife, I must close. I am enclosing a piece of tartan off the Pipe Major's pipes. He was so brave and was killed, but we managed to get the pipes back.

Goodnight my dearest, all my love . . .

JULY 12TH

My dearest wee Pettie,
This is about the 20th time that I have commenced to write to you and every time just as I get settled down someone has come in or something has cropped up.

I expect, dearest, that you know all about the great push, the papers are full of it and as usual have made, in many cases, a botch of it, for instance the Tyneside pipers are said to have played certain Scots regiments into action. It was our own pipers, not the Tynesiders at all. They came over hours after we had got to the German fourth line. It was our own Pipe Major Anderson who led us with the pipes, and who afterwards distinguished himself marching up and down playing 'Cock o' the North'.

Certain regiments seem to have come in for no end of limelight; the Gordons had a very tame correspondent, indeed. Mind you the Gordons did magnificently well, but look at any regiment on that terrible day, everyone did more than any group of men could be asked to do.

We took four lines of trenches in our first assault, we also led the assault, and passed thro' that perfect inferno of machine gun fire. Our men dropped like flies, but not a soul flinched and not a soul had one regret, I'll wager. We got to the fourth line and held it for three days. Why did we have to hold it for three days? Just for the one reason,

Pettie, that no one could get through to relieve us. The same inferno that we had crossed in No Man's Land was holding them all up, and it continued to do so for three days. Our men were just magnificent, wonderful fellows they were and the four waves swept into that inferno just as on parade.

We now have confirmed that poor old Major Bruce[5] whose death is now announced was killed very early in the fight. He was hit in No Man's Land, but reached the German wire, where he was shot by a German officer who was shot on the spot by one of our corporals. Elder was killed in No Man's Land, Brough and Pinkerton were both killed there too, also Reid and Gibson. Lawrence had a bullet through his ankle and was hobbling to the dressing station when he was buried by a shell and a bomb in his pocket went off. His foot was blown away and both legs badly smashed. I dressed his wounds and remained with him for a long while. Gee and Douglas too all gone, all shot in NML. Reid got as far as the German front line, was hit; he was alive at 2 pm but sat up about that hour and was shot through the head by a sniper, the dirty brutes shot all our wounded. Brand, poor boy, got to the third German line, but was killed instantly with a shot through the neck, and is now buried in the land he was helping to save. Dougal and Grant were killed at the same place Brand was hit. Brown was hit seven times and is now in hospital in England. McArthur was hit in the groin, Hole and Major Stocks are both wounded and missing, we hope they are both prisoners of war. Stocks will show the Hun a thing or two about how to win at bridge! I have a task ahead to write to all the loved ones, all the time wondering if someone will write about me some time. I am so sorry for the Brands and will write to Mrs Brand. Geof was with me at 1 am on the morning we went over, and when we parted and said goodbye he was quite cheerful and confident of coming through. Mrs Lawrence I am writing to today. I thought that he had a chance of pulling through when I last saw him, but he must have failed soon after. It is so awful.

Well dearest, no more about the war. I love to get all your dear letters, telling me all about you two most precious beings. It restores me like a great tonic to hear what you are doing, it helps so much to wipe out the noise and death and the fear.

[LATER]

I was just so tired I turned in to bed and slept for a few hours, and now feel a great deal better. I see I have told you all the terrible things again, I think I am so tired I keep repeating myself. Apart from all the noise, the killing and fatigue, I have so much work to do. All the packs of the wounded and killed had to be gone through, all the officers' kits investigated and certified and sent off. On top of all this we had a reinforcing draft of 400 men[6] landed on us and all the work this entailed; however we are again a fighting force and another 200 will bring us up to our fighting strength. The new draft is made up of splendid fellows and the battalion will again do well; but one misses horribly the old faces, especially men like Hole and Reid. I am writing to all their people, and what a rotten job.

My dearest wee woman, I don't see any chance of leave in the immediate future; at present we've the Hun thinking he is in for a right good hammering and a richly deserved one. Mind you we are so close to them we can hear them thinking, some trenches are actually in front of some of their trenches. Don't look forward to big advances. All is well but it is tough going. The Hun machine guns take a lot of doing in. The noise of their death dealing is something we will never forget. Goodnight my darling, let's look up at the same old star again together, it is a link, but even the stars have a job to shine their friendship through the gloom of hatred where I am.

All my love . . .

JULY 15TH

Dearest wee Pettie,

No letter today but one came yesterday telling me that you had seen poor old Lawrence's death announced. I am so sorry too for Mrs Lawrence. Poor old chap, I dressed his wounds twice and he was with me for about six hours, he was so game and uncomplaining and so badly knocked about. Gee wrote to us from a hospital in London, at least his wife did, he too is badly knocked about and won't be out of bed for four months and even then will be a cripple all his life, poor chap. It was a splendid lot of officers and men we had, I do miss them all so much. At times it makes one feel very blue, they were so keen, so smart, and took such an interest in the men and wouldn't they all just be so pleased to know how well they led the men and how grandly every man followed them, not a slacker, not a soul who flinched. I can honestly say that we did our bit and will be doing a bit more some day I hope. We are, man to man, miles ahead of the Hun; but he is so cunning and resourceful. When you get near he bawls out 'Pardon Kamerad' and up goes his hands, you pass and and he turns around and fires at you or turns a machine gun on to your back. The bayonet is the only tonic for them, and they hate it.

I think, in the push up to date, we are the only regiment that actually charged as a regiment, 'got in' with the bayonet. Of course there was any amount of hand-to-hand bayonet fighting but we went into them as a regiment. Things are going quite alright and we are making a big impression on the Hun and I have a sneaking feeling that he is feeling the pressure far heavier then he admits. Anyway, prisoners are coming in at a great rate, and for the most part are overjoyed at their capture. Some of the wood fighting has been terrific, the whole woods just wired up with invisible and terribly strong wire entanglements that are only observed when one stumbles on to them. We are very busy reorganising and now I'm glad to say most of it is done.

Well, my dearest, it will soon be the 28th, won't it? I am feeling quite excited about it and only wish that I could be with you and our dear wee son to celebrate it, the most wonderful day of my life. We will hope and pray that we will be celebrating many many together. I'm afraid that there is little or no prospect of so doing this time; until we are definitely held up or outrun our energy and manpower everyone of us has his job to do and now that we are on the job and the Hun is about to be on the biggest run he ever had, we all want to be in it together! It will be so funny and strange marching peacefully and quietly over the ground we helped so materially to win, the ground where men fell like flies and lay for 48 hours suffering the torments of hell. It's quite safe there now and the only sign of life is the Salvage Coy clearing up the battleground; a truly grim and awful job. I do wish we all could get to some decent baths, everyone is positively lousy as can be, big horrible whoppers they are.

I wish we had a monkey as a mascot. The mascot we have just now Deckie would love, it is a lively wee tabby kitten that the Sgt Major caught in the Hun lines and carried throughout the scrap. Such a lively, playful and pretty wee one. If the war is soon over I will get it and give it to our dear wee son. Now my dearest lover, my gladness bundle, I must say goodnight.

All my love and kisses to you both . . .

JULY 17TH

I cannot understand why up-to-date you have not heard from me. Major Rose has had replies from Mrs Rose to his letters that were sent off the same day as mine. Poor dear little woman, I know that you will be anxious and I'm so sorry that no word has reached you yet. Well the fighting is still going on and tonight the artillery is most intense. A shell burst in among some of our tents and killed two and wounded two transport men.

Dearest wee sweet, I've just discovered that the mail is to go out earlier. Captain Greig just came in and told me so to get moving. I must conclude such a tiny wee note but dearest, it carries just as much love and thoughts for you and dear wee Deckie as I've ever sent.

Goodnight dear heart . . .

July 20th

You will be most surprised to hear that today I went out to see Bobby Taylor, Blue Harper, Walter Stack,[7] Peter Graham and hosts and hosts of my old Varsity pals. Bobby was asking after you. It was strange and warming to meet them all in this dreadful place. Aussies are just everywhere, makes me so homesick. What fine chaps they are, so fit and tanned. They are ready for anything. I do hope they meet fewer of the Hun machine guns than we did. Let us hope that all the battalions did as well as we did.

These wretched Hun have just thousands of machine guns. We captured 24 in one 24-hour period. I hope the authorities allow us to send some home to Edinburgh as trophies. I did not bring any trophies or souvenirs. Some day when this is all over, I do not want anything to remind me of what Hell is really like. But there are lots of German helmets, rifles, cat-o'-nine tails and thousands of things lying everywhere, but it is safest not to remove anything, for the penalty for looting is death. The men look for pistols, watches and the like and we have to discourage their endeavours. I was wearing a German helmet of French design, having lost my own steel helmet when I was arrested and marched with fixed bayonet to the chateau as a suspected spy. Thank the Lord, Bunkey was on duty there and identified me. I, in turn, was able to identify Major Temple, who was also under arrest. I don't wonder that I was arrested; I only had one puttee on, was covered in mud up to the waist, and had not washed or shaved for four days; all that and a German helmet to boot. 'Bloody Aussies!' they said, which nearly precipitated a new war.

My dearest, I am so glad that my letters are getting through, I had begun to wonder if I had the right address.

Deckie sounds to be talking so well, the dear boy. How I wish they would hand out a bit of leave. I honestly think that we have earned a decent respite as we are so busy trying to lick the new drafts into shape. They are all from Egypt, and have done no trench work or bombing. We have lost so many experienced officers, all replaced with young inexperienced officers, that I have to take all the bombing classes as well as all the adjutant duties. I have a new assistant, Lt. Mortimer, a very decent and helpful sort which is a great relief. I was beginning to wonder how much more I could take.

I have a new mare, she came the day we came out from the push. I don't think I told you about her. She is black with two white socks; not very pretty but a beauty to ride though full of nasty tricks, rears right up and roots out if another horse comes near, but she has just met her match!

Wouldn't it be just too lovely if I could get leave for the 28th, what a dream but I'm afraid it is not possible. Dobie, Robson, Beech and Dickson are all out first, as they have been here for seven months and so far have had no leave at all. Robson and Dickson were in the push. Robson did wonderfully well. He is a splendid chap, full of pluck. He will certainly get the DSO. I do not expect to get the Military Cross for which both the CO and Major Rose recommended me, but I did nothing dramatic, nothing that makes a thrilling story. I don't know if I will be made Captain; Dobie and Pagan have both been given companies, which necessitates them being Captains. Tod, Lodge, Russel, and Harrison are Captains, on our strength but are all on sick leave, but will probably return to us soon. The new Second-in-Command is a regular, Capt. Perry, who will soon be Major so that is all the Captain vacancies. But dearest I would sooner a day or two with you and wee Deckie than any promotion. Bobby Taylor tells me that Dora Barbour is expecting a new family addition in Egypt. Any day, Bobby says, seems a bit vague on that point as I expect he should be.

Fancy, dearest wee lover mine for three years and a good bit longer than that too, heart body and soul you've been mine and me yours. How happy those days have been, dear little woman, and how I'd love to be with you next week but never mind, anticipation will shorten the time and then I'll be with you, and we'll be able to forget all about this war, and all its awful sequences.

Nothing further has been heard of Major Stocks or Hole. I am having the most frantic and pathetic letters from all the officers' and men's families, it is so sad. I write to every one of them, so I am kept writing till the small hours every morning, but it has to be done, and I am so thankful that the letters are not about me.

One piece of good news is that the Pipe Major is in hospital in Wales, hit twice through the body, through the arm, through the shoulder and through the thigh. We are all so glad he is safe. He is to get the VC. He just piped away all through the battle with those terrible wounds.

And now my darling dearest, all my love to you and our lump of love . . .

JULY 21ST

Pettikins mine,

Just a tiny wee note as I have only just returned after a long and tiring field day.[8] It was so hot. I have never felt the sun so hot as in France. Well my darling, things are once more arriving at something like the ante push days and with the new drafts the battalion is once again resuming its former self but one will always miss the old faces that one was accustomed to see around every corner.

Lice are awful just now, everyone from Major Rose down is alive with them. When we come in from parades we always strip and sit on the grass pulling the beastly things off our clothes. It is really a funny sight to see little bunches of men sitting everywhere all doing the same. They are awful wee things; somehow or other, if one is talking to the General or anyone else of importance and trying to be just the thing, one of these big fellows commences to crawl up one's collar or along the neck it's really too discomfiting. Fortunately we are all in the same boat. Well dearest wee sweetie, this is just a tiny wee note to give you and darling wee Deckie all my love.

Goodnight, dearest two . . .

JULY 23RD

Dearest wee wife of mine,
I got a nice long letter from you today and also the snapshots of dear wee Deckie. The ones of you are very nice and I just loved getting a picture of the two dear ones that I love so well, but the ones of Deckie are not very good, he does not take a very good picture yet.

Well my Pett, things are a bit quieter just now as far as we are concerned but the fighting is going on just as heavily as ever, and the guns at night just make one creep and thank heaven that they are sending the stuff in the other direction. I've seen nothing further of Bobby Taylor or Peter Graham but I have seen a great many other old pals; Taylor and the rest of the AMC people will be more than busy. You will be sorry to hear that poor old General Williams was killed,[9] he was caught by shrapnel and a piece went through his heart and he died instantaneously; he was very efficient, a great fire-eater and a tiger for work and had the satisfaction of exacting the last ounce out of the division and I must say the division has made a great name for itself.

You asked after Dobie — he did not go into action, we were only allowed to take 23 officers into action and by the papers and reports you already know the fate of most of them, only four of us came through. We can get no information on the fate of Major Stocks or Hole. Hole was splendid and was last seen leading a counter-attack, with fixed bayonets against the Hun. Stocks was hit three times. Poor wee chap, we used to have so many rows but he was a real pal. He really wanted to visit us in Bundaberg after the war!

The honours and awards are out. We got seven MMs, one DCM and five MCs. I got two MIDs.[10] Gee got the MC, which was richly won and earned. He is very badly wounded and at present in London, and will most probably be a cripple for life, which is a long time for a MC! He has a terrible injury to his knee and ankle. Douglas got a MC and is in hospital in Boulogne, having lost his leg from the hip. Robson got the MC but certainly deserved at least the DSO. He saved the situation and was mainly instrumental in enabling us to hang on for those three awful days. The men who won the MM were splendid and won it time and again, one cannot adequately reward these gallant fellows. The 16th Royal Scots only got five medals all told, but to judge from the press one would think that they did everything. Old Sir George is an excellent advertiser.

It's nearly the 28th, dearest little wife. I expect neither of us will ever forget that day. I don't think there is one detail I forget, even picking up the confetti from the carpet, what a dear wee little tiny girl then and not a big grown-up woman with a dear wee son; she was also a wee bit shy too, wasn't she, but what a woman, what a day, and now here am I, a war away, miles of trenches and death. If only the authorities would convert my MIDs into leave! But there is not even a whisper about it, and I don't expect there will be any leave while the push continues, and there is no chance of the push letting up, but when it does come, I will fly to you both. I expect you will be back from Troon by then, but I am so pleased that you love Kilmalcolm.

Deckie's appetite sounds good, if only you can continue to get good food. Are you still taking your tonic, and how are my two little ladies, plump and ready for their dear old daddy to love, and he certainly will. Goodnight my dearest, love to you both. How useless words are in times like this.

All my love . . .

July 26th
Somewhere in France

Dearest little Pettie,

I never got the chance to send a line yesterday, we had been out all day training and arriving in camp found a draft of 62 men[11] waiting to be disposed of and no accommodation available. So I had to set about and chase all over the countryside searching for tents and bivouacs. At last, at about 9 pm we found a deserted camp and managed to get a party up and sneak off with ten tents and by the time we got back there was no time to catch the mail.

A very welcome bundle of Australian mail. The picture of all the Sydney push bring it all back, but it seems to be unreal, perhaps another world. Do they all exist? Are they real? Am I real? We are all so tired it's hard to know. We are like Rip van Winkle, when we get back to Australia, they will all look so much older than us. You will look so wonderful and fresh, as I'm sure time is standing still.

You will see by the papers how the ANZACs are doing over here. It is very funny the way we are not expected to mention places and regiments, but the press is allowed to do so. I've seen a great crowd of the Australians, they all look very fit but are having a great deal of hard fighting. The fighting is just now intense, the guns are just roaring all day long, one wonders how the supply of guns and ammunition lasts. There are no end of small woods and villages hereabouts and these make fighting most difficult and deadly. The woods are so strongly held and wired that one can only get them inch by inch. A little further back the country is more open and once we get them there things will move apace.

The Hun is fighting with the tenacity of despair just now, but he cannot help but recognise that he is up against it. He has hurled his best troops at us in the most awfully concentrated counter-attacks and whole battalions of Hun have been wiped out. It's such a weird and uncanny sight to see thousands of men in lines jump up from the trenches opposite, move forward and then just vanish into the ground as if caught in quicksand.

Our guns are wonderful and the Hun cannot get through. I saw two big motor lorries coming along with a big load of men with German helmets on. At first I thought it to be two loads of lightly wounded prisoners, but when they reached me they all called out 'cheerio, Jock!'. They were wounded Australians with their trophies and all in tremendous spirits.

We are just at strength now in the battalion, and no doubt we will be in the thick of it again, full charge into the killing-and-be-killed game. We are quite famous now as a fighting unit and everyone is talking about our wonderful charge.

Well dearest little lover, everything is going alright, please don't worry about me, but how I wish for two or three weeks' leave and love. Just fancy, it is almost the 28th of July, and all the joys and troubles it has brought us, but we soon forget the troubles, completely buried by the joys, the unforgettable joys of love, of friendship, of wee Derick, and all the troubles bundled together don't even outweigh one tiny single joy, and there are so many more joys to be lived. Leave I'm afraid is a long way off, so long as the push is on no one can be spared.

Look after yourself my darling, make sure you get and eat your ration of all the nourishments. Fill up those wee legs, such shapely wee legs and I should know something of them, oughtn't I?

All my love my dearest . . .

JULY 28TH
In the field

Sweetheart,

So many, many happy returns of today.[12] I so wish, little girl that I was with you and dear Derick and what a real, long, happy love day we would have, but as it is, I am getting ready to move up into the thick of things as we go up and into action tomorrow. Last time we all went up with such confidence as we all knew each other so well indeed, and we knew every man and what he could do but now although we have been very lucky in getting such excellent material to work on, we don't yet know all the men and officers, many of whom have never yet been under fire. I will be both adjutant and acting Second-in-Command Major Rose put up his Colonel badges yesterday; although he is not yet in the Gazette, the Brigadier told him to do so.

Dobie had a letter from Mrs Gee yesterday, poor old Gee is in a critical condition, and has lost one of his legs. Douglas, too, had to lose a leg, and I'm rather of the mind that Lawrence died following an operation for amputation. I've seen nothing further of Bobby Taylor or Peter Graham but I saw a great crowd of other Australians I knew. One lad, Townley,[13] a Lt in the Light Horse was at Maryborough Grammar School with me. Did you see in the casualty lists that Lt E.R. Manning,[14] attached to the RFC has been wounded, that is the second wound. I expect Manning will forsake medicine for the Flying Corps when the war is over, there will be any amount of scope for light men with the Flying Corps, as he is very keen. Personally, I will be very pleased to get out of khaki for a long time and wax fat in the family circle of my wife, my son and any other wee babies and of course dearie, not forgetting to mention those two dear wee brown young ladies of ours.

Thrilled to hear that Deckie is looking so well, an that you are still enjoying Kilmalcolm. How much longer do you think you will be there? If I wired you when I got leave, I wonder if you could come to London to meet me. We could then travel up to Scotland together. I'm sure Deckie would give up his mum to his dad for a few days.

It would be grand to step out of the old leave train right into your dear brown arms. Last time every man on the train had someone to meet the train but I didn't and it felt so lonely. Fortunately I had to ask about how to catch the train north so the time quickly passed, but it would be heavenly if you could meet me in London and we could have a couple of days together in London. There's just a chance that after all our hard work and anxiety they may give us ten days' leave instead of the seven; but of course it is only a very slim chance. I wonder if old No one is anywhere near here, I expect he had gravitated to this area, but I forget the number of the Battery he is with.

The new kitten is growing famously. You remember what a playful thing Turka was, well this one is just the same only it is much more original and rushes up one's legs and away again.

I am glad you are going to see Mrs Greig, she may be able to give some news that I've missed. He did awfully well in the push, in charge of carrying and store parties and was also responsible for ammunition getting up, and he worked so hard. He was done up by the end, but he is quite himself again.

We had a long letter from the CO yesterday, he has been warned for some home duty, I expect he will be given some depot. The poor old chap was far too old for the hard life here, and went away just looking a wreck, was mentally fatigued and broke down crying on several occasions in the line. He was a very decent old fellow and was quite good to me, but was very hard to get on with at times, when he became tired.

The big guns are at it, the ground is shaking continuously. I think the Hun is working up to a counter-attack. He is really a most tenacious fighter, fighting over every inch of ground, as though it were his own. However he is being pushed back and very soon he will be out of the last wood and then he will have to shift faster. In the meantime he has his top troops against us, the heroic and classy Brandenburgers and their friends, but nothing can match the endurance and bravery of our tremendous fellows. The press is giving the Australians any amount of notice, they are up against a tough crowd, I know the spot to an inch.

Well dearest wife, if only I was with you, but wishes won't get the job done and one day we'll be together again. Why don't you go shopping with Mrs Greig, get some lovely pink pyjamas and a smart tailormade suit. We will have lots of snaps made when we are together to send home, how they will be so pleased to see us. I must close, my love.

Love to you both . . .

JULY 29TH

Just a tiny note dearest to tell you that tonight we are on the move, that is we move up[15] at dawn and I expect by this time tomorrow we will be hard at it again, so if the mails are very irregular you will know that no opportunity has arisen to get any letters away. It will be an anxious time for Major Rose and myself this time, as so many men are new and so many of the officers have had no experience, some have not even been under fire. However there is a fair sprinkling of our own men left and they will be invaluable and have a most reassuring effect on the others. Just at present the old faces are thoughtful, even sad, no doubt they realise what they lost on the last occasion.

The new men are very excited and everyone is having his hair cut short like a gaolbird, it makes such a difference in the condition of head wounds. I am going to try and have a decent bath tonight, have had Richardson and a pioneer building me one all day, so as soon as I can get it fixed up, I'll bath, and jump into some new clothes and burn the others. The lice are just the limit and breed so quickly in this warm weather. I hope we don't have too hot a time this time, but we are going into a much disputed position, where the fighting has been so hot that there has been no time to bury the bodies, which makes the hell even more unsavoury, if that can be possible.

All sorts of rumours are rife here today about Austria suing for peace, but I expect they are only vale rumours, though, no doubt she must be in a bad way. We had a wire from General HQ saying the Russians had captured Brody, and 10 000 prisoners.

The troops opposing us are, on the whole, very good. They fight their machine guns with tremendous tenacity and will fire them to the last gasp but they won't face the bayonet. There are not a great many of these troops and we gave the Prussian Guards an awful hammering on July 1st, a hammering those who survived will never forget.

Well my dearest, we are now in the fourth year of our married life, aren't we getting old! My grey hairs are multiplying very rapidly, you will never keep up. I dreamt of you the other night, you were brushing your beautiful hair, one of my jobs for the rest of our life, there were some grey hairs and I was teasing you. I dream of you and dear wee Deckie, such warm dreams, so friendly, and suddenly the guns roar more loudly, or suddenly stop, and I am snapped awake, to realise that it's all a dream. The guns roar so unceasingly and continue the same blat and blast all day that one misses them if they stop. We can tell by the sound if new, or bigger ones have joined in, or an old grannie has dropped out to have her throat sponged.

Well my old married woman, I will try to get letters off, but don't worry, just remember, my darling whatever happens, I love you heart, body and soul. I want and need you so very much, just to hold on to you both.

Goodnight, all my thoughts . . .

La Boisselle

51 Highland Division

until the p.c. arrive
Daddy wants to
to the two dearest
Just fancy dearest
the fateful night

when we a
weetie is
hear see
so lonely
the last two
and the
is at
at the Chur
ely lately
chiefly ladi
they are
at I do not
is in un
little abo
one of wor
an awful
ing great
how the
reply se
y lucky. W
Duthie
ght nai's p
morrow as
ins are du
own to di
we played
quaranta

Dervickes Daddy
up for all little
Today the letters a
Australia are. I wo

MESSAGES AND SIGNALS. No. of

	Words	Charge	This message is on a/c of:	Recd.
...m.			(D)	Date.
...ructions.	Sent		Service.	From.
	At...m.			By.
	To.			
	By.		(Signature of "Franking Officer.")	

19.1.16

Day of Month | In reply to Number

d little Sweetheart now
may note as I have not
y. For we have a big
rrow and I have to go
Yesterday
but a
result
before. The
at Sutton
weeks here.
a rare
having
not had a

August

AUGUST 1ST

My dearest wee wife,

Here I am right in the thick of it again. Oh, what a time we have had the last two days. We are now about four and a half miles ahead of where we were when we pushed and what a revelation it is to pass over the fields where there has been such woeful fighting. The ground has been just torn to pieces by the shells, great huge craters in every yard; to see it one can realise what the Hun sat out. The whole ground is like a wire mesh, the guns did wonderful work. The night before we moved into this area we bivouacked in a wood and got the most awful shelling, everyone scuttling about like rabbits trying to find some tiny hole or shelter. The new men were very good under very trying circumstances. It is very funny to see all the tents all over the area where the Hun was in occupation and where previously one had only to show a periscope and get it shattered.

Well my dear, my fountain pen has just gone dry. We crossed straight overland to where we are now and the traffic, over what was once the Boche lines, is marvellous. Horses and limbers everywhere, Australians galloping about after stray mules, all the time huge clouds of dust arising from the roads that were inches thick with dust and the Hun hurled some huge 5.9s at us. We were moving along the road when two huge crumps just screamed overhead and down in the dust we went. The crumps landing fifty yards away and a huge piece of shell killed two mules and a limber. They were sideways on and about 200 yards away and it just walloped both on the head and killed them outright. All the way along the route they crumped at us and have been at us ever since. The Hun has moved a great many big guns up on the front and he hurls his weight about, I can tell you. I was never in a worse place for shells. All the way over one sees graves, just shell holes filled in and little wood crosses on top. Some have just the simple inscription, 'Twelve Germans here'. We found Brand's and Elder's graves and marked the spots down on our maps. You could not imagine a more desolate and devastated looking place, every tree is cut off about midway up and there is not a green leaf in any wood, the shelling has been so terrific and so thorough.

Major Rose had ridden forward to see the General and I was in charge of the battalion and was riding along with Anderson when I ran bang into old Horrie. He would have passed me without recognising me as I was wearing a steel helmet but I shouted out to him and he nearly fell off his horse. He rode back with me and we had a chat for about an hour. He is just the same, only a bit fatter if anything. I was in charge of the battalion and very busy so was sorry I could not have a decent long yarn but now no doubt when we come out I will see something of him.

The weather here is just sweltering and water is very short. Every drop we use we have to carry, and fighting in the heat and dust is very thirsty work. We are to be up for about ten days and then I hope we will go out for another few days' rest. It is about time our division had a rest. We have been in action since the start of the proceedings. Of course, we ourselves had a rest but then there was no alternative and all the while we were doing training and reorganising and personally I have had precious little rest. The Germans here are cracking up and are surrendering each night in little groups. The night before last night a party of fourteen or so came over. Their guns still have plenty of punch yet and no shortage of ammunition. At present within ten yards of where I am sitting there are five great big 21 cm guns that we captured from the Hun. I don't mean our regiment, I mean the army. Great huge things they are and beside them are thousands of huge shells which I hope will one day wobble across to the Hun with our compliments.

The trenches here are only mere scratches in the ground but in a few days will be in order. The Hun snipes us all day so the only digging and moving that can be done is by night and oh ye gods, the stench. There are dead bodies everywhere. Some in almost every shell hole along the wire entanglements and on the parapets and in the open. There are crowds of dead Hun all black and mouldy and smelling all day and all night in the most awful manner imaginable. If we try to bury them the Hun shells us, so the best we can do is sprinkle chloride of lime on them. There are very few British dead about. I have not seen any at all recently.

Well, old woman, it is three months since I had leave now, isn't it and I am sure that I have earned a fresh leave just now but of course it is quite impossible with so much at stake. The new men are doing very well but they are not used to trench routine and do not understand the art of making themselves as comfortable as conditions admit. Not very comfortable, I agree.

The Russians we hear are still making big hauls of Austrian and German prisoners. There can't be many Austrians left. I don't expect we will see a paper for ten days, so by that time they ought to tell us the Russians are well on the way to Lemburg.[1] Horrie tells me that Manning had been sent home at one time for sick leave and was in hospital for four months with shell shock and mental trouble due to shellfire; it was after that that he transferred to the RFC.

Yesterday a great many Boche flew over us and our fellows went after them in great style. One Boche was cut off and rounded up by five of our planes and made him descend on our lines. When we last saw him he was slowly flying to earth with our planes all around him. They just rounded him up like a stockman does cattle. There have been no end of duels in the air but it is so hot and sunny that one cannot look up for long and follow the scraps.

Well sweetheart I have written about as long a letter as I can under the most trying circumstances so now will try and get some rest. Goodbye my dear little wife, give my love to our dear son. Bless you both.

My heart is always with you through prayer. Love,

AUGUST 7TH
Somewhere in France

Sweetheart,

We are fighting for all we are worth. We are fighting for our very life. Fighting in the woods and bombing, it's terrible work and we are all just about done, my feet are fearfully sore, I've not had my boots off for nine days. Let us pray that we will be relieved soon. The Hun attacked us twice and got into our trench[2] once but we biffed him out. This wood[3] fighting is awful, there are no trenches or dugouts, just holes in the ground. German dead lie everywhere and the sights and the smells are just sickening. The Hun has brought up a lot of new big guns and is shelling us day and night with tremendous stuff. Still, with our guns we can hold him easily enough. Any quantity of Huns are surrendering to us voluntarily when they get the chance.

The Hun is using a new big phosphorous shell and it showers burning phosphorous on everything which burns anything it touches but it is really far more terrifying than effective. He gave us a gas attack on the 5th but the helmets saved us all. There are hundreds of dead Boche here in all the woods and in the open along our trenches. Horrible they look, been lying there since the 14th of July. The flies too are all in favour, the rotten things!

We are alright and fit and very weary and worn and will welcome a change to more comfy quarters. The weather is still continuing hot, fine and very dusty. Hun planes have been coming out more frequently but our RFC puts them at discount. We hear we are to be relieved by the 15th of this month. I hope it is sooner, it is so hard but if it is the 15th I expect we have to stick it out and trust to luck.

All my love to you both, my dearests. Goodbye . . .

AUGUST 11TH

We came out of the line last night and are now back at the place[4] I met Horrie, that is almost at the very spot we pushed from. It is so funny to sit here and look out over the very trenches we took and to wonder how we did it. I was going out this morning to search over the ground and to look for and identify the graves of any of our officers. We have located Brand's and Elder's so far. I had a most heartbroken letter from Mrs Brand. The Indians are now occupying the trenches we captured from the Germans on the 1st. It is so strange not to get shot at as you move about here. Of course they shell us all the time but it is only the long-range guns that can reach us now and as soon as they commence we just hop into the trenches and wait until it is over. For the rest of the time we are out and about and sleep in the open. It is such a treat after being cooped up in the most awful trenches that we have been in this time. They are not trenches, just little holes in the earth amongst the trees. Fighting in the woods is about the hardest of all the fighting and everyone hates it. It is terribly nerve-racking to be shelled in a wood at night. The Hun set the wood on fire in three places one night. We had to put it out otherwise we would have all been roasted and all the time we were putting out the wood fire he shelled us and shrapnelled us. Men get very jumpy in woods, the shells burst with such a roar and the splinters make a great fuss amongst the trees and trunks.

We had all the men bathed today and they got a clean shirt and socks and are all terribly pleased with themselves. Ever since the 1st of July I have had on what I am now wearing. You see, before the big push on the 1st all our clothes and kit were sent back to a base depot and we went into the line with fighting kit only and ever since then we have been in the line or in support. Even when reorganising we were in support and liable to move at an hour's notice. Now we are in support but on the 15th, so report has it, we are to be taken out for a good long spell. I do hope it is true for our division has been in the line since July 1st and not only that, it fell to our lot to make our own preparations for the push whereas most of the divisions and brigades came up the week after the push. However everything comes to him who waits, but one does get fed up with the long wait.

There is of course no question of leave whilst we are in this sector, no doubt when we are drawn out we will get a job at the old game of trench warfare in some quieter sector and then leave will come as a routine. The news is uniformly good from all fronts just now and no doubt old Kaiser Bill must be feeling a bit sick with himself although not nearly so sick as the old rake in Austria. The Italians are at last making a bit of a show and seem to have fairly rattled the Austrians in and around Gorizia.[5] The Hun is having a great deal more artillery here, all big stuff too. He must have moved up any number of big 5.9 guns which are the very devil and most powerful things and shoot with tremendous accuracy and the burst of the shell is fairly awful and the scream of the shell overhead is like an express train coming out of a tunnel. I had a letter from Ray Norris[6] (Jessie Martin's brother) yesterday. He is just near me somewhere and is a Lieutenant in the 2nd Australian Battalion. I do wish I could run across him. He was in the Poziers scrap when the AIF did so well. He was lucky to get through.

Last night I went into the 12th Australian Ambulance to see if there was anyone there I knew and I met a host of Sydney fellows including Dr Wilcox-Kennedy and Colonel Ross[7] from Queensland and also had a chat to some German wounded prisoners, miserable flabby wretches they were. One, a student with a badly shattered leg, had imagined he was going to be shot or crucified or something dreadful. When the padre gave him a cigarette and a light he burst out crying. German prisoners are all saying that the war will end at 1 pm on August 17th and that Germany will win, everyone has the same story. I wonder what new stunt they intend to work on that day, some more frightfulness of a new kind I expect. They are very keen on working up new and horrible stunts like this new phosphorous shell they are firing at us. It is one of the latest inventions, and it is a very terrifying thing. At night it is a glorious sight too wonderful to be described, but so long as one gets the chance to get some shelter from the burning phosphorous it is nothing very alarming. Just now they are hurling thousands and thousands of gas shells at us and they are pretty dangerous. The gas is so deadly but our helmets are alright if one gets the chance to whip them on. I got a dose of gas as did the CO and I did feel beastly all the next day, a most violent headache, vomiting and diarrhoea, a most unwelcome lot in the trenches where one gets shot at every time one moves out.

Well, dearest woman, what do you think about coming to meet me in London? I think it would be just the most wonderful thing if it's possible but as the leave will come at a moment's notice I guess a telegram would only reach you after I did. But what fun we could have with 48 hours in London. I got the snapshot of the family at Thirroul and also one of the aqua-planing, I would love a chance now to do some aqua-planing. I am sure the wee beasties would get dizzy and all fall into the water and be drowned.

Well now, my darling wee sweetheart of mine, I must get some work done, casualty returns are the big job these days. The names of officers and men have to be checked and sent to the base and there are no facilities for office work.

With all my love . . .

August 13th

We all thought that when we came out of the line the night before last that we were in for a nice long spell but last night we got orders to go up again tonight[8] until further orders, but we only expect to be up until the night of the 15th and then we all sincerely hope to go back for a decent rest. I really believe we will go back on or about the 17th. I feel awfully nervous about going up this time. One always does when leave or a spell is close. The shelling has been perfectly terrific the past few days, the Hun has moved up a great deal of heavy stuff and shells us with all the heavy stuff that he's got.

Great excitement here yesterday; a captive balloon broke away and flew up sky high, the poor observer had to jump out of the balloon with a parachute and we watched him, most fascinating, he came down alright in our lines but the balloon was drifting over to the Boche. Our aeroplanes, two or three, went up to try and shoot the balloon down but it got away over the Hun lines. A few minutes later an aeroplane fell from the clouds nose first and crashed into the Boche line. I don't know if it was ours or the Hun's, we could not tell from the markings as it fell too fast to be able to detect them in the failing light but I rather expect it was one of ours as there were a tremendous number of ours up at the time.

The Zeppelins seem to be very busy just now in England, it's a pity they cannot get a big haul of the gas bags one night. That would get their wind up and keep them home for a while. Well dearest sweetheart I must now close and say goodbye and get ready to go up for the next stint.

All my love . . .

Yesterday the first mail for over a week and I got four letters all in a bunch. Since about the 4th all inward and outward deliveries were stopped for what reason I don't know but we were instructed to send no mail and also that none would be forwarded and so yesterday I got your loving bunch of dear letters. It was so nice to hear all the details as it's been so lonely without your letters. I am sure you have been worrying why none have come from me.

Well, we have had a most fearful time up in the line, we went in on the last day of July and were in until the night of the 15th of August[9] and were fighting all the time. On the 4th in the night we attacked a German trench[10] but failed to take it but we killed lots of Germans. The next night the same trench was to be attacked and just as we were getting ready to go over the top the Hun attacked us instead and got into our trenches.

We counter-attacked and soon mopped him up and so on and on, the wood fighting is terribly trying and gets one very nervy. At the same time we had a tremendous amount of digging to do, as when we took over there were no trenches, just scrapes running into the various shelter holes and the German dead lay about as thick as flies, and when the wind blew to us it was just purgatory.

Some of the bodies, in fact hundreds and hundreds had been killed on or about the 12th of July by shellfire. We could not send men out to bury or bring in the wounded because the Hun fired all day long and we shelled him all the time. He mixed up a great many more big guns and shot with extraordinary accuracy, great twelve foot craters. If the shell fell near a party of men, they were never to be seen again. Our own guns gave the Hun a dreadful time.

Some of the prisoners and wounded had been lying out in No Man's Land in shell holes for as long as eight days and came in doddering idiots. We found two dead Boche under an old collapsed dugout and buried them where we found them. An awful task.

Well, we were relieved on the night of the 15th and had to march to the support lines and stay there the night. There was a terrible strafe on at the time. We were shelled all the way down and had to rush the men out in small parties, watching where the shells fell and then dodging from hole to hole. We had full packs[11] on and it was devilish work. Once we had the men on the move the CO and I went through the wood along the train line that runs through (an old German line) and they commenced to shell it just behind us with great heavies. These big shells just fell right plum in the track one after the other and followed us down the track and we had to run for it. After staying one night in the support line we moved back about five miles and all felt very done up as we commenced at 5 pm and the day was very hot indeed. We stayed the night in ——[12] and I had the first decent sleep in seventeen days and my boots off for the first time since we were brought out and washed; when we had the baths for one day and went up the next. It was like heaven to get into sheets again. I was in billets with John, I took the bed and he the floor with a mattress.

We were up at 3 am and at 4 am on the march to entrain, getting aboard the train at 10.30 am. We travelled all day and night arriving at a most lovely spot, quite the prettiest place I've seen, at 3 am. We then had a march of seven miles to our billets where we stayed for one night and left at 5.30 pm last night arriving at the rail head here at 3 am and then marching a further seven miles to where we are now and that brings us back to the old spot where we were before we went south.[13] In fact it is like coming back to an old friend. We did four months here and now here we are after all in the same old billets and just now things are said to be pretty quiet here. Anyway they can never be like the south, at times there it was just too awful for words. The noise, the smell, the screeching shells made one quite stupid, so stupid that one became insensible to danger and didn't care if the next one ended it all.

I hope that things are all quiet here and we get the opportunity of a decent rest, really we have earned it a thousand times and all of us are really feeling the effort, the frightening was bad enough, God knows it was a nightmare at times and then on top of it all comes the moving, the worry of the entraining and rations etc, and to cap the lot we go direct up to the line tonight. However there are compensations. There will be the usual trench routine, life at least will be freer from the everlasting scream and roar of the guns and one will not have to be in a shell hole with three or four dead Boche, three feet below, nor will one gaze for days at an end at the same hideous swollen figures that lie just at the parapet, then when our front line and support line spell is over we get the chance of a bath and a billet.

I am afraid I was writing pessimistically dear wife but I am not a pessimist, really I am a great optimist and the only excuse at present is that I am tired, dead dogged tired and it will soon pass off. I was so sorry to hear that Mrs McOmie had been so unwell, I do hope she is well again. And how sweet that you are writing her to cheer her up.

I do wish you had been with me to see the pretty village[14] we stayed at one night. The village itself is built alongside the Somme and is surrounded with the most beautiful woods and parks and where there were not trees loaded with fruit there were the most quaint gardens and lovely dahlias and roses. There was the usual chateau, a magnificent one on this occasion in superbly laid out grounds. We had 300 men billeted in it. I was billeted with the schoolmaster at the communal school. The new second, Major Clark and I had splendid beds and enjoyed every minute. Major Clark only joined us the day of the 15th of August, he seems very decent and come from the 1st Royal Scots, his arrival relieved me of a good deal of toil and detail. The people at the village were very nice and much better class than those who remain around the war zone to collect the soldier's pay. There was a very nice *estaminet,* quite a small one, and we went in and ordered a dinner and Madame gave us a splendid turn out, vegetable soup, then a priceless omelette as only the French can make omelettes, followed up with a magnificent pork chop, cabbage and potato chips with a bottle of Champagne each. There was a snow-white tablecloth, serviettes and nice clean cutlery. Oh it was too delightful for words to sit down once again in comfort and forget all about the war and frightfulness.

Now that we are here in a more or less quiet neighbourhood I hope and expect something in the way of leave will be discussed. I am so hungry to get home to you and dear wee Derick for a while, you poor little soul, I am afraid you are having a lonely time but it will soon all be over and then we can have a lovely loving old time. Deckie must be growing into such a man and is sure to be full of his own wee importance, dear soul. I do wish I could get away to look after both of you.

Now my darling I have written quite a long if very hurried letter and I hope it gets off by the mail by tomorrow at least; it won't go today as the mail will be collected too late. At present we are resting in a big laundry and there is every chance of a hot bath and so a chance of nice clean clothes.

Goodbye for the present my love . . .

AUGUST 22ND

Dearest wee sweetheart of mine,

Here it is just 12.30 am and as there is a gas alarm on and we are awaiting developments I am taking the opportunity of telling you what a dear wee woman you are. I was working pretty late and just at 11 pm I was going to turn in when a wire telegram came in saying that there was a Hun gas stunt or something precious like it working up so I had to rush out information and instructions to all the chickens under my wing and am now waiting acknowledgement of orders received and understood. It is a glorious night outside, clear as crystal and just a mild breeze blowing, in fact an ideal night for a Hun gas stunt, so we cannot take any risks. Gas is not so bad if one gets the opportunity to whip a helmet on, but a few seconds without a helmet is fatal and I don't want to die yet, leastways by gas.

I got a tiny wee note today enclosing a cablegram which to me is very cryptic indeed. From the contents I gather that Gordon Alford[15] has been wounded and is somewhere in London and that enquiry through the bank will find him, so I have written in that direction to Gordon care of the bank so maybe I'll track him down. I hope he is not badly hurt, he is a splendid fellow, one of the nicest cousins and one of the best of good fellows. He may call on you when convalescent but of course, you've met him. As to the rest and the photographs I don't exactly know what it means. I am hoping if I can find Gordon he may clear it up. As a matter of fact it is quite a rest here compared with down south. The work of course in the orderly room is as heavy as ever but the fighting is very quiet thank goodness and I hope will remain so.

I had about my share down south. I wish they would give us leave and then you could meet me in London. We could hunt up Gordon who would then tell all the Australians just really how nice a wee woman I have got all to myself; but on the question of leave at the moment there is nothing doing. The CO and I are ragging Captain Greig about it every time we see him. Even the General can't get it, less therefore a poor hard and overworked adjutant. Let me see, don't you go back to Troon at the end of this month or am I only dreaming about it? It is probable because I dream so often about you that my dreams get a bit mixed up with the reality.

It is getting so cold here at nights and in the mornings real autumn weather and already the strawberry beds, or rather what were once strawberry beds, are beginning to turn that pretty vieux rose colour. Mulberries too. Today I actually had some nice ones from a tree just near my bivouac. No one here knew what they were and when I commenced to munch away at them everyone watched me to see when the convulsions would come on. When I stated they were mulberries everyone carried on and said that only silkworms ate them. Rats are very bad here in all these old and deserted houses. There is every scope for Mr and Mrs Newly Wed Rat to make themselves comfy and sit down to the homely and reasonable occupation of rearing large families, quite an interesting and charming hobby, isn't it dearie?

I see by a paper dated 18th August that at last England has an aerial fleet of air ships, it may be not as up to date at the moment as the Hun's Zeppelins but it is certainly a step in the right direction and I only hope that they are powerful enough to get as far as Berlin and drop some bombs on that sinkhole of iniquity, it will give old Bill something to worry about. I have meant so often to write to Nancy so I really must get off a letter to her this time. She is really a dear wee kid and is very good indeed to Deckie.

Well my darling, at this hour I was called away down the line so had to put away the letter and it was after 2 am before I got back. Today it has been very dull all day and I think that we are going to have some heavy rain. The CO and the MO are both laid up today with a sort of French fever, following the course of influenza. Many of the men have it too, it is equally a reaction following all the exposure and work we had down south.

I heard today from Captain Greig that there is every chance of leave being commenced at the end of the month. However like Mr Asquith[16] I'll wait and see. Please let me know if you think there is any chance at all of coming to meet me in London. It will have to be at fairly short notice. The best plan would be for you to write and arrange with Hotel Russell and then wait there, I could wire you again from Folkestone saying at what hour the train would arrive in London and could come straight along to the hotel and find you there all snuggled up. The train usually arrives somewhere about midnight.

Well dearest, home to bed . . .

AUGUST 25TH

I really did not get the chance to send you a few lines yesterday as I was going full steam ahead all day and most of the night trying to get the casualty returns more or less up to date. It really is a most complicated business. Since the push, dozens and dozens of our men who are now returning to duty after more or less light wounds are being sent to other units and dozens of them are writing me for transfers, it is all very muddling. In addition we got a big bunch of regular soldiers from the KOSB and they are all just time expired and claiming all kinds of bounties and privileges which one can understand. It would be ordinary routine work in peacetime but it is an awful nuisance out here at the present time. I had a long letter from the late CO. He is getting a home battalion that is not yet in harness. He wrote about four pages telling me how the push ought to have been conducted.

The papers are only one day old when they arrive, we depend on them to find who is winning the war!

I saw one of our aeroplanes brought down by the Boche anti-aircraft guns, however he whizzed and whizzed about in the air out of control but then managed somehow or other to get control and landed in our lines and I believe he is not hurt, so was most fortunate.

The front here is still cool, calm and collected, and we are all hoping that it continues. I am busy making a great comfy and snug dugout. The floor is wooden, the insides are bricks and plaster and were papered, it really is like an underground house. We have propped up the roof with big logs, then sandbagged inside and out. I had three prisoners carrying bricks, so it will now keep out a 4.2 shell and any amount of whizz-bangs, but not a 5.9. It is so comfortable that I would be happy to chance the 5.9 and stay here all winter. I must to bed, I have a terrific headache, not enough sleep, I got called by phone seven times.

All my love, my lover, and my strength to go on . . .

AUGUST 27TH

Dearest wee Pettikins,

When I last wrote to you I had a most awful headache, in fact a touch of what is known as trench fever due no doubt to the continual work and worry combined with the result of too long continued proximity to too many dead bodies. I am not the only one, the CO was off colour, the MO and four other officers have all gone to hospital and many of the men are feeling and looking pretty bad.

However, here things are quieter, the air at least does not absolutely reek of putrid smells and one has not the continual worry and some sleep and rest can be obtained. We are still in the trench and will remain in the line until Monday week and then go back to a village for eight days' rest.

Not counting the four days' trek, we will have been in the trenches for 32 days in succession, and of course we were brought back on the 12th of August for a bath and left for 36 hours in the support line but we were shelled most of the time there and so taking everything into consideration the past three months have seen every one of us doing our bit and a bit more. However I'd sooner remain for three months on end in the trenches here than five days down south. It was just perfect hell let loose down there, sometimes one could almost feel oneself going dotty, the continual noise of the guns, the awful shelling and the ever-present putrefying Boche lying blown up, fat, black and gaping at one.

The countryside around here is much nicer now than it was when we left here. All the trees are out and fruit are to be had in a great many places for the picking, and one can get fresh vegetables and so some change in diet.

The Australians are on our right, a pretty fresh division, so I don't know yet if I know any of them. So far I've not seen any of them that I know but of course being in the line one does not get the opportunity of seeing anyone. No doubt when I get out of the line and go back I may see some I know.

It is raining today and has been raining for one or two days with the result that the trenches are very muddy and uncomfortable. One drawback here is the lack of dugouts, the water is too near the surface so that we cannot go down deep and if we raise up a structure, the Hun forthwith blows it down. Down south we lived sometimes in fine deep German dugouts, some quite underground houses with several rooms and 24–40 feet of solid chalk overhead, it gives one a fine sense of security. Even the 24 feet deep dugouts however were blown by such shells. A 5.9 shell at the moment of bursting exerts a pressure of 240 tons, so you can imagine that it takes a good dugout to stand up after a 5.9, yet some of our dugouts get direct hits, all lights out, showers of chalk and debris flying everywhere and the concussion was just something awful, almost burst one's head. If one is in the open and a 5.9 falls one mile away the roar and the concussion is terrible. At night it seems as if they are ever so much closer. You can only imagine what our 12 inch and 15 inch must have felt like to the Boche and he got plenty of them too. Pipe Major Anderson has been awarded the Croix de Guerre, he ought to have got the Victoria Cross. Both he and Robson deserved the Cross if anyone did. No doubt in a few days you will see the whole story in the press and I want you to keep it for me please. Quite a number of the exploits of our men are appearing in the press now although the regiments are not referred to. You will not see or rather recognise them. I am glad that poor old Stocks[17] is a prisoner of war but ye gods what a truculent wee prisoner he will be and no one to argue with. Wouldn't it have been too funny if he and I had both been captured together. I expect adversity would have made us wondrous kind to one another if we would have lived like brothers. He was tremendously game and kept going after two wounds.

I see that Hughes[18] is stirring up the conscription racket in Australia and I think public opinion will demand it, so many returned soldiers and so many relatives of soldiers will demand it. What with the continual Zepp raids in London and the home counties will all become a most unhealthy region but I'd still like to take the opportunity of risking it.

A German 'commercial' submarine, the *Deutschland* (or words to that effect) put up a good performance;[19] still it is a mere flash in the pan and she won't make many successful trips, and after all, it is only another conclusive proof of our blockade when a whole nation can go into ecstasy over a small cargo of £50 000. The chief thing is that it gives Bernstorff[20] direct communication with the desperate Hun.

I wish our own Zeps would drop a cargo of HE on to Berlin. I believe we have quite a few now and I hear they are 'some' ship.

Well dearest wee woman of mine, there is not a great deal of news to gather here. Things are normal and quiet and may they so remain. Give my very fond love and kisses to our dear son. Can we survive this terrible thing? Leave is still no closer but at some time in the future it must come.

In the meantime all my love . . .

AUGUST 30TH
BEF, somewhere in France

My dearest wee wife,
I am sure I don't have any idea why it is you have not received any of my letters, for the first opportunity I got I wrote and have written every day. I can only hope that you have at least received the most recent ones by now. Your letter that reached me today was dated the 25th so I really cannot understand the delay. The mail has been very irregular and it has been a very difficult job, not only collecting mail for dispatch to England but delivering it has been a nightmare. I can only hope that you have now received the letters I have written.

Well here we are still in the line, a long, long spell at it we have had this time but we come out on the 4th of September and then go back to rest for eight days. It will be a welcome change to here compared with down south, it is comparatively speaking paradise. All the same just when one is least expecting it they send over a salvo of whizz-bangs and 4.5s and they play up a bit. The weather the last two days has been absolutely wretched, rain and wind. All the time the trucks are feet deep in mud, our dear cursed old Flanders mud.

Of course there are no dugouts here, there are trench shelters that protect one from splinters but they are no protection against HE. Young Mein, a grandson of Sir Robert Cranston and one of our best junior officers, had his leg and arm badly fractured owing to his dugout collapsing when a whizz-bang landed just near the top. He was badly buried beneath the debris and was extricated with difficulty but was wonderfully cool and collected, a very good lad indeed.

I had another letter today from Ray Norris,[21] he is up north of us but not very far away. I am sending your address to him in case he gets leave so he can come up north and see you. Mother gave him strict instructions that he was not to come back to Australia until he had seen us all. Ray is really a very good fellow and I would like very much to arrange our leave so that he could be in London for 48 hours with us. Of course, Petty, I am counting on you coming to London to meet me, but I fear that there is little chance of leave before the end of November as Captain Greig's report that leave won't open until November the 1st seems to be correct.

Today we got the excellent news that Roumania had joined in the war, and now no doubt the people of Greece will make up the feeble mind of Tino. It sounds very like the beginning of the end of Austria Hungary, if not the whole business. Russia will, I expect, just pour troops in Hungary and Bulgaria over the Roumanian frontiers and the greasy Bulgar will soon pay heavily for his treachery. I guess the peace policy of Germany will commence to assume some definite shape. Anyway after all, the Salonika picnic party is at least going to see some real hard fighting, for the Bulgar will have to draw back from the Salonika front.

The struggle still waxes hot and strong at the southern point of interest, I hear the weather has been holding things up. I can just imagine what it is like there in wet weather, the roads would be impossible. They are nearly one continual succession of looped-up shell holes and every one is a grave.

You seem to be having a nice time at your picnics, I wish I was at them, as our picnic here is of a very different type. I did not get a chance to write yesterday so I sent a postcard. I was around the front line system all the time trying to arrive at some drainage system.

So far no word from the bank as to what the text of the cablegram meant. I sent the wire, or rather cable to them. I expect I should hear from them any day now. I do wish I could see Deckie, fancy people admiring the dear wee soul's hair. Do you remember how we used to despair about it ever growing into anything save tiny wee rat tails? I think that you are just a lovely tiny wee mother and know how to manage little babies. I would love to see Deckie and his little lady friend. He is starting very early calling on young ladies, isn't he? No doubt he takes after his young mother. I know two dear other wee ladies that I would love to call on just now.

We must have everything cut and dried about what you are to do when I know what day my leave is due. I'll write to you as soon as I know, hopefully three or four days beforehand. Wires take three or four days to get through but I will wire as soon as I arrive at Folkestone. I will wire again if I can do so and not miss the train in the meantime. Please come direct to London and go to the Russell Hotel and then I'll fly up to the hotel and eat you all up. It is a pity you did not keep in touch with the Flapper. You could have stayed with her a couple of days ahead and then come with me to the hotel, that is if you wanted to. Now you must get some nice new clothes and show them all what a lovely woman has been waiting all the time in Scotland whilst her old man has been working so hard over here.

I notice that Hugh Rayson and Keith Grieve won the Military Cross. They won it here during a raid for something or other. There will be no holding Keith now. Wasn't it great old Pipe Major Anderson winning the Croix de Guerre, I thought he would win the VC as he was tremendously game and went into battle with nothing but his pipes. I am sorry Mrs McOmie is ill again, she seems to have very bad luck.

Well my dearest I must close now telling you just how very dearly I do love both of you. Give our dear wee son such a kiss from his daddy who just loves to hear that he is having such a good time and being such a good boy.

Goodnight both of you . . .

La Boisselle

MESSAGES AND SIGNALS.

No. of M

Words | Charge

This message is on a/c of:

Service.

(Signature of "Franking Officer.")

Sent

At. m.

To.

By.

Recd. at

Date

From

By

19:1:16

Day of Month

In reply to Number

September

SEPTEMBER 1ST
BEF

My dearest poor worried sweetheart,
I really cannot understand how it is that you are not getting any of my letters and so today I sent you a wire. I do hope by now at least some of the letters will be turning up. The mail has gone mad and all services seem to have fallen to pieces. I sent you a letter the same day as I sent the one to Mrs McOmie and you never got yours. Major Rose's are all arriving okay but Beech and Black's people have both wired asking for news as no letters have arrived.

I sent my passbook to Cox to have it made up and at the same time I sent under cover of another letter two cheques to Cox to be placed in my account. So far not a word about them and the passbook has been out and it is back. My credit at Cox's is in a very healthy position, there is £178 in the bank to my credit, in addition to that there is £114 for the first year's gratuity pay and £60 for the second year up to date making a grand total of £342 which will fix up a lovely dear wee home for you and Deckie and who knows, Lyndal. I really cannot understand the mail arrangements. They used to be so good and regular but since our move they are all at sea and yet some of our mail gets through alright.

Things are still nice and comparatively quiet here and we are coming at last near the end of our spell in the line, we go back on Monday. Your letter enclosing one from Mother and Bobby came today, I am glad Mother heard from Robert, it will buck her up. She does not appear to have been well at all. I have written her several times since coming on the line but no doubt the same fate is holding up her letters.

I had a letter from the bank today telling me of poor old Gordon's death from wounds. I am so sorry. His people will be broken-hearted. Would you be a darling and write to Aunty Lilly or Uncle Charlie. The address is care of the Bank of New South Wales, Sydney.

This morning I was wandering about outside our HQ in the mist and searched an old strawberry patch and came on some nice ripe ones. The grounds and houses here have at one time been very decent but now of course they are nothing more than ruins and a few standing walls and perhaps a chimney stack here and there. It is so nice to hear that you and Deckie are both well and looking forward to having their daddy home but it looks almost certainly like it will not be before the end of November.

I see the Kaiser has put Hindenberg into a sort of Kitchener job. I think it means that the Hun is going to shorten his line and Hindenberg will claim it is for tactical reasons. I think it is all the beginning of the end, anyway I hope so. I am off to look up the Australians now to see if I know any of them.

No more just now, Petty. I found some copies of the *Parisienne* of which you have heard so much so I am going to post a copy to you. It is a very celebrated and a very naughty paper, I don't really think you are old enough to read it! I really don't, so I'll only send you one copy, some of it is at times very clever. The advertisements at the back are pretty hot stuff aren't they? I don't think you had better let Fanny see it either. Isn't the girl on the back sheet a naughty wee girl, very bold, young hussy?

Goodnight my dear,

SEPTEMBER 8TH

My darling wee wife,

Today I got your nice long letter with the photo of dear wee Derick. The two with the dog on the steps are awfully nice. He does look such a dear sweet little chap, so keen and wide awake too, isn't he?

He will never know, thank God, about this war. The one with his dear wee finger pointing is nice but the one standing up is spoilt by his finger. Oh what a boy he is growing into. No wonder poor old daddy is turning grey. You never tell me about your own grey hair now, I really believe that your grey eyes must have gone back to their original colour. Wee Derick looks nice and fat in the pictures and I think he has really nice fat strong legs like somebody else I know but you would never guess who that is.

The CO has just been called to take over the brigade[1] temporarily during the absence of the General, who looks well but has gone on leave. No doubt leave might open earlier than November. It looks as if we are going to stay here for the winter. The Hun did quite a lot of shelling yesterday and killed many poor civilians.

Well my darling wife, all my love . . .

SATURDAY, SEPTEMBER 9TH

Isn't it too bad my dear, I've never been able to find my lovely fountain pen. I'm sure the forward observation artillery officer must have taken it and not by mistake either. I am watching him pretty closely when we go back into the line, he's sure to come to us again as he is permanently attached to us. He is called FOAO and through him we keep in touch with our covering batteries.

We go back into the line[2] for another eight days on Monday and we will be back for four days into the second line. We go up forward again for eight and then come back here again for eight, at least that is the idea at present. Whether the arrangements will be adhered to or not is hard to say.

Today the Second-in-Command got an awful toss off his horse. I thought at first his neck was broken. We had been up to the front line to see the trenches as we go into a different sub-sector of same sector this time and we went up to see the disposition of the battalions that we are to relieve. We had left our horses near a haystack in a stubble field and on the way back were galloping across the stubble full speed, when his horse came down turning a complete somersault. I thought he had gone west but he jumped up with blood streaming down his face which was dreadfully skinned, bashed eye, and bleeding nose and hardly any skin left. Otherwise he was more or less intact but naturally very shaken. The CO is acting Brigadier just now and the second is really the CO and is most worried at his appearance.

I've got a very nasty headache at the moment and have not felt really fit since I got the dose of gas down south, it is either that or French Fever. Some days I just feel fit for nothing. However there is too much to do, so that one soon forgets the minor details.

I've been watching a party of civilians today, 'real lydies' from the neighbouring village. I think they have come over to see the 'sojers'. There are any number of civilians still left in this town, the majority of whom are working in the rope and yarn works, you know the type of flossie that works in these kind of places. There are no men here at all and somehow or other there are plenty of wee babies and going to be lots more by the appearance of most of the ladies. I have a fear that most of them will talk with either an Australian twang or a Scots accent, however they will I am sure be an improvement on the local product. The wee French kids here are awful-looking brats, all ears, flat big donkey ears.

The old Boche has been very uneasy here the last few days, I think he has got the wind up about the gas and soon as the wind blows from us to him he shoots off Verey lights and star shells with great gusto. If red flares go up it seems to mean 'look out for an attack', while green flares or rockets, we think, mean 'gas' or 'gas expected'. The gas we do use now is very deadly stuff — I saw the effects of it down south. I am enclosing a little picture cut out of the daily paper showing an old French windmill down south. Such a landmark it was. We lived just near it for about six weeks and on the night of the 29th/30th of June, that is the night before the big push, we bivouacked in the field just near it. There was a very big flying base just near it too.

I have not met many Australians I know so far. I did meet one of two and I know that Hughie Rayson, Keith Grieve, Packer and Charlie Parkinson[3] are all here just near me but so far I've not met any of them but I had a letter from Rayson. He married Doris Waterhouse and has a daughter, a delicate wee thing suffering from a constricted stomach, isn't it bad luck on him or rather on both.

Well, you will have received the naughty *La Vie Parisienne,*[4] but I might add, Petty, ones I sent you are very very mild compared with some of the ones. To my great delight I had a visit today from my favourite old friend Chaplain Crottee, who has left us for some considerable time but who has once again joined us, a rare old sport. Tomorrow I am going to have dinner with the three padres. There are more New Zealanders here than Australians. A New Zealand officer named Wells lives next-door to me and he seems a very decent chap, he comes in to see me a great deal and today at dinnertime he and I had a swim in the canal.[5] It was quite a treat.

I sent a runner out to buy some young corn yesterday from a farmer a little way out, and I roasted some when I got it, covered it with butter, salt and pepper and everyone ragged me about the wild Australian dish. However after they tasted it everyone roasted some and most of them have been at it all day. I notice in the paper that the Australian casualties are coming in and are very heavy. I thought they would be, the fighting down south was indescribable. The pressure is still being kept up and the Hun is having a rotten time but he deserves it and a lot more. I can really appreciate the time he is having. I never want to see the south of France again.

Troon is certainly good enough for me my dear. Just four walls, you and Deckie is the sort of scenery that would cheer me up no end and all I need. I try not to think about when the leave will be, let us pray that it will not be too long.

All my love to you both . . .

SEPTEMBER 12TH

My dearest wife,

I got your letter today, it is wonderful to have them so soon after they are written and to hear all about you and our wee bundle. Yes I think that you are quite old enough to read the *Parisienne.* I don't know if you are old enough but you have proved by being such a lovely wee mother and such a sweet wee wife that you ought to be allowed to read anything. You do make a splendid and loving girlfriend and you don't really know how your poor old soldier man appreciates just every quality that you have.

We are just getting ready to move back into the line after a tiny rest and of course it is not a very inviting outlook. The line is comparatively quiet. There is a good deal of intentional shelling all the time. It would have been great to have come back here with all our old officers and all our old men, but things are so changed now, all new officers, all new men, and lots of ghosts. You can count the old soldiers on the fingers of one hand. We don't go into the same sub-sector this time but go into the same sector. There are four sub-sectors to a sector. I don't know how long we will be up there but I suspect for eight days.

You will be pleased to hear I am being promoted to Captain, my name has already gone with the War Office but there will be the usual delay before the Gazette comes through. It is very satisfactory and it means an increase of four shillings a day in pay and as I am to be antedated to July the 1st it will be very acceptable and will swell the already flourishing bank account. As soon as the war is over we will take a lovely wee house and be so very happy, dearest and by then Deckie will be able to look after dear wee Lyndal won't he? I see in today's *Times* the official report of Gordon's death, poor chap, I am very sorry for them all.

Well dearest wee wife, all my love . . .

SEPTEMBER 14TH
BEF

My darling wife,
It is awfully cold today and yesterday it rained very heavily and we spent most of that day crouched down behind the parapet to avoid a very respectable artillery strike. It is certainly most unpleasant but at least the Hun is having similar unpleasant weather. His sandbag breast works and his parapets went sky high and his wire was blown to pieces; every now and again you could see a Boche bolting past the breaches in his line and the men and machine guns took flying shots at him. I think many an old Boche got it. He retaliated pretty heavily all along our line and blew us in, in quite a number of places. Fortunately our casualties were not worth mentioning, none killed, several men were buried but were all dug out safe and sound. If we would let old Fritz alone here I don't believe he would fire a shot but we absolutely get him mad continually hammering at him and then he looses off at us for about an hour and then gets it back harder than ever.

I am afraid if today is any indication then we are in for a very early winter. I was awfully cold during the night and the wretched dugout leaked badly, so badly that it disturbed the rats and they scampered all over the top of me all night.I have not had my overcoat off all day and now that the clouds are covering the sun I think it is even going to be colder.

Great excitement in our world here as leave has been reopened, a very few at a time, about eighteen in the brigade, that means about four allotments to a battalion a week. That will be about one officer every other week for us so that it will be about the end of October at least until I get leave, somewhere about the 26th or 27th of October. Of course that is not absolutely certain and is liable to be changed. Selby, Beech and Dickson have not had any leave at all yet and so they will have preference. Then I expect the CO will go before me and then I am the next in turn.

You just don't know how excited I am to think of seeing you again soon. I just long for you both and love you both all the time. I don't think I will ask you to come to London to meet me for now, what I know of the train arrangements and the boat times I will get to London about 10.30 pm and just have time to catch the midnight through to Glasgow and then on to Troon. Last time the boat was just too late for me to catch the Glasgow train and I had to go by the Edinburgh train.

The CO is still in command of the brigade during the General's absence and Major Clark is in command, he is quite a decent chap and a very good soldier and he and I get on well. He backs me up in my rows with the company commanders. My promotion to Captain has been sent in for confirmation, it will probably be some weeks before it is gazetted but the rank's badges are already up and I feel very pleased about that. I kept Sergeant Duthie, my orderly room sergeant, out of the office on Tuesday and have promoted Stocker (the trusty) in his stead. Duthie let me down very badly over a return and then told me a lie about it so I held him out by the scruff of his neck.

There are quite a lot of nice gardens or the remains of them in the back of the lines here but nothing doing in the way of strawberries or anything else. The Tynesiders were hereabouts so you may reckon there is not even a pale or frightened strawberry left but at the other place it used to be quite a diversion looking in amongst the old ruins for strawberries.

I love Derick's note in your letter and his drawing seems to show a leaning towards Impressionist work, don't you think? The dear wee lad, I could just imagine him drawing it whilst his young and pretty mother sat and watched, I am so proud of you both. Goodbye for the moment. Do you remember September three years ago? I think we would fancy you going for a swim. I wished I could have been there.

All my love . . .

SUNDAY, SEPTEMBER 17TH
BEF

Yesterday I missed the mail. I have to go out of the line to the brigade headquarters to conduct a court martial against one of our men. My case was the third on the list so I was kept hanging about for a long while and then when it did come on I was kept at it all the afternoon and finished too late for the mail. It is a nuisance to have to leave the line to do these things. It means going out in daylight and as the Boche has the high ground here, he can see every movement at the back and his snipers chip away at me; it's a case of trusting to his bad shooting. The result is that when one spends any time outside, a court martial is the last thing one wishes to conduct.

Today is a perfect autumn day. The night and mornings are getting very frosty but the days have been perfect the last two days. The result is that there is, to quote the word of the armchair war correspondents, 'increased aerial activity'. Everything is very satisfactory here and as well down south and the Boche is getting it pretty swift and sore on the neck. The progress will be a bit quicker now the Hun has not had time nor the heart to put in his wonderful defensive operations, besides the men are so fed up, whilst our men are just dead keen to get to holts[6] with the square heads. Here we are shaking him up all round and he is getting very tamed. He put up a notice the other day: 'English man, why do you strafe so much'. Some of the stunts here have been quite lively, any amount of heavy shelling, guess the Hun must be absolutely staggered at our supply of shells and the quality of them. If the war goes on through the winter we will have just a colossal supply of big guns and shells to pass over to him in the spring. It is amusing how he always squeals about after unprecedented shellfire, etc. The beggar knows what superiority in gunfire means. He only got this far thanks to the self same factor, but now we are level, soon he will be hopelessly outnumbered and then the end as far as personnel goes, we can biff him any day. Well our eight days in is rapidly coming to a close now and soon we will be out for another rest in billets and a good clean-up.

Leave has certainly opened but we are only as yet allowed four vacancies per week. Dickson went off this morning, that leaves Selby and Beech to go now before me, of course. The four vacancies a week are not for officers only and the CO does not want too many officers to be away at once. So that if I do get away it will not be before the end of October. Colonel Rose is going on the 19th, he has got a month's leave on compassionate grounds which is on account of his business.[7] He tells me his business has gone to pot during his absence and he is down in the mouth. He has been very depressed about it all, quite unlike what he used to be, at present he is acting Brigadier. I do hope I can manage leave before the winter sets in.

Derick seems to be growing up so fast doesn't he? I'll notice a tremendous difference. Did I tell you that I had a letter from Mrs McOmie enclosing the snaps? They are a bit out of focus otherwise not so bad. I see that the tiny wee legs in the picture are still holding their own.

On Saturday next week, God willing, I am racing the Roman Catholic padre for 100 francs. He has a horse that he reckons can beat mine so we have arranged a match along the river bank[8] and the Presbyterian padre is to be judge. Charlie Anderson is the starter. My mare is a real flyer and if he beats me, his horse can gallop. Padre Black was up here for lunch yesterday, came up to conduct some funerals, I was out at the time so missed him.

Well my dearest wife and son, all my love . . .

SEPTEMBER 18TH

My dearest, much missed sweetheart,
It is raining most heavily today, started last night just at midnight when we were commencing a great stunt against the Boche and it has come down consistently ever since

with the result that the trenches are becoming the usual quagmire. It has been really cold along with the wet so that we are looking somewhat like a mob of pigeons on the roof of a house on a wet day. Everyone and everything looks droopy but the gunners are still busy and every now and again a few yards of Fritz's parapets go up sky high. There is no mistake, he has been getting it on the necks from us. Our eight days is up tomorrow and if it only fines up it will be great. The eight days in seems an eternity when one commences but the fear, boredom and the pig-like life is completely obliterated by the eight days out. It is so wet that I am afraid my race with the padre will not come off.

When Vera's other letter came telling you she was at Gunnedah, I meant to tell you then that they were Harry's relatives. Poor old Mary seems to have made a great hit with Vera, she really has wonderful spirits and is no chicken in size or age. Mary always called Horrie and I the spurious knights after a play we once saw in Mudgee. I have met all the Hoskings, some are very nice and some are the limit, wild outbackers. Fancy you dreaming about me. I'm rather afraid I've often dreamt the same thing, sweetheart.

The CO left on a month's leave last night and I believe he will not come back at all once his business is set up a bit. I think he will get some administrative job at home where his organising and business methods would be invaluable. I believe his business has gone to pot but this is strictly confidential. Dickson is away on leave, that only leaves Selby and Beech ahead of me now, but until the next allotment comes out I cannot even judge when I will be together with you. However I am still hoping for the 26th of October. Now my dear I must stop and take some rest.

All my love . . .

September 20th

Fancy young Deckie blossoming out into speech all of a sudden, why he will be toddling off to school in no time now. What a shame that I am to miss all his babyhood, the dear wee thing. Why I might almost have married a widow and had one wee child to commence with I've seen so little of him, but you have been both a mother and a father to Deckie, always playing a double role for his sake and mine. How many wee sons and daughters of all the chaps out here are going through the same life? How many young men and women of the future will grow up with a handicapped childhood, or worse how many will have no father to look to? You are so good at looking after the wee boy, you will want another dear wee bundle to look after soon won't you? It will be wonderful to watch Derick and Lyndal growing up together. I think that it ought to be Lyndal's birthday on or about the 21st or 22nd of November don't you dearie? I mean tell your poor old man if he is right.

We came out of the trenches last night and it just poured with rain the whole time and has more or less continued to do so. Just at dusk the Boche gave our headquarters a rare old bashing with his two heavy guns, some dugouts were blown in and some trenches blown up but no one hit. We were just having tea when the first one came over with a vicious scream and landed without bursting in the trench. That of course put us wise and we took every piece of necessary cover and then the fire commenced and he paced with us for a long while. However he seemed to cool off at dark and our relief[9] went on. We are in a farm just behind the line. Of course, there is the usual old hag and a decrepit old man, otherwise it is nice and quiet and still but a great many machine gun bullets whistle around the orderly room after dark. We are only to be out about six days this time and then in for another eight. Eight days is a long while and one gets bored to death with the monotony but the longest spells out compensate. When the weather comes really bad, we won't have to do eight days in. There are great rumours about the increase in leave allotments, I do hope it is true. Captain Greig thinks it will be increased on the 22nd. Let us hope so as at the present rate it will take three years for every man in the battalion to get leave. I am just longing to come home.

I've got another wretched court martial on, it's an awful nuisance and they are looked upon so seriously here and the punishments are very severe on service, I hate them. Still it's my job and I've got to prosecute the delinquents. Well my dearest all my love again and again and again. Tell me if I am right about Lyndal's birthday, dearest, do tell me dearest.

All my love . . .

SEPTEMBER 23RD

Again I missed the mail, a thousand curses. Major Clark who is acting as CO during Colonel Rose's absence is ill in bed, in fact he has been in bed since we came out of the trenches. We are all feeling so blue and down in the mouth, we came out expecting to have eight days out and were just settling down to the idea when we got orders to go back into the line so it is on again tonight.[10]

I had a tremendous day yesterday, in fact I was going until 2 am in the morning. I had to go up to the line and arrange for the relief and then had to come down and call the company commanders together and tell them all about the relief, and then on top of that, get orders out. In addition there was all the ordinary routine work to be got through and now we are getting ready to move into the line again.

I got your wonderful letter yesterday, my darling, how I look forward to receiving them and how I enjoy reading them. Looking forward to letters is the only joy in this place.

And now we are about to shift back into the line just as we were starting to get a little bit comfortable in the rain and mud. Several men are away on leave, Selby goes the first week in October and then Beech and then it ought to be my turn. However with the CO sick, my prospects are not too bright. I'm trying to persuade him to go when we come out of the line this time, his going does not interfere with the leave vacancies as COs go on special leave. Captain Greig is going on Tuesday I think. I am still hoping for October but please don't be disappointed if I don't get there before the first week in November. There is no one here who can take my place. It seems a silly thing to say doesn't it but it is true. It is really extraordinary how many of these officers here, who have all had good educations, cannot write a decent letter and I have had four on now as assistant adjutants and none have been any good. Black is on now and is useless, Beech was worse, Mortimer promised alright but was worse than the other two and Brown about the worst of the lot. I will try someone else soon, we have so many new officers that at last I might get one suitable. Robertson who was adjutant of the 16th was asked by the brigade to resign, he made an awful mess of his casualty returns during the push. I think my horse would do a better job in the orderly room, in fact I may even promote him and get him in the trenches next week.

Things still seem to be going alright down south. The Germans appear to be counter-attacking in desperate strength but their morale seems to be breaking. Fancy me sending back to you the letter you sent me. Really sweetheart, I think I must be in love and I really am too and I've got the dearest wife to prove it.

Goodbye now my two loved ones . . .

SEPTEMBER 26TH

My darling,
Yesterday all I could do was send you a postcard as I was at a planning conference all day. The engineer headquarters were discussing how to render the trenches more comfortable and habitable during the winter months. The meeting was suddenly arranged, we did not get finished until well after 7 pm and I did not get a chance to write.

On Sunday I was out almost the whole day conducting a field general court martial against one of our men who left his sentry post to get his breakfast, so that I had almost two full days away from the camp.

This is to be a shorter spell in the line than the last one, as we came out on Thursday night. The arrangement is slightly altered now and we won't do any more spells of eight days in, five at the most for the future. I wish they would send us back in to rest for a while so when we do come out of the line we go out into fighting billets. True enough one can get off for a ride in the stand-to area but one is only 1500 yards behind the line and one moves about very cannily.

Our brigade has been hard at it now since the last week in April. Ever since I got back from leave I've not had a spell but my leave will soon whisk around and in about three and a half weeks I hope to be home with you and dear wee Derick. What a time it will be. I'm longing to see you both. I got a letter from you today in which you say you got two of mine at once. I expect the post has been hung up somewhere.

Today is another bonny day, not a cloud in the sky and just a nice autumn touch in the weather. Brother Boche must be feeling in fine key too as he has been shelling us most promiscuously all day, sending them into all sorts of unheard-of spots which have never been shelled before. He has increased his anti-aircraft guns to a great extent here, he has got something on the go at the back. If any of our planes take a peep over he nearly strafes the heavens back and I've seen him bring two of our chaps down in his own lines. It's a very queer feeling to see a plane fall from a great height.

Today eighteen of our big battle planes went across to see what tricks he is up to at the back and incidentally to do some bombing. Fritz got highly indignant and shelled them tremendously and got one on the return journey. After about an hour the planes returned for a second trip across. The night before last several of his planes came over at midnight and dropped bombs on us but did no damage, nearly all the squibbs fell in No Man's Land, indeed three fell just outside his own front line barbwire.

Great news yesterday about the two Zeppelins, two isn't a bad bag is it. No doubt the remaining swines will soon think the game isn't worth the candle and that our anti-aircraft guns are not so bad after all. I only wish that the whole crew of the second one had been done in. Good news came in too from the south today, reaching us at dawn by wire and is confirmed so things are pretty satisfactory all round.

The Boche is living with a perfect hell down there, no one knows it better than we do. Isn't it a funny thing that on our first push and on the first day we went 2000 yards and hung on for three days and then the Boche had all the pick of the artillery positions and was right above us. He has increased his gunfire there, we notice the increase each day but now he can only shoot from the rear, we hold all the good observation and he will just be slaughtered. He has paid an awful price down south and so have we, but the losses now are nothing compared to his. We have taken about 40 000 prisoners and his dead lay about just like flies. I saw hundreds and hundreds, some shell holes and dugouts had as many as thirteen to seventeen dead and the open ground over which he has counter-attacked was in places littered with dead. He is no doubt sorely tried and I think very sick.

Weren't the old caterpillars[11] a joke, we used to see them clamouring about and crawling over the trenches in the back area long before the push was made, the secret was well kept. It's very amusing to see that the Hun is complaining about their introduction, saying that the machines are inhuman, and their use should be banned. Coming from the monsters who invented asphyxiating gas and liquid fire the complaints are ludicrous. Even the imperfect sense of humour of the Boche must have felt that the claims were absurd. Gas is alright if the other fellow isn't ready but now with the respirators so perfect, it is not very deadly, but if it gets one unawares it is awful and tends to make men panic.

I hope when I get home on leave that we can get a chance to see the picture of the battle of the Somme, I believe it is very good and is not a fake, at least not all of it. The actual infantry attack is quite genuine. I was so sorry to know in your letter, old sweetheart of mine that you had a nasty old bad back. I hope it is now on the mend, poor old thing. I should have been there to look after you, shouldn't have I? You didn't tell me in your letter if the dates of my leave would suit you. I could wait a week longer but I could not get away any sooner. I am getting so excited about my leave, looking forward to seeing you both. Tell Deckie all about me so that he will know who I am. I think you would be working very hard to be making him so many suits and pyjamas too. Fancy the dear wee might only want one extra pair of pretty pink ones dearie to complete the picture.

Now goodnight sweetheart, all my love . . .

The September letters end here, due to the sudden arrival of the much longed for leave and LWN's return to Scotland.

la Boisselle

MESSAGES AND SIGNALS.

Words Charge

This message is on a/c of: Service.

Sent At m. To By

(Signature of "Franking Officer.")

Recd. at Date From By

19:1:16

Day of Month In reply to Number

October

This is the only letter that exists from Doris and is to her mother-in-law, Jeannie Nott, in Bundaberg, North Queensland, and refers to the period of leave mentioned.

TUESDAY, OCTOBER 17TH
The Bungalow

Dearest Gran,
Last week Lew wrote you a long letter, so you will know that at last he had his leave. A fortnight ago today we were in at breakfast when a voice said 'Hullo, you people' and there he was looking round the door! We hadn't even heard the front door open and didn't think that he could get away till the end of the month. Wasn't that a glorious surprise? And he had twelve days till the Thursday of the following week. What a happy time we three had together but it was all too short and now it seems an eternity to wait till he comes again.

He looked very well, only his eyes were tired and somehow different like all the other soldiers who have been through such an awful time — it's a marvel he looked so well but he looked even better when he left, the good rest and change and the happy loving time with his wee wife and son did their work well. But, oh, Gran it was so hard to let him go again and now I am so lonely and wanting him so much. I'm sure Derick knows it too, for today I had a backache and he said 'Deckie can't get Daddy', dear wee lad. He knew Lew at once and called him Derick's darling Daddy and wanted to love and hug and kiss him all the time. But Lew is not inclined to spoil him anymore than I am and the lad hated Lew to speak sharply to him, his little mouth went down and he said 'Derick will not cry' but he was close. Just now he and Bobby are playing trains on the floor, they both love them.

On Monday we went up to Glasgow and Lew had his photo taken, went against the grain. I am waiting for the proofs now, and hope they are good. On Tuesday we went to Edinburgh to see Mr Hole and his family. Their son was with the RS and was killed on the 1st. At least they have his identity disc and compass but no other trace of him was found. His poor mother, I think, is hoping against hope that he is a prisoner. That afternoon Lew went to Glencorse Depot to arrange for his men.

On Wednesday, the day before he had to go, we had a lovely quiet day together, sitting in front of the fire and talked about the happy time we are going to have when all this awful time is over and we have a little home of our own to love. I have had a little note from London, but have not heard from France yet. I do hope that they stay in their present reasonably quiet sector, I don't think any of us could stand it if they had to go through another time like they had on the Somme.

Here is a letter he had some time ago from Gladys, which he wanted me to send on to you. It is best not to write to her as it may get her into some trouble. I wrote to her and the letter was returned with a note from the censor saying that no letters were to be delivered to enemy or neutral countries.

Well I must stop now and say au revoir, *with much love to all the family, from your loving*

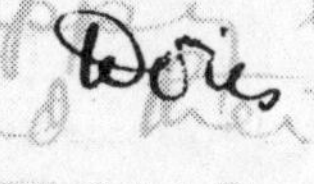

October 14th
Somewhere in France

Pettikins, Pettikins mine,
Last night I just arrived in time to send off a few lines. I had a very very rotten trip right along, put in almost a whole day in sitting in the train at various sidings, whilst trains hurrying anxious, grim troops south ran through. We were dumped out of the train at 2 am, waited shivering till 10.30 before we got on board and completed our journey. When at last we reached the rail head the mess cart met me, and I came straight up into the trenches. It is just too rotten for words to get back, I feel as homesick and miserable as one could possibly feel. The weather is still fine here and delightfully sunny but a bit muddy. I've been very busy all day trying to overtake the work I've missed. The CO has done a fair bit as he knew how I would feel on my return, but I don't feel a bit interested in the work, and all the time I am thinking back to you and dearest wee Deckie. Oh how I love you both. I can hardly bear to write, was it all a dream, can there be such a beautiful life so close to this rotten war?

There have been a few changes, for whilst I have been in Utopia, a new doctor, and three new officers[1] have arrived, whom I have not yet met. Captain Greig just phoned, he is leaving the brigade and going to the Corps HQ. Everyone seems to be leaving the old ship. It isn't a promotion for him, he said and he will certainly return at some time, but in the meantime will be DSA and QMG, sounds alright but is no catch. 'Blanco' White will probably get his job.

All my love to you both, words are so empty after a leave like that,

October 17th
BEF

My own wee wife,

I got your two lovely letters, one yesterday and one today, and it was so nice to hear from you so soon. You did not say if you had a letter from me which I wrote from the Buckingham Palace Hotel, which is a jolly nice pub, clean and cheap, as well as near to the station. Next leave let's spend some time there.

The weather is so cold and I have a severe cold in the head, I think I caught it in the train, and as well, I had an awful spill last night, fell over a railing and ten feet into a ditch. I think I have sprained the wrist that caught Mr Boche's shrapnel on the big push! Still I'm not too bad specially when I recount that yesterday we saw one of our planes get a direct hit; both the pilot and observer fell out, what a sickening sight, to see them going round and round in the air, like two big frogs, falling, falling from ever so high. They both fell into No Man's Land, and must have died instantaneously.

Winter is setting in apace, and already the trees are almost bare of leaves and sniping is beginning to warm up; when there is a lot of foliage there is good cover and now that it is thinning the men are forgetting, and getting sniped.

I do feel like a fish out of water and never took so long to settle down. I told the CO that I intend to drop out in the New Year, and he said he would do what he could. We examined the regulations and found that there is no single obstacle, and I will get away alright. Most of the officers get back to England much sooner than this; I will have done 12 months in the trenches, and except for a few of the senior officers, I have nearly made the record.

All our promotions are held up. Lodge[2] is the only one that will go through, as Russel, Harrison, Dobie and Ross are still on strength, but it's a bit tough on us all.

Dearest wee mate of mine, there is nothing to tell you except the old old story that we both love so well, I do love my lonely little lover and our wee son.

Do keep well and look after yourselves . . .

OCTOBER 19TH
BEF

Raining, raining, raining like the very Dickens, commenced the night before last, and has not let up for a moment. Fortunately we were relieved last night and are in fighting billets[3] just behind the line, and they are none too comfortable, the rain beating in everywhere and making a terrible mess. The trenches will be in an awful state and I'm glad we are not in it now.

My cold is on the mend although it shouldn't be, got an absolute drenching last night, and have been dripping, and frozen since. Life is just awfully miserable, everyone looks down and out, we all have the miseries. Its dark by 4 pm, and your poor old man is most disconsolate and wants his two wee treasures more than ever.

No mail today. I was expecting a nice letter from you today but for some reason no letters arrived at all. I expect that movements of troops have upset the train service, as they are sure to be getting this awful weather down south, and it will certainly upset the offensive. No infantry could do anything in the torrential rain we are having. I'm afraid that it is going to be a long, hard and very wet winter.

There is a deadlock in the matter of promotions, and it looks as if they will be held up indefinitely. I do long to hear all about you both, I need to know your every doing, it is the only thing that is sane in this world. Nothing else matters to me, darling, and it's all I can think about.

This place is a hole, it's dead, and there is no news, absolutely no news. I do hope it fines up a bit tomorrow, so I can get out for a bit of a ride. I am feeling very blue, I just hope the Boche is feeling worse. If you do have any spare time, dearest, could you see Mrs Stocker, she has had a wee son and Stocker is so worried as he has not had any news, and fears she may not be too well.

No more now, my dearest, all my love to you both . . .

OCTOBER 22ND
BEF

Pettikins, Pettikins tiny wee wife and sweetheart,
This is to be a very tiny note just to say what a dear wee gypsy sweetheart of mine you are and what a darling wee boy you and I have.

I received your dear letters and just love getting them. I was glad to get the Australian mail, fancy the Craigs coming over, it will be great to see them, but not a very nice time of the year to come. Mother, I'm sure, will come too in January, I certainly hope so. Doesn't little Phil write a beautiful letter? The parcels arrived today, everything alright.

Great excitement here, we are occupying a billet that has been continuously occupied by the British and there was only supposed to be two old dames living in the house. The Sergeant-Major noticed an extraordinary amount of food going upstairs and took a peep in and spotted a man in bed; there was intense excitement, and one of the old dames rushed in and tried to blow the light out. The matter was reported to me, and in my best and politest French I questioned the dame, and she admitted through a great many tears that the man was her brother, and was quite mad. He was not too mad to look at, as far as I was concerned, nor did he look much like her brother. I told him to jump up which he did, and I sent for the APM and the Gendarmes, and after a great deal of Gallic cursing, shouting and screaming he was removed to the asylum. I think he was a French deserter, who had found a cosy nest, with all sorts of side benefits.

Boche has just dropped a bomb on us, but missed everything, I think if it had not been for Isaac Newton and the power of gravity he would have missed the ground altogether.

Goodbye for now darlings . . .

There is a gap in the letters of one week at this point. The battalion was not doing anything of great interest according to the Unit Records, although it was up into the line for five days. There may be letters lost but I expect that none were written for those few days.

October 29th
BEF, somewhere in France

We were relieved last night,[4] and returned to the old billet we were in last, and whilst there is nothing fancy or elegant about them, there is a certain amount of comfort that is not to be had in the trenches.

The Boche gave us a regular pasting yesterday, hurling across a great deal of material. He has brought up some new 5.9s and has been searching promiscuously with them, and at times got dangerously close to our HQ. The worst of it is that all the shelters such as cellars, which would give good shelter are flooded, and no good. We dodged about and trusted to luck, which has lasted so far! Our guns responded, but he nevertheless continued to heave those infernal 5.9s at us, reducing a dozen houses to rubble and brick dust. Today we are burning with indignation as he tried to shell our billets, just our luck, on the day we come out of the line, but he fell short and no damage was done.

I had a long letter from the old CO today, he is still doing nothing, and the poor old man is down in the dumps.

I got your two letters today, they were held up by some stunt in the Channel, the particulars of which we have not yet heard. I hope no boats were torpedoed, as we have men coming and going across the Channel. The people were so sick on the boat I came back on from leave that most would have welcomed a torpedo to put them out of their misery.

I got the Australian mail today, and when next I write to Vera[5] I won't mention Geoff as she seems pretty sick over his departure. I do hope he comes through alright. I seem to know the name of Failes but in what connection

I don't know. Send along the splashes that contain the picture of Auntie Nancy, I will return them.

The weather is cold and wet with very high winds, which is miserable, but saves us the worry of gas.

It was special to hear all your thoughts about us and about love, aren't we just the luckiest people alive, or for certain I am the luckiest man alive. My luck was to marry you and that luck is holding in this terrible place. I swear that I will never be cold again.

Well, my darling, I'm off to have some sort of bath, to try and rid myself of the beasties.

All my love . . .

PS. *I know the people Cis spoke of, Fergus McIntyre, a decent fellow, his brother married Mollie David's sister and he is living somewhere in Scotland. The father was a judge in Tasmania, but is now dead. Stocker was so overjoyed that you had been to see Mrs Stocker. He wept about his wife's condition. She wrote him her first letter all about your visit the other day.*

OCTOBER 30TH
BEF

Dearest wee girl,

Just a tiny note, as there is really no news at all. I got your letter today, and what a day it has been, raining and blowing a hurricane without a pause all day. The big guns have been adding to the row too, very active all night and day. Almost all the ground is under water. We have been issued with our new leather and flannel jerkins and they are nice and warm, the men have them too and are looking very warm and contented, especially when they are compared with a line of Hun prisoners we saw yesterday. They regarded their captors with envy, they were in thin grey tunics, many without underclothes, and were all shaking with cold.

Today you are in Glasgow, and then go to Edinburgh. I hope all is well at No 3. Give my kindest regards to Mrs Greig and tell her how much I miss Captain R.B.G. All the old hands are leaving the brigade and the various units. Derrick will love being in a house full of children, they will notice a difference in the dear wee fellow. Everything I hear makes me want to be away off from this place and to be with you. Pouring outside and there are men waiting in the rain to get their orders.

All my love to you both . . .

OCTOBER 31ST
BEF

My darling,

I can't see why my letters are not arriving, they must be hung up somewhere. Yours are arriving here and thank heavens, I couldn't stand it if they were held up for a second.

Not a great deal to write about here, old girl, just the same dull routine, the same dull and wet rain, the same dull and cold weather. I had hoped to get out for a ride to clear the head, but too wet, so I worked in the orderly room, copying some maps. The guns are going all night, all they seem to achieve is to keep us all awake. I saw a very game pilot today, in the only aeroplane up. I suspect it was not so blowy up high, but all the same he was having a very rough passage, and hardly seemed to be moving against the wind. Very brave.

You will be in Edinburgh now, I can imagine you there, only a few miles away, but really as good as a million miles. I met 'Blanco' White today, and he tells me Captain Greig is so busy with paperwork, he is not getting out on his horses at all. That would make him very depressed. Major Osborne is away on a six week course, the brigade is not a bit interesting just now. Padre Crottee is coming over to dinner with me tonight, which will liven things up.

We go up into the line again on Thursday. It's about time we had our rest, it's been front line or stand-to billets for a long time now, hasn't it?

Well my dearest lover, all my love to you both . . .

la Boisselle

MESSAGES AND SIGNALS.

Words | Charge

This message is on a/c of:

Service.

(Signature of "Franking Officer.")

Sent

At.......m.

To.......

By.......

Recd. at

Date

From

By

19:1:16

Day of Month

In reply to Number

November

November 3rd
BEF

It seems a long time since I last wrote to you but it is because the last day has been raining and blowing so hard and we had to come into the line yet again and relieve.[1] The day of the relief is always a long drawn-out and boring affair and it is in no way made more pleasant by the wet. Today is Friday and the weather has improved considerably, in fact it is quite a decent day but the mud and water lie everywhere, and the duck boards are as slippery and treacherous as they can be. There is a good deal of shelling on both sides and the Boche is shelling all round very systematically, with those devilish 5.9s which makes one very windy.

I heard from Colonel Rose yesterday, he has got his extension through alright. I am sure you will hear all about the push when you see him. Padre Black is just back from his leave, and I hear he has been delivering most dramatic sermons in Edinburgh.

We have had no English mail for some days. I hear that the weather in the Channel is atrocious, bad enough when I returned but now far worse.

Now, Pettie, whilst you are in Edinburgh, keep your eye skinned for a little place for you, me and the wee Deckie. You know the sort of place, cosy and warm and not too big. I don't mind where it is, so long as it is connected with some services, train or tram, as I must get to the infirmary. It is so exciting to start thinking again of the world, and our future. Two years so far out of our life together.

Would you please send me Aitcheson Robertson's *Jurisprudence and Public Health*, and if you can get it, a secondhand Hale Whyte *Materia Medica*. It won't take me long to fix these two exams, which I would sit at the first opportunity. I reckon three weeks would do me, and the rest would not take long. I'm beginning to think about the work ahead, and it soon comes back. Anatomy is going to be the big thing, and will require any amount of hard work and long hours, but time will fly. Imagine being able to come home every night, to my two treasures, clean and dry!

Goodnight my dearest, love,

NOVEMBER 4TH
BEF

Sweetheart wife of mine,
No letter for the past two days, but I expect the fact that you have been on the move will account for that. I hope you find Mrs Greig well. The Colonel wrote me the other day and told me he expected to see you in a day or two. We are all wondering when he is coming back. Major Clark has returned from leave and wears the usual fed-up look.

A better day today, quite fine and even sunny at times and both sides are taking advantage of the fact. There has been a great deal of shelling in either side in fact, quite a heavy strafe has been on for two days, as the papers glibly put it 'an unwonted activity by air and in artillery duels'. Our batteries have managed to cut the German wire in preparation for a stunt, and the machine guns have been so active to prevent the Hun repairing their wire.

I see the Italians have made another bit of a bound, which is good for them. The French are going well down in Verdun, aren't they?

Stocker is off on special leave, which I got for him, as his wife is very ill again; her case has gone wrong, septicaemia or something like that as far as I could read from the letter he had.

My dear little bright eyes, have you been able to find a love nest for us yet, and how does Deckie like a house full? Probably in his element.

Another wretched court martial tomorrow, a very serious one, man absolutely refused to obey a command, refusing in a very defiant manner. I hate doing the prosecuting but one has to do it.

Otherwise things are going alright. I see that conscription has fallen flat in Australia, but I don't think Hughes will leave it at that. I'm afraid he will work some other lever.

Well, my darling, all my love to my two treasures . . .

NOVEMBER 5TH
BEF

My own dearest wee woman,
I see that I have been addressing letters to you to 39 Clurey Gardens, as I thought that you would be there, but I'm sure that Mrs Greig will send them to you, as she knows your address. I am using some ink I made out of some ink powder we found, it is not too bad, is it.

Great old shelling match is on, there is a high wind blowing and the shells are fairly screaming as they tear through. Ours are tearing over me as I write, very low and sound very very businesslike. The Boche is heaving it back at our batteries but he only has an idea where they are and the wind is not helping him so that he is making poor shooting and as long as he keeps at it where he is now he can go on for 24 hours on end. They have not been able to repair their wire.

No aeroplanes have been up for the past few days, the wind is far too high for them, so things are not what one calls exciting but I am very content to wish for nothing more exciting at the moment.

I'm so glad that you like the new dress you got, I can hardly wait to see it on, you look so pretty in all the dresses I have seen, I'll bet this one is no exception. I do hope when you are in Edinboro' you see some decent theatre, there is generally something pretty good each week, even in the middle of this terrible war. There must soon be an end to the madness.

Richardson is getting so excited about his leave. I was censoring his letters last night, and he was full of his plans, he ought to get away any time now.

Well, my two dears, all my love, hope to be able to bring you more news soon, all my love . . .

NOVEMBER 6TH

My dear little girl,

This is the only paper I have left and the whole book has been stamped by Stocker, so please excuse it. I am also using the ink we made out of the ink powder so it is likely to blot, as it was made yesterday and gradually seems to get thicker and thicker.

I am dreadfully tired today, never got to bed at all last night, had lots of excitement that kept us all out of bed all night. A real stunt led by Selby, Eric Sandison and CSM

Park and about forty of the men. They came up in great secrecy and set off from our trenches after midnight. When they were in position, the guns sent in a terrific bombardment, after which the raiding party charged on to the German trenches. Selby shot three Germans but took a blow to the chest from a rifle butt. Sandison's party rushed along the trench in the other direction, and had a bombing fight, with Boche mortars being destroyed. Poor Sandison was wounded, how bad we don't know.[2]

I was going to hop off to bed at the first opportunity but the wind has died down, the rain cleared off and there is a lovely moon, so I felt more like having a chat to my own dear woman, than lying in my old flea bag.

Oh, Pettie, you are a joke, why you won't even let me have the proofs of my own photos, fancy keeping them like this. I think you must be in love with me. I was keen to have some postcard-size enlargements made of the snaps as I have been asked by several of the fellows to give them one, and it is not so expensive that way, as the big ones.

When are you going to Mrs Greig? I imagined that you were already there, she will think me touched in the head, or perhaps a little shell-shocked. I do so miss Colonel Greig, he is such a fine man, and always a gentleman. 'Blanco' White might be more or less effective but I don't think his best friend would perjure himself about 'Blanco' being a gentleman. Everyone seems to be leaving our brigade. Major Osborne is away on a six week course at GHQ. It used to be great fun going up to HQ and see Greig and Osborne but now the General seems to be surrounded with a very queer-looking brood. Osborne and Greig looked well and were smart but I don't know from where they are digging up some of the ones they are getting. The General remains the same, thank goodness, a fine chap.

It seems a long time since any Australian mail came to hand but I expect you will be having some, next mail. There is not really much to say or tell you, but I do love to scratch off a few lines to my own dear lover. It somehow makes it seem less lonely, and sad. Give our dear wee son of ours a big love from his daddy, and tell him I hope he is being a good wee lad and looking after his mummy, till his daddy returns.

Goodnight now, my little gypsy love, such a crowd of loving thoughts to you both . . .

NOVEMBER 11TH

Sweetheart,

The last two days I've been going against time, not a moment to myself.

All day yesterday I was prosecuting in a court martial case that involved a death sentence and it is a rotten job, I hate prosecuting the poor devils. This man is such a fool, a good fellow too, who flatly refused to do as he was ordered in the trenches. He was warned and replied he'd take the risks. There is nothing to be done but prosecute, for it is part of my job and the service must be upheld. Discipline is a total thing, and his action could seriously endanger all his mates. Still it's an awful job. To make matters worse, Stocker is away, and Sleath, my other clerk, would go and get sick.

We are out of the line but go in again tomorrow. The last time in was a very lively one, stunts every night. Four men won Military Medals, and there are some more to come out yet. I've had to do an awful lot of office work the past few days and then the court martial threw me behind.

Fancy old Mick[3] arriving in England. I do hope we see something of him. If only he was in the Infantry I could get him a commission easily enough with us. Selby and Lodge have both been invalided home, Selby did wonderfully well the other night and surely will be decorated but we will never see him out here again. He is a big blow to the battalion as he was an excellent officer.

We go back into the mud tomorrow. I was hoping against hope that I would get a bath this time, but there is not a ghost of a chance now.

Keep a lookout for a house in Edinburgh when you are there, just a wee nest, preferably with no stairs. It may mean you should advertise, we should try for a little garden front and back if possible.

No more now, my darling . . .

November 12th
BEF

Darling,

Here we are back in the line,[4] again slopping about in the mud. Very misty, and a depressing sort of day. There is a quiet foreboding in the air, and all is quiet and the world seems to be waiting, meanwhile we are trying to tidy up.

I got a lovely letter from you today, I just love hearing all the news about you both, two little Aussies in a foreign land. Fancy Mother coming over again, I think it is wonderful but sounds a bit risky. The Huns have just torpedoed another P&O liner, still the P&O have been very lucky. I can just picture Mother's surprise and joy when she sees that dear wee son of ours and all the credit rests on your shoulders, my sweet. What a wonderful, good person you are, how was I so lucky? You have been a wonderful wife and I am so longing to get home so that we can all be together again. It will be just lovely to have a home again and all your love and your loving ways, and for good this time, no more sad departures after ten days and a trip back to France to spoil our time. I'll have a chance too, of loving and seeing something of our dear son that you gave me in your great love. How I appreciate all you have given me and all you are going to give me, in return I will look after you forever, comfort you, love you, look after you till time ends.

It's funny that you have heard no more from Mick. However he has your address, and he will be in contact.

I met an artillery subaltern today, he came in with Captain Knox-Gore to call on us. Gore commands the battery that covers us. I thought I knew the face of the subaltern. I asked him where he came from, and do you believe he is one of the Loneragans from Mudgee. You will remember we met them in Mudgee. They are the rival business people to the Marks.

The Craigs will soon be arriving in London, it will be Vera's turn next, and then I am afraid that Deckie and his dad would be forsaken, but what joy to see her.

I'm sitting at a tiny wee table in a tiny wee (and wet) dugout and the mice are scampering all over the place, one just ran over my foot and then commenced to come up my leg. Cheeky wee presumptuous thing, but he is a friend, 'a wee cowrin timrous beastie' and does not threaten me, like our friend the Boche.

I hope Mrs Greig has sent on my letters. Col. Rose has had his leave extended until 5th December, which I hear is his last extension, so he will rejoin us then. He will find it hard after such a long time at home. He has been lucky, and on full pay all the time. I was speaking to the brigade Major about my leaving, when I was up at the brigade for the court martial the other day. He said, that is the limit, 'Once you are away you will claim to be an Australian, and then go home and leave us out here'. *Claim to be!!* what a rabbit, but it made me think, I had never really thought of going home as soon as I qualified, it certainly would be possible.

My darling and truly dearest cosy wee wife, here is all my love, and kisses for you both . . .

NOVEMBER 14TH
BEF

Your dear old letter came this morning, with lots of news. I'm so glad that you caught up with Mick, poor man, he ought not be laid up too long with the mumps. Sorry to hear that Mrs Stocker is not so well, poor thing seems to be having a pretty tough time. Stocker will be about due to leave England tomorrow, which seems pretty unsatisfactory, leaving and knowing his wife is in such a low condition.

Great strafing going on, from both sides. We look right into a cemetery, which is not such an inspiring view. The Boche just landed three shells right into the graves, which will make more work for the gravediggers. They don't take long to disappear once the shells fly in, but who would blame them? They are usually very old time-expired men and as dirty and grubby as they are old.

Good news comes from the south today, we seem to have made a very decent haul of Boche prisoners, with more to follow.

Today my resignation and application went on from the brigade to the division, from the division it goes to the corps and then to the army, on to the War Office, and then the reverse process commences and eventually back to me. I don't think they can upset the application as the need for MOs is so serious.

Yes I think a place somewhere in Liberton or the Braid[5] would be delightful. The best thing for you to do, dearest, is to send an ad to the *Scotsman*, saying that we need a small furnished house for six months, with a front and back garden, without stairs preferred. It would be helpful if it could be on a bus or tram. Why not take Mick house hunting, he would help in getting fair play. It will give him a chance to see Edinburgh, and to say the usual things about the trams.

Darling, I have been doing some figuring and I think, after paying lectures, my hospital fees and getting a couple of new suits, I ought to have left a clear £100, so that won't be too bad. I hope you are drawing your £17 a month regularly. It's going to be so strange being a civilian again. Sometimes at night I lie thinking, planning and get no sleep, it all seems too good to be true.

No more now, darling wife, all my love . . .

November 16th
Somewhere in France

Dearest wee lovebird of mine,
I love you so much, and send you this brief note to send a kiss.

It is so cold, wind, then icy rain and then our first snow, and still snowing. What was mud is now frozen furrows and jagged mounds, all frozen hard as a rock. It is now impossible to dig graves, but the cold makes it less urgent, but does not render it less obscene; to slip or fall in what was mud is dangerous. It doesn't seem to stop the wee beasties, just makes them snuggle closer to their unwilling hosts. Thank you for the singlet, it will be a big help with the beasties.

I loved Vera's letter, she and Geoff must have fixed things up. When we get our house fixed up, we must ask him to come and stay with us on his furlough. Vera ought to come home here, marry him when the war is over, and we could all go home together, and what a help you could give Vera, now as an experienced wife and mother. Geoff is a very lucky man, getting such a wife, nearly as lucky as I was.

A great bombardment last night, we watched it from the dugouts; the sight was reminiscent of our days on the Somme. No sign of the weather letting up, some parts of the trenches are waist-deep in freezing water, no fun to move about. Nothing here to write about except the cold.

All my love, all I can think of is a warm cosy bed, with a warm, cosy wee woman . . .

NOVEMBER 17TH
BEF

My own dear sweetheart,

What weather we are having, no more snow but very hard frost each night, which continues to solidify the mud. To make matters worse the wind at night has been favourable to the Boche for gas if he felt disposed to send it over, and that rather increased the anxiety. The days have been perfect if one was not here, clear blue skies and no wind to speak of.

The Hun aeroplanes have been very busy, all the time dashing out, dropping some bombs and away again. We were relieved today[6] and are out for five days but what an exciting relief. The Boche planes spotted the relief going on just as we were nearly complete and he commenced to shell us with a vengeance, all around our HQ, the huge crumps landed and knocked things about; all the time his planes hovered about over the top of us, gad, we had some close things, one big fat chap gurgled over and fell about twelve yards behind the orderly room, which is only made of some corrugated iron and a few sandbags. There are two windows in it and both were blown in and one side of the old caboose fell in, so we went out and moved to the right a bit and the next one went just over and blew in the front. At last the relief was complete and we commenced to file out, that is my HQ people, and away we went down a shallow trench to the road, but he spotted us and shelled the trench ahead of us so back we came and had to go by another route, then as soon as we got to the road towards the trees he dropped three on the road, one behind and two in front, so we came across a field. It was very methodical shelling indeed and we were lucky to get off as lightly as we did. I caught three shell splinters, one in my left elbow, one in the left ear,[7] and quite a nasty graze on the scalp, but nothing much to worry about. Our own guns have been giving Fritz fits, day and night, not light stuff either, and today is the first day he has been stung into severe retaliation, but he got it back with a Jew's rate of interest, and will get more yet.

Things have warmed up here considerably, and on the whole the Boche is having a thin time. We have had great rumours out here about a huge Zepp raid in Britain, forty Zepps taking part and ten having been brought down. The casualties are said to be 2000. When I had no letters from you I thought it must be true, but we got yesterday's paper today and there is certainly no word, so I felt much relieved, it is no doubt an ASC rumour. I got several *Bullies* but no letters, which is why I got so worried.

My resignation has reached the division, keep your fingers crossed. Do you remember Major Locke of the divisional staff? The day of the gymkhana at Sutton Veny, he and his charming daughter rode over to us and watched; well he has been very badly hit, and will not survive. I am terribly sorry, he was an awfully fine chap and so pleasant to work with.

I wonder how Mick looks, he must be a big fellow now, what a pity he arrived in Troon at this time of the year; it can be a mournful place in the cold.

Now, my dearest, I must close and get a letter off to Selby, who is wounded and won the Military Cross, a very gallant fellow. Five men won Military Medals at the same time.

Goodnight my darling . . .

November 20th
BEF

Today I got two nice letters from you, and a bunch of Australian mail too. Fancy Mick having actually arrived in Troon. I wish I had been there, I'm so glad he thought you were just the same dear wee fresh young lady that I ran away with, and that he does not think that you have been knocked about. I don't think that I knock you about much, or tire you do I, my darling?

The weather has quietened a bit and today it is fine but very cold. Anyway I took advantage of the absence of rain and took a ride over to ——,[8] and did some shopping, had hair cut, a bath and then some tea and rode home; it was about seventeen miles altogether, and was very nice and now I feel lovely and clean but very sleepy. Biddolph came with me; he cannot ride much and had a very rough passage and cannot move now he is so stiff. Had a letter from Stocker, his wife is still very bad and he appears to be most distressed. He went to see Colonel Rose who worked out an extension for him. It was jolly good of Col. Rose to use his influence, but it is typical of the man, so human and thinks of every man, big or little.

All the talk here is of transfers and resignations. Major Clark is transferring to the Machine Gun Coy, Robson and Beech are doing the same and of course the *pièce de résistance* has been my resignation, which is moving through the circles, and has reached brigade level. A special form is now required, which has to be sought from the War Office. Old John Anderson is to be the new adjutant in my place and his recommendation should hurry the War Office along. Lieut. Walker is attached to John for this week and then on Monday next John comes up to HQ to be attached to me. John has had a very soft job up to now, and to tell you the truth, he has not spent one night in the trenches. He is in for a shock. I've not written to Col. Rose yet, it would be best if you don't discuss it with him. I am writing to him tonight. In the meantime keep on the lookout for a wee cosy nest, I only wish I was there right now, so we could do it together. Make sure that it has a huge bath, I am never going to be without a bath again, may have two a day, to make up for this year.

We go up to the trenches again on Wednesday, I can tell you that I get less and less keen to immerse myself in trench warfare as the discharge nears. My darling, I am counting the days till we are together again, as a loving family, evenings at home, never to have to sleep in mud and snow and ice again, to live an ordinary life, and not feel obliged to help kill people, and run no risk of being blown up. In the meantime we are starting to prepare a great beano and blow-out for Xmas for the men. I will probably not be here then, but life goes on.

All my love . . .

NOVEMBER 21ST
BEF

This is to be a tiny note, my lover, as we go into the line again[9] tomorrow I am getting more and more apprehensive about going up each time. I am sure I must get out soon, there is a limit to what a person can stand. There is no time to write as there is so much to do when moving up; half the day is lost packing up and then unpacking, followed by the usual flood of work and bookwork to do. Stocker is away as you know and I only have Sleath, who has only had three weeks' training in the routine returns, still we are managing.

I have another wretched court martial again, not such a serious case this time, a man back late from leave, he will not face the firing squad.

Brigade told me today that from what they can judge, my release should come about a fortnight from the time it is received, so maybe I have another week or so.

What do you know, I had my passbook back from Cox's today, and I have a balance there of no less than the grand total of £210! That is pretty good, isn't it? I think it ought to see us through, it includes pay and all allowances to the end of November. Unfortunately I had to buy some new shirts, some underpants, also a pair of trench boots, and a new fleabag; it has been terribly cold and wet and my old ones were done, so we can count on £180 which is still a good bit. I will have to pay Richardson about £6 and £3 to my groom, but when I come home my only expenses will be clothes, and hospital fees. My fees, I reckon, will (including hospital ticket) be covered by £15, clothes will be about £12, and then I don't see what else there is. My books will be no more than 30/-, our house should be no more than £4 to £5 per month, just a tiny nest just big enough for the three of us and lots of love. If we offer to pay on the nail for six months in advance we may get a pound or two knocked off, although you know what they say about the Scots!

All I want is to be with you and Deckie. It's going to be just fine, if only they would tell me when. We'll buy up all the sugar, potatoes and coal, put them all in the cellar, and maybe get a pussy and a dog for Deckie. I've a mind to bring home one of the wee ginger cats from the trenches, they are a wee bit wild and I cannot vouch for their house manners, specially if they have been in the trenches with the Boche, who don't have any manners at all.

Must close, a big day tomorrow, may be the last time to go up. . .

November 23rd

Dearest wife of mine,
Biddolph has just come back from sorting the mail and tells me it is quite ridiculous that there are no less than three lovely letters from you. He seems to think that this is not quite fair. Fair or not it is wonderful and has quite taken my mind off the shelling, which is severe. We are back in the line and we are all praying for the dark, when he will lay off a bit. To make it more uncomfortable, our aeroplanes are busy and low over our lines, which irritates Fritz, and he fires lots of low anti-aircraft shells at them, and what goes up, must come down. There is a constant hail of hot metal splinters on us. It pays to keep one's metal hat on.

No word as yet from the division, it's now a week, and my patience is thinning, but they keep talking about the War Office, and delays and the War Office, etc. etc. There is no reason for you not to tell Mrs Greig now, as I have written to Col. Rose. Bad news today, Sandison, one of our best young officers, who went on Selby's raid, has died in hospital[10] at the Base, and Selby is now in England, recovering from a bad knock-about. You will remember I told you he was in a hand-to-hand scrap and had his chest knocked in by a German rifle butt. Lodge too is there with para typhoid fever. I feel so sorry for Sandison's people, the father is dead, his mother is very delicate, and the only brother is at home convalescing from severe wounds he received in Gallipoli. Eric was one of the finest of our soldiers, and one of Britain's best. It was entirely due to his efforts that Selby was got back to our trenches.

Goodbye now, my absolute dear, all my love . . .

NOVEMBER 24TH

Dearest,

I am just recovering from a rotten headache, but I snatched an hour's sleep and some good strong mugs of tea, and I'm pretty good now. We had a stunt on last night, which judging by all the shelling we received, the Boche knew something was on, at least he seemed well prepared, and things fairly hummed for a couple of hours. The 102nd Brigade had a stunt on our left, which produced more dead Germans.

All my papers came back from the Corps HQ last night. They had been to the division. My resignation was quite clear, I asked to resign to complete my studies and quoted the War Office authority. The corps returned the papers with the note added 'Does this officer wish to transfer to the RAMC?' The brigade asked for all the papers to be filled in again. My God, how do these people expect to win a war!! So I filled in all the papers again, and said — No, this officer wants to continue his studies, become a doctor, and then perhaps join the RAMC. (Probably never.) It is quite absurd, they never read anything I had written. I never mentioned the blessed RAMC. I believe the corps can settle the matter within a few weeks, so let's hope.

Charles comes into the line on Sunday, it will be the first time he has ever slept in the trenches. It will take him a while to get used to all the strange noises, the smells and the rats, which are really the worst thing of all.

Please remember me to Mrs Greig, and keep an eye skinned for a wee home, all my love . . .

November 26th

Dearest wee mate of mine,

There is no real news to tell. Yesterday was mostly used up in another court martial, which came off today. The wretched man fortunately pleaded guilty, which saved a lot of trouble.

Whilst there, a Boche plane came over HQ so low we all thought he would hit the ground. We all rushed out of the court in time to see him drop two bombs on one of our batteries. The guns had thought he was one of ours, so low was he, but as soon as they saw the bombs, all hell broke loose — six shells burst right above him, and the seventh scored a direct hit. He went into a tailspin, and then nose-dived into our lines about a mile away. The brave pilot appeared to have met his end instantly.

Charles Anderson is in the trenches tonight for the first time, and it's my job to turn him into an adjutant. I was speaking to the brigade Major today, and he feels sure that all the correspondence will have reached GHQ by now. I am in an awful state, picked up a horrible lot of beasties in a new dugout, not the mere body lice like we all get all the time, but an awful biting crowd. The itch makes one nearly tear oneself to pieces. I am at the moment almost entirely packed up in sulphur ointment; what I really need is a great scrub in a hot bath, then lots of the sulphur The doctor came down yesterday to rub the ointment well into me. I had a parcel of socks from Leslie Blair, and this time I have acknowledged them right away. Well old girl, I must beat these beasties before I see you, otherwise I won't be able to come near you.

There have been several resignations to complete medical training, so my case is not too unusual, if only they would tell me something. How did you enjoy the Xmas card which I designed all on my own, it's quite artistic isn't it? Hidden talents, but really well hidden.

Sir Geo. McCrae was called home yesterday, he won't be here again. Stocker returned this afternoon, he does not look at all fit, the poor man. I believe his wife has improved a bit, she must have been bad. Poor Stocker cried when he heard I was leaving the battalion, he is going to apply for a transfer to the Transport Branch–Canal transport.

There is nothing further here my dear little brown wife, such a heap of burning kisses to you and our dear son . . .

November 27th

I got a wonderful letter from you today. I am thrilled that you are having such a nice time, and that Deckie is enjoying himself. The change should do you both good. Well here we are, out of the line again[11] and in the same old billets with the same evil-smelling muddle in the centre of what is left of the farm. The farm is now called Greig's Farm. We tried all we knew to condemn it, sent in a medical certificate and all kind of complaints about it so the division told the brigade to look into the matter and Captain Greig hurried down in a very important way to see it and said it was no worse than any other farm, as if he had any idea, so it's now Greig's Farm! and he is welcome to it. As we came out today, the countryside looked like a fairyland, all sparkling with fresh snow, and decked out with thick frost, turned into a myriad of diamonds, then up came a thick ground mist, which provided such good cover it was as if the war was over, and we had a nice quiet day.

Tomorrow I am going to the theatre, a new show, really excellent I hear. The combination of artists is a very good one. John Anderson joined us at HQ last night and is very busy trying to get the hang of things, and is shaping well. Charles did not like being in a dugout after the comparative safety of the transport lines. He finds the rats the biggest problem, as have we all, but the awful thing is that we have all grown used to them, almost consider them a normal part of life. It is even possible to imagine one could come to take the war as the normal thing, as the normal life.

There was a great burst of machine gun fire just as he went to his dugout, bullets whistled and sighed over and whacked into his sandbags. Charles came rushing back, white as a sheet — 'Did you hear that?', 'Yes,' I said. 'Some MG stuff.' 'What in the name of God can be the matter?' It sounded so funny, it goes on all night, every night, it's when it stops one wonders what is the matter! I will leave most of the work for Charles and I will just swank around, superintending.

My main task for today will be to try to get a bath and a good scrub, to try to get rid of the beasties. They have been giving me a bad time, the vicious wee devils, I only hope they are giving the Hun as much trouble. They breed so quickly, and bury under the skin like a cattle tick.

I noticed them one morning when I was in bed and by the middle of the day I was almost frantic, and had to shave all the hair from my body and rub in the sulphur, which seems to have worked as it's not so bad today. I hope I don't get any more as I am getting short of clothes, I had to burn all my underclothes, and breeches.

I am keeping the pressure on the brigade about my resignation, trying to keep them on the mark, but so far nothing.

All my love, my wee darling . . .

NOVEMBER 28TH
BEF

Sweetheart of mine, dearest wee girl,
Banish all the dark 'cirkies', banish everything but love, all my papers came back today, from Army HQ, saying that everything was in order and that my release would be granted as soon as I forward a certificate from the Royal College certifying that I was a final year medical student.

Isn't that lovely, dear wife, it's over, the Hun didn't get me, and now you can, forever. I am longing and longing to hold tight your quivering little body and soul for all time. Now I'll be able to come home, and stay home. Kiss our dear little son and tell him his daddy is on the way home to see him. It cannot be long now, I wrote off immediately. We will need to bustle to find a house, it's going to be so perfect, not just twelve days' leave, followed by the sad parting. I'm afraid the 'cirkies' will be a great deal darker for a wee while. We have not had much of one another since the war started, and we have so much to make up. What a wonder you have been to Deckie and me, all alone, away from home, husband at the war, how you have come through, my God, you are the one who deserves the DSO. But we will have to be careful, as you say, my darling, but our love will weather the storm, won't it. Oh my darling, it seems too good to be true, can it be a dream, no, as I can hear the 5.9s and the MGs and they are not stuff dreams are made of.

Must close now, this is just a wee note to tell you the news, and to tell you of my love . . .

[Same Day]

Sweetheart mine,
This is the third attempt to write to you, but each time I get settled down someone comes in and interrupts me, but I think for the next hour at least I have no fear of more interruptions.

You will have received my rather incoherent letter telling you that the papers have all come back, with a request for a certificate from the university, showing that I am a final year medical student. I wrote off at once, so a reply should be here soon. It takes a few days for the letter to get to Edinburgh, and a few days for the return, I only hope the boat does not get torpedoed. Once the certificate reaches me the rest of the planning should take no more than three days, I can still reach you by December 14th.

I have only one more turn in the trenches, I am so excited that I find little interest in the work. I long to get back to you and wee Deckie, to sit by the fire, and talk, or read, and plan. I wonder how the house hunting is going, just look for something quite small, three bedrooms, one for us, one spare and one for the lad, he is quite big enough for a room of his own, and he should not be in with us, he is far too observant now, but he can scuttle in in the mornings for a cuddle, Oh! it is going to be grand. If you advertise, it gives you a chance to form a sort of opinion, and saves a lot of visits.

Now don't go and run about too much and tire yourself out, I will be home by December 14th, I reckon, at the latest. I am going to stay one night in London, to see Selby, and will catch the day train home. Perhaps we could meet in Edinburgh, look at the houses and then wait at Troon till the house was ready. But don't let us waste any time, with other people, I have been two years without you. We have been apart for most of our married life, well, nearly two thirds of it, and that is much too much. But we will have to be so careful, won't we, but never mind, Darling, we will be just too happy to notice anything. But please don't run about too much and tire yourself out.

I could not sleep at all last night, head full of plans for our life, and then, when sleep came, you filled my dreams. You were with me in the dream, and I could hear you whispering to me but couldn't quite make out what you were saying, but we were together, and then to wake up in the ice and cold, with the rats, really cruel. I wonder if you dreamt of me last night, because you were really with me.

I do hope that Mr Eadie does not delay in sending the certificate. The sooner it comes, the sooner I am home with my loves. No more now, my darling wee gypsy, soon we'll be together, and you just don't know how I'm longing for the day, and longing and longing for you and your love.

You are such a dear sweet desirable little wife and mate,
goodbye, dearest heart, see you soon . . .

la Boisselle

MESSAGES AND SIGNALS.

No. of

Words | Charge

This message is on a/c of:

Service.

(Signature of "Franking Officer.")

Sent

At.......m.

To.......

By.......

Recd.

Date.

From.

By.

19:1:16

Day of Month

In reply to Number

Daddy wants to

Just fancy

the fateful night

Australia

little Sweetheart

not as I have not

For we have a big

and I have to go

December

December 1st

I had two very special letters from you today and one from our dear son. I am so glad you are continuing to be on the lookout for a home. I was most surprised to hear that so many people are after houses just now. The flat sounds nice and most attractive and I wish I could do more than wish you best of luck in finding something for us. I had a letter today from Mr Eadie, the Registrar of the Royal College. I had written and told him that I had applied for release and also that I had told the authorities to apply to him for verification as to my statements and in his letter to me today, he states he will be delighted to confirm my position as soon as the authorities write to him. Today he will get my letter telling him they require a certificate and I asked him to send it by return. It should only be a matter of three or four days after the certificate arrives.

I go into the trenches[1] tomorrow and I hope it is for the last time for a considerable time or perhaps forever. Charles is doing fine in the orderly room and is picking up the work in great style. I am easing off and letting him do almost everything and this time in the trenches I am going to take things easy.

I had a letter from Colonel Rose today and am enclosing it for you. I asked him if he would like me to stay until he came back but he said no, not to bother, just to do as I like. We expect him back on the 8th, as a matter of fact I don't expect to be away before the 8th. As soon as the certificate goes I hope to get straight across to London from here in one day but at present the service is a good deal interrupted by weather and some of our men have been held up for two or three days at Boulogne. I am writing to our old Sergeant Major Burchell to be on the lookout for me and will be glad to see him although he is quite deaf now. In London I will stay one night with Selby who is now out of hospital and convalescing and will come up via the day train but I want to hear from you just to know exactly what you want me to do. I had a letter from Captain Harrison today, he expects to be out this week but has been sent to the HLI which is very bad luck for him. Russel has never yet come out, he is one of the lucky ones. He was hit in May or April, it was only a scalp wound too but he has been in Blighty ever since.

There is great excitement here about my departure, everyone gasps and says — oh you lucky devil, and sometimes much stronger descriptions: but anyway I have done my bit and as soon as I qualify I can do a bit more but at the same time I more than realise just how lucky I am coming home to my tiny wee home and my little family. You have been so brave and it's now my turn to do some of the hard work. It's amazing to consider that I've only received four or five wounds, none of them particularly serious and I guess, in looking back any one of them would have got me some sick leave in Blighty. It could be so wonderful to watch Deckie growing up and then there is dear wee Lyndal or have you forgotten about her, sweetheart. Do you remember the time when we first started housekeeping when you told me something one day when I came home from the hospital, wasn't it all so wonderful? I am just longing to see you both and it will probably, can you believe, be within the next fortnight.

All my love,

December 3rd

No mail today for anyone, I expect the Christmas mail is beginning to pile up and proving a nuisance to deal with. It is bound to be a stupendous affair.

I am still anxiously awaiting the necessary certificate to arrive; if it was posted the same day as my letter reached Edinburgh, it ought to arrive here on the 5th or 6th but perhaps it will be delayed a little bit too with the Christmas rush. I hope not. I am most anxious to hear how you are getting on with the house hunting. I hope you will find something that will suit us. It certainly is so exciting to be waiting for the certificate.

Colonel Rose will be back next week, he will be so sick at the thought of having to come back. It's bad enough being out in the winter but to get three months out of it and then come back to the full blast of winter isn't a great catch.

It is dreadfully cold here now but we have had no rain, thank heavens. It is colder than I have ever felt as there is a constant knife-like wind to add to the frost. This, however, doesn't stop the shelling which seems to be never ending with lots of trench mortar activity and to set it all off we had a gas alarm. The wind is against the Boche so I only hope it keeps in the same direction.

Charles is in the trenches this time and I am leaving most of the work to him. He had no idea how much work there was to be done and he seems almost to despair of getting on top of it. He is doing quite well really and if only I had had him as my assistant all along my work could have been halved. Major Clark goes straight to take out another battalion when Colonel Rose returns.

Lodge is very ill and away so that he will have a busy time for a while when he returns. Well my dearest this is just a hurried note to say I am thinking of you both.

All my love . . .

DECEMBER 4TH

My dearest family,

No letters yesterday. We are still in the line but the weather is quite decent today but the shelling and raids are the order of the day and I think all goes well as far as we are concerned. Poor Low was killed by a flying splinter, poor chap, he has not been here more than a few weeks. A mortar shell dropped only twenty feet from him, killing him and one soldier and seriously wounding three others.

I am crossing my fingers that tomorrow my certificate will arrive and then I should be able to leave within a couple of days. The brigade Major was down in the line today and called in to see me and he asked me if any certificate had arrived. He also told me that he thought the papers would have to go on to GHQ as he did not think the corps could settle the matter. Anyway he said that it would probably mean a delay of two days. This is a sort of psychological torture that they are trying I think but I will triumph over it. This is only a very brief hello, goodbye, all my love.

Love from . . .

December 7th

My darling,

I was very delighted today to have your two dear letters but was equally disappointed not to receive the certificate. I was so hoping it would arrive, however no doubt it will come tomorrow. The reason it did not come today is probably due to the fact that the 3rd of the month was a Sunday and no doubt my letter to Mr Eadie the Registrar would not receive attention until the Monday. I only hope that is true.

I had a wire from Colonel Rose and he is due to join again tomorrow. It will be so nice to see him again. I will feel for him coming back to this frozen wet hell on earth. I hear that he tried for a resignation but the War Office would not sanction it.

You have certainly been doing a great deal of running about looking at houses, you dear wee thing, your poor thin legs will be worn out. It is bad luck Deckie getting so nasty a cold. I hope that Troon soon blows it away. I got one myself now, the dugouts are fearfully wet and clammy and it is a wonder we all keep as fit as we do.

So Fanny has sold the 'Bungalow' or rather the 'Bungalow' has been sold. She will miss it, won't she? You seem to have two very decent wee homes under consideration and if you can strike a bargain either sounds nice. I don't mind much what they are like dearie, anywhere with you and Deckie will just do beautifully for me. The house near the Cluny Gardens seems to sound very nice as does the one at Colinton. I have heard of the Dell[2] but never seen it. I think the one near Cluny Gardens would be the nicest for you as you would see more people you know and it would not be so lonely. But the one at

Colinton appeals to me as I so like the country where I can potter about with Deckie in the garden and mean to keep some patriotic hens who lay most beautiful brown eggs. You say you will close for January and take the house for six months which ought to be quite okay.

Padre Black had lunch in the line with us yesterday, he buried Lieutenant Low, one of our officers who was killed in the last stunt. An awfully nice fellow Low was, his father is a parson in Glasgow. I also had a note from Harrison yesterday telling me he was due to arrive in Boulogne today so we should see him soon. It does sound like he is being warned for duty with the HLI. Lodge is, I hear, home and sick, he is about the luckiest man that I know. He always manages to get great hospital leaves and all the rest and has actually done less work in the trenches than any man with the battalion.

I forgot to tell you that I received the wee photo of you in one of your letters. What a dear wee round thing you are. I almost could see the picture of little Lyndal in your own little face. I do hope you are remaining well and that it's not too much for you. I can hardly wait till I see you, let us hope that certificate is hurrying to me.

All my love . . .

DECEMBER 8TH

Well, my darling tiny wee gypsy wife,
I feel in great fettle today for the certificate I wanted has arrived. It reached me at 11 this morning and by 12 noon it was in the brigade and ought to go on to the division tonight so now at last I feel as if something in the nature

of finality is being reached. I was so disappointed yesterday when it never came that I almost wept. Anyway it came today and I do hope they buck up at the corps and get simply moving. As soon as that is done the army will sanction my release and I am out of this place. We came out of the trenches last night and at the moment am back at the old familiar billets,[3] a billet I hope to have seen for the last time.

Colonel Rose got back yesterday and looked a bit down in the mouth, the usual return from leave expression and is a good bit thinner than when he went on leave. He took over command again today and now I am letting Anderson do everything. I am now in the state that I cannot sleep at night for the plans and castles in the air that flood in my brain. We are going to be such a happy family, I do hope the house is okay.

Sometimes I think that my luck is so great that it cannot really be going to come off and that every second I am here my luck must be running out. But my papers are in order and the War Office authority cannot be disregarded so that the worst it seems they can do is delay matters but at least all the time the pay runs on so that is one compensation. I am afraid that I will be a very rough and selfish husband for a while, my dear, but I have really not had much of my little girl, have I, and I do always want her so much for she is really when all is said and done, the one little girl in all the world for me. I hope to see something of Mick and it is just possible that I may. I was awfully nervous in the trenches this time, the time just seemed to hang and would not pass at all and each day I built up hope and then I was disappointed when the mail came.

Last night when we were coming out it was a very dark night with the only illumination being a great deal of machine gun and rifle fire and our big guns were belching out the old story of hate and the Boche receiving a lot of shrapnel about, the result was that there was a great deal of stray stuff and splinters flying about. I was just out of the communication trench and was on the road with John and Major Clark when a whizz-bang screamed on us and plunked into the mud five yards from us. As soon as we heard it coming we went flat into the liquid mud on the road and lay still waiting for the crash which we wouldn't have heard as it was so close we would have been all dead for sure. It was a dud and did not burst so after waiting for about five seconds, we up and ran for it to where our horses were and then away at a gallop until we passed our batteries and were out of range of stray bullets. It was a relief and I guess my luck is still holding. I just want you all to myself and for such a long time, we are going to be so happy, the three of us.

All my love and thoughts from your husband . . .

DECEMBER 10TH

My dearest wife,

Here I am just waiting to hear from the army now and waiting and waiting and trying to keep out of the way of the Boche metal. The battalion goes into the line again on the 12th but I am not going in this time. My luck is tested to the extreme and Colonel Rose agrees that I should go to the transport lines to wait the result of the report. He said he is not going to take me up into the line this time. I asked Colonel Rose why and he said, 'No jolly fear — you are bound to be knocked out, just in spite, so make arrangements tomorrow to go down to the transport lines till your discharge comes through.' Wasn't that topping of him?

Today I had a court martial to conduct in the most infernally cold and wet day. I was kept hanging about all day, Charles was with me and did most of the work under my instructions. Being a lawyer he got along quite well. I only hope that I have never to conduct another one. I hate prosecuting men who have volunteered for service and it seems to me so hard on the poor beggars but it has to be done.

I do hope I am not kept hanging about here too long. I can fill in my time by going for nice long rides but all I want to do is to go home.

I am so glad that I am coming home to you and feel so sorry for those of my friends in the trenches who have no one to come home to, and most sorry for all those comrades who will stay here forever. What wonderful people, all dead, but in a very selfish way, I am so relieved to be one of the lucky ones who can return home. Guilt is a fairly common feeling amongst us all for not getting killed, but thank the Lord we weren't.

I am glad that you have arranged about the house at Braidburn Crescent.[4] Colonel Rose and Charles say it is a delightful spot, they know it well.

All my love . . .

December 12th

Dearest wee treasure of mine,

Nothing further yet as to my disposal. Today I am going away on a new job. Charles is now installed in my place. Of course I am still nominally adjutant, but at 2 pm I leave for —[5] to take over a draft reinforcement of 200 men who arrive tonight. The place I am going to is about eight miles from here and I expect to be there for three days. We are very short of officers just now. There are plenty belonging to us in the country but they are nearly all on detached duty and attending various schools of instruction so that for regimental duties we are very reduced. A wire came in to send an officer on the job and as I was not going into the trenches I asked Colonel Rose to let me go. He was so good telling me that he did not want me in the trenches that I was glad to have the opportunity of filling the job.

As soon as my papers come through the CO says that I am to leave immediately, a substitute will bring my ticket out and I will leave the same day. I am so glad of the arrangements, it would have meant otherwise that I would just hang about the place waiting and getting in everyone's way. I will be quite happy looking after the new men at R. till the magic word comes along.

Yesterday was a day of more excitement than we need, it was very cold and cloudy and I was walking along the main road to — when the Boche commenced to send over some 5.9s searching for a 12 inch gun of ours.[6] I had to run for it across the fields and ran with two other officers and we lay in the ploughed field and watched the shelling. The Boche were making wonderful shooting but did not hit the gun, they landed one and demolished an old billet. It went down like a house built of cards but no other damage was done. Later I was on the same road and suddenly a Boche plane appeared from the clouds flying at about 300 feet, so close we could see the men's faces in the plane. The engine stopped and as there was a perfect fusillade of rifle fire and anti-aircraft guns going we thought he was hit and was coming down. He was heading straight for one of our batteries; everyone thought he was hit and the firing ceased and he looked as if he was going to crash on top of the battery; he was then only sixty feet up but just as he reached the battery his engine commenced again and away he went in a climb. A perfect uproar of firing commenced, men firing from the trenches and from the stand-to billets and on he went and right out the line back to his own side and never climbed higher than 100 feet. I grabbed a rifle and put four shots in at him but though he was so close he was not brought down and continued on his flight as if he was doing a show stunt. The bullets fairly zipped and plunked all around us and as they fell it was very reminiscent of the 1st of July. They were bullets falling from our own rifle shots from the men in the trenches. It was about the cheekiest piece of flying I have ever seen. Very sporty, the plane was for most of the time less than fifty yards up.

It is terribly cold and slushy today and the snow has been falling very heavily all the morning with the result that everything is in a terrible muddy cold mess.

The battalion goes into the trenches today and I have very mixed feelings. I see all the preparations going on for the usual move and I must say farewell to the battalion. It is the first time I have not gone up into the trenches with the battalion since January, to look back over almost twelve months of incessant trench warfare. I don't envy them the trenches on a day like this. If only some of the 'stay at homes' could be here and go into the line today after all the snow and rain with the intense cold and the shellfire, they would realise a little what the Tommy has to put up with out here.

Well dearest wee love of mine, today I hope that all the papers come to hand. I'd rather hoped to be with you by the 14th but this is not possible now but any day will do. How I am longing to see you and hold you so tight you can't breathe and our wee son. Goodbye my darling, will be with you soon.

Love . . .

December 13th

Here I am nine miles behind the line in charge of a reinforcement camp. I reported to the A and QMG at the rail head at —— as I was ordered and was told that there were 1100 men coming by train and I was to take charge of the 400 for our brigade. The train arrived in a blinding snow storm at 6 pm. It was pitch dark and of course no lights were allowed. The sorting out in the snow and slime was a big job, I almost envied the battalion in the trenches. I had only one sergeant with me and I'm afraid I used the most awful language, the Australians and New Zealanders gaped at me. After getting my lot together I had to march them three miles and get them fixed with billets. The billets were farms forty men here, fifty there and so on all spread out over sixteen billets, it was an awful job but by the dint of much heavy swearing I got through by

11 pm and when I got here to the farm I'm billeted at, Richardson had managed to get the old lady (about 103) to make some coffee and some omelette and off to bed. It was really a tremendous job and I only had a map reference to go by and it was the most dreadful night. The poor men had been travelling all day and were done. The roads were dreadfully heavy and snow fell all the time. Then there were cooks to be detailed, rations and messes to be allocated and fixed up, straw requisitioned as the men had no fur coats and no blankets but it all worked to my plan and Colonel Tonson-Rye was very complimentary about my organisation this morning. But the job is impossible without at least six more officers, even now there are over 400 letters just come in to be censored and I am not going to sit up all night censoring letters for anyone.

I was delighted to find twenty of our old men in the reinforcements who had been wounded on July 1st so I called them out and put them in charge wherever I could as I knew they would not fail me. It was awfully nice to meet them again, splendid fellows they are. One (Corporal Harlech) I saw on July 1st lying in No Man's Land shot through the neck and the hip. I gave him a drink but never expected to see him again. I've made him acting quarter master sergeant. Sergeant Scott, another of our veterans and a priceless fellow, I've made camp regimental sergeant major and so on, but it is too big a job for one man. However it won't be for long and no doubt before you get this letter I will have heard when I am leaving. Witcherton is cooking for me and doing a marvellous job. We went down and got four frozen mutton chops from the rations, bought some tomatoes at the canteen and he gave me a good lunch and now he is busy getting my dinner; oxo soup, some fish he bought and some hard-boiled eggs but it is very lonely, no one to talk to, just work and off to bed. There are many Australians about here and there are six Australian officers down in a billet about half a mile from me and whilst I was out one of them called to see me.

I fly a little blue and white flag with Camp Commandant on it but it's my own wee wife and son I want, nothing else counts, I am just longing for your company, warm and understanding, safe, and calm, and to be near our wee boy.

Goodbye for the present, my lover . . .

DECEMBER 14TH

Dearest sweetheart,
Here I am still commanding the reinforcement camp, sent 200 men up to one of the battalions today and on the 16th that is the day after tomorrow, I leave myself and take up the party that has been drafted to us. These will be handed over to the CO and surely by then I will have some news of my own movements. I've not had a single word from any of the authorities and believe I've been completely forgotten about. I sent an urgent wire for my horse and groom to report tomorrow morning as the riding shall keep my mind occupied.

Last night another 400 men arrived. The roads here are in parts under water and in some places the water is over three feet deep and in one way it is a good thing as it keeps the men from straying about and getting into mischief. The majority have had no pay for a fortnight which is also a blessing and saves trouble with the drunks, but they are very pally with the Australians and of course they have plenty of money and always plenty of beer, no one knows where they get it from. Many of the men are out in France for the first time and one gets a certain amount of pleasure or rather amusement from censoring the letters. All are of one mind as to the generosity and fellowship of the Australians.

I am pretty comfortable and have a big double bed and last night slept in pyjamas for the first time. The room is very cold but convenient and large. Richardson who is looking after me is in great form and gets along very well with the old lady. There is an extraordinary looking priest living at the farm. I've never seen such an evil face, like one sees in a picture of Lindsay's when the villain is a Chinaman. Some of the big guns were hard at it today and the newcomers stood in silent groups and listened, obviously very scared whilst the old hands looked as if this was quite normal, looked on indulgently and made sarcastic remarks. I heard one Corporal (an old stager of ours who was wounded on the 1st of July) tell a group, 'Don't just stand there gaping, don't you think you had better have a look at your rifles and ammunition, this is an attack developing and they'll be over here in about an hour.' The men could not make out whether he was pulling their leg or not but they floated to their billets and commenced to get busy. From here we can see the star shells and Verey lights going up in the distance and it is amusing to see the interested way the crowd of new men gather and gape. I expect we did the same. Some of the new men are very homesick and write very homesick letters whereas the old men of the 15th who have joined us again are just delighted and cannot speak of their luck in glowing enough terms.

I went into a very nice house today for tea; one of the officer's tea rooms run by two refugees and they make most excellent cakes, etc. I palled up with a New Zealand ASC man from whom we draw our supplies and went in and enjoyed the good things of life immensely. In addition the women make wonderful fine lace and we were examining a table centre and I asked one of them what she would take for it and she replied 105 francs per metre, of course the bargaining ceased when it began. It seemed to me to be a pretty stiff figure.

Well my dear, I am so longing to be back and so keen to get into our wee home together. The days won't pass nearly quick enough. I am sorry you have been having so much trouble with your tooth but it is best to get all that needs sorting out settled at once. I was so glad to hear in your last letter that reached me that you had not forgotten about dear little Lyndal. She is such a real dear little person to me, just a tiny wee gypsy thing, I so wish to see her and can hardly wait, but wait we must. I am so pleased that Deckie is behaving like such a wee gentleman. I certainly understand that everyone thinks he is wonderful. It is amazing to think of him staying there on his own with all his friends, he will be forgetting what his dear wee mother looks like if he does not get back soon but not if he takes after his daddy, who never forgets about the dear wee girl and always sees her pretty little face before him.

Now my dear I must close, all my love . . .

December 18th

Here I am back just about two miles behind the line and still waiting to hear when I am to leave. The battalion came out of the line last night and I went up to see them. I had moved into this town with the draft the day before and in the morning I handed them over to Colonel Rose and so now I am going to stay down here where I am until I hear definitely when I can get away. It is ten days now since I sent my papers down the long, long trail that leads to the War Office and I'm so disappointed I've not heard anything yet. The brigade Major told me when I put in the papers that it was just a routine matter, that I would hear in a day or so, that everything would go automatically so I do hope that they shake it up a bit and let me know.

I've not had a decent chance to send you my love, to have a chat, dearest wife as I've been very busy looking after the men. I was the only officer and the billets were so split up that I was never finished. Drawing and superintending the distribution of rations was an awful job and then came the censoring of letters, no light job to censor the letters of so many men as one had to be careful for one is totally responsible. So many of the men were new men and knew practically nothing about the censorship regulations.

However, here I am now almost free from any responsibility. I have my horse here and no men to look after so I can have some decent rides if the weather holds. Dearest little woman of mine I am so longing to be home with you and our little boy. I thought at first that by now I should have been in Troon with you and though the time is short I still hope to be home for Christmas.

I will come home just as fast as it is possible as soon as I get the go-ahead.

It is very cold and very foggy just now but no rain. This afternoon I am going to have a lovely hot bath and will put most of the afternoon in at the baths and then go up to the HQ for dinner with the lads. I had a wonderful long solitary ride today, went about twenty miles and found one isolated German who imagined he would capture me, but his heart wasn't in it and I took him prisoner and brought him back. He didn't seem such a bad lad and I think he is quite happy to be out of it all.

There is nothing fresh to write about my darling, just expect me when you see me and I'm going to close now, walk down to the quarter master's store to see if the mail is in.

All my love . . .

So end the letters from Somewhere in France.

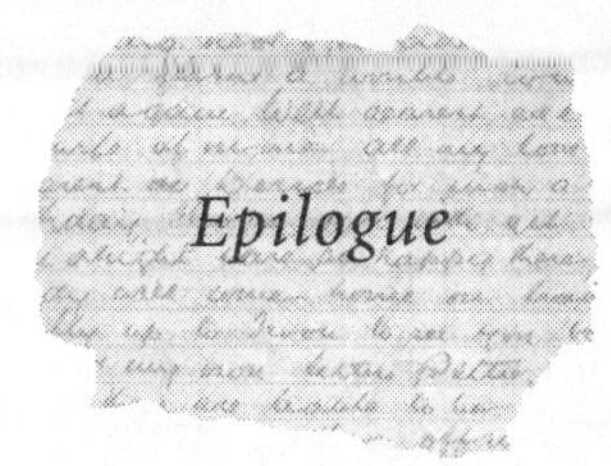

Epilogue

By December 1916, Captain Lewis Nott, adjutant of the 15th Battalion, the Royal Scots, was tired. He had spent almost a year in the trenches, with only two weeks out of France on leave. He had been in the front line for almost all of that time and had lived through the first Battle of the Somme. He had spent months separated by only a few metres from an enemy intent on killing him and his comrades. He had done more than his bit for King and his far-away country, and had applied to relinquish his commission in order to return to his wife, his son and his medical studies.

This request was approved and he received his orders on 18 December and was reunited with Doris in Edinburgh on 20 December. It is sad to relate that Doris had lost the baby they were expecting just a week or so before. The family were able to celebrate Christmas together, after which Lewis (Lew) recommenced his studies, graduating with first class honours in June 1917. He immediately joined the RAMC and was posted to the War Hospital, Thorpe, near Norwich in Norfolk, a 6000-bed acute military hospital, as Senior Resident Medical Officer and Surgical Registrar. During his time in Great Britain he also served as Senior Resident Physician at the Royal Infirmary in Edinburgh and at the Pilkington Orthopaedic Hospital, St Helens, Lancashire.

The family, now four with the arrival of their second son, John, returned to Australia in 1918 as crew on a cargo boat: Lewis as ship's doctor, Doris as stewardess and the two boys as rather small cabin boys. They set up house in Mackay, Queensland. Lewis was commissioned by the International Health Board, a part of the then recently formed World Health Organisation, to take charge of a survey of the incidence and treatment of hook worm in Central and North Queensland. He was appointed Medical Superintendent of the Mackay District Hospital and, showing his already developed interest in politics, became Mayor of Mackay, a post he held from 1923 to 1926.

In November 1925, Lew burst into politics after a tense battle with the former Queensland Premier, E.G. ('Red Ted') Theodore. Theodore had aspirations to become Prime Minister, which required that he enter Federal Parliament. He selected Herbert, then about half of Queensland, as a suitable electorate. He imagined this would be an easy way to gain his federal dream, as his opponent was only a 'minor local government boy'. The *Bulletin* considered the seat would be a 'gift for the ex-Queensland Premier' and Billie Hughes wrote a few days before the poll that, 'barring a miracle', Theodore would win the poll. The local 'lad' was Lew Nott, Mayor of Mackay and he enjoyed vast popularity in the region. The election was hard fought and the result very close, but Lew won the day and went to Canberra, thus having the honour of sitting in the Federal Parliament at its opening by the Duke of York in the brand-new Parliament House in 1927.

His fight for federal representation for the citizens of the Australian Capital Territory began during that first session of Federal Parliament on 20 June 1928, when as the member for Herbert he moved the adjournment of the House of Representatives to discuss the petition of the residents of the Territory for representation in Parliament. Prime Minister Bruce stated that it would be impractical to grant representation in Parliament to an electorate of only 4000 persons. This was the commencement of a fight which culminated in Lew Nott, a long-time committed Independent, being elected to Federal Parliament in 1949 as Canberra's first member. During his first term in Federal Parliament he served on many committees and was a key member of the Royal Commission inquiring into the Future of the Motion Picture Industry in Australia.

In the period between the wars he played a major part in the life and times of the developing city of Canberra, being involved in the dramatic arts, citizens' rights and, during the Great Depression, running soup kitchens. He continued for years to help the disadvantaged as a member of the Canberra Relief Society. Always aware of the great suffering and difficulties experienced by many returned servicemen, he became President of the ACT branch of the Returned Servicemen's League (the RSL) in 1932, a position he held for many years. His interests and hobbies were manifold and in all of them he played a germinal part in their development in the city. He was a life member of the St John Ambulance, a foundation and life member of the Canberra Horticultural Society, and a founder, first president and life member of the Canberra Kennel and Trial Dog Association.

Within three weeks of the outbreak of World War II, Lew tried to enlist as a medico in the Army. When it was decided that he was in a reserved occupation, he pestered every person from the Prime Minister down to get him into the Royal Australian Air Force, but to no avail. In February 1940 he attempted to raise an Australian Field Hospital and Ambulance Unit to take to Russia. He was inundated with applications from doctors, nurses and ambulance drivers, and he embarked on a national campaign to raise the Unit. Robert Menzies, then Prime Minister of Australia, wrote to Lew on 11 March 1940: 'The War Cabinet was of the opinion that it would be unwise to authorise a further effort of the nature suggested in your proposal, and . . . I regret that approval cannot be given.'

Lew Nott was one of Canberra's most distinguished pioneers, devoting almost half of his life to the city and its people. In 1929 he commenced his long association with Canberra Community Hospital by being appointed Superintendent, a position he occupied until 1934, and again from January 1940 to October 1949. During that time he developed the hospital into a fine example of a country hospital. He established the School of Nursing, many of whose graduates are in senior nursing positions in Canberra and around Australia. He was the only doctor in the hospital for most of that time. He ran Casualty and Outpatients, took the X-rays, delivered the babies and helped the Secretary, Mr Anderson, with the books and finances. Lew Nott died suddenly in October 1951.

Doris, the only child of George Edward Ashbury and Millicent Helena Aspinall, was born on 6 February 1893 at 'Arden Lea', Woolwich, a solid sandstone mansion on the Lane Cove River in Sydney, where her parents had been married. Her mother died when Doris was only 10 and she grew up with her first cousin, John Alvarez, almost as brother and sister. She remained with the Alvarez family until her university days, whilst her father travelled all over New South Wales as a district postmaster. Doris was a most accomplished student, winning a gold medal for her pass in the final school exams and gaining entry to Sydney University where she read honours in classics and languages. She was swept off her feet by the handsome and somewhat impetuous young Queensland mining engineer and then medical student, Lewis Nott. They were married in July 1913. Their honeymoon was spent in Edinburgh and included the period when Lew was studying medicine, as well as the Great War.

Throughout their life, Doris provided constant support for the arduous and testing medical and political life that kept them occupied for forty years. Canberra was an exciting place in its early days, and the pressures of a public life had many consolations, especially the whirl of Federal Parliament. Stanley Melbourne Bruce was a frequent visitor and was my godfather. Lew and Doris had five children, Frederick Lewis (Derick of the letters), John Hillhouse, Joy, Lyndal and David Bruce. Derick died of meningitis in 1927, aged 13, and his brother John died the next year from the same disease, aged 12. After Lew died in 1951, Doris opened a bookshop in Canberra, offering good books, cheerful company and conversation with coffee. She died in 1970.

The Nott Family

Appendix I

In the 1860s, Lew Nott's father, Frederick Lewis Nott, and his uncle Henry Oswald Nott travelled north with their father, John Nott (at the time, all established merchants in Maitland), to settle a property on the Burnett River in the Bundaberg district in Queensland. The original plan was to breed cattle. A site was selected in 1871 and called 'Windermere', after their home in Maitland. (The house, still standing and classified by the National Trust, had been built in 1821 for Thom Winder, an English sea captain, said to be the son of Arthur Wellesley, the 1st Duke of Wellington and Lady Mary Melville.)

Although the Burnett River plains appeared to be fertile enough, Fred, Oswald and their younger brother, Eb, set off on a tour of North Queensland in February 1878 to get the feel of the country and establish if there was better land for raising beef cattle.

Travelling by ship from Sydney as far as Townsville, the intrepid brothers raised an expedition of horses, men and cattle and struck out west. Starting off along the Ross River, they crossed the Burdekin and made good and rapid progress all the way to Lyndhurst. Then, striking north, they passed through Lynd and crossed the Copperfield River. The expedition avoided the very difficult Newcastle Range by keeping north, but there still remained much hazardous terrain to negotiate. The party headed west for the Gulf, first moving north to cross the Einasleigh River. They were now in the Gulf country, with the only real progress being possible along the course of the many rivers. The travellers arrived in Normanton on 17 May.

After resting for a week or so and spending a few days taking in the sights of this small Gulf town, the party embarked on the return trip. They retraced their tracks for the first few days until they reached Mt Jack, then headed north-east, towards Port Douglas. From Rookwood Station, which was a pleasant respite, they moved on via Thornborough to Port Douglas, arriving on 19 June. The diary kept by Fred Nott is brief and factual. It is clear that the amazing seven-month trip of well over 1500 km in the saddle was not considered to be of any great note. Here was an expedition, in Far North Queensland, nearly 120 years ago, on horseback, in mid-summer, from the east coast to the Gulf and back, which would be a test today, even in four-wheel-drive vehicles.

They returned to Bundaberg by sea, having decided that most of the country they had seen, apart from the region of the Etheridge and Einasleigh Rivers, described below in an extract from the diary, was not as tempting for farming as the Bundaberg area.

April 24th 1878.
Followed down, still good grassed ridges and splendid flats. Nice lagoons. Splendid country.

April 25th 1878. Thursday.
Still travelling down, splendid flats, lagoons 1 mile long by half across. Very deep, camped alongside one, and had a swim. 8 to 10 feet deep.

Friday 26th April 1878.
Travelling over very good but narrow country, a good run for 2 or 3 thousand head, camped about 3 or 4 miles from the Etheridge.

And later, approximately 32 km east of Gilbert Station:

May 8th 1878.
Camped at Crooked Creek, crocodiles, mosquitoes and blacks very bad. Killed a beast.

After their trip, the Nott brothers settled in Bundaberg, at 'Windermere'. It was a most significant property, about 600 hectares in all, with 260 hectares under cane. The first cane was crushed in 1882. By 1887, 70 hectares of cane were crushed, the juice being pumped to the Milliquin refinery. To enhance the production of sugar, the Notts applied modern scientific knowledge to the process, building the first complete plant for its production. The plant had a capacity of 50 tons a week and was one of the most advanced in the district.

Fred Nott courted Jeannie Blair, a very strict and upright Presbyterian of even stricter Scottish parents. Jeannie was born in Sydney but always remained a true Scot, keeping in touch with the Scottish side of the family, which is the reason Lewis went to Edinburgh to complete his medical degree. Fred and Jeannie had married at the Scots Church in Sydney in 1872, well before the great trek, and had eight children. As the family grew up, the children became well versed in the Kirk, in their Scottish ancestry. Meals were ceremonies, conducted in absolute silence, with the children's table manners being watched by Jeannie who was ready with a long cane to touch miscreants on the back of the hand.

The eldest son, Frederick Lancelot, was a member of the Queensland State Parliament for many years. He was one of the first graduates of Hawkesbury Agriculture College and gained a Science degree from Brunswick University in Germany, putting these skills to work on cattle stations at Charleville. He died in 1928. The second child, Arthur, died in infancy. Lilian and Jean Irene followed, and the next son, Frank Beresford, died aged 13. Archibald was a grazier in Queensland and had a great deal in common with Lewis, who was the next born. The last child was Gladys, who married a German national, Frederick Jacobi, just prior to the Great War and moved to Stockholm.

Appendix II

The Royal Scots
A brief history

The Royal Scots, The Royal Regiment, is the oldest regiment in the British Army, having been formed in 1633 by Sir John Hepburn. Sir John recruited a body of tough Scots to serve in France under Louis IX. Scottish irregulars had served for many years in Europe prior to this time with great distinction. So renowned had they become, by the end of the Hundred Years War the survivors formed the Scottish Archer Guard (*Les Gardes du Corps Ecossoises* sic), the bodyguard of the King of France, and the Scottish Men at Arms. King Charles I granted a warrant in March 1633 authorising men to be raised to form a regiment in Scotland, and Hepburn combined other groups of Scots, including the famous Green Brigade, with the two Scottish units in France to form a force of nearly 8000 men. Hepburn's claim of precedence for his unit angered some of the French military, who nicknamed the unit 'Pontius Pilate's Bodyguard', an opprobrium that the regiment has proudly used since. Hepburn was the first and one of the greatest colonels of the regiment and was only 40 years of age when he was killed at the siege of Saverne in 1636. In 1871 the name of the regiment was changed to the 1st or 'The Royal Scots' and about 10 years later to The Royal Scots (Lothian Regiment). In 1920 the name became The Royal Scots — The Royal Regiment.

The regiment has had a most distinguished history, as can be judged by the battle honours including: *'Tangier,* 1680; *Namur,* 1695; *Blenheim; Ramillies; Oudenarde; Malplaquet; Louisburg; Havannah; Egmont-Op-Zee; St Lucia,* 1803; *Corunna; Busaco; Salamanca; Vittoria; St Sebastian; Nive; Peninsula; Niagara; Waterloo; Nagpore; Maheidpoor; Ava; Alma; Inkerman; Sevastopol; Taku Forts; Pekin,* 1860; *South Africa,* 1899–1902. Mons; *Le*

Cateau; Retreat from Mons; *Marne.* 1914, '18; Aisne, 1914; La Bassee, 1914; Neuve Chapelle; *Ypres,* 1915, '17, '18; Gravenstafel; St Julien; Frezenberg; Bellewaarde; Aubers; Festubert, 1915; *Loos; Somme,* 1916, '18; Albert, 1916, '18; Bazentin; Pozieres; Flers-Courcelette; Le Transloy; Ancre Heights; Ancre, 1916, '18; *Arras,* 1917, '18; Scarpe, 1917, '18; Arleux; Pilckem; Langemarck, 1917; Menin Road; Polygon Wood; Poelcappelle; Passchendaele; Cambria, 1917; St Quentin; Rosieres; LYS; Estaires; Messines, 1918; Hazebrouk; Bailleul; Kemmel; Bethune; Soissonais-Ourcq; Tardenois; Amiens; Bapaume, 1918; Drocourt-Queant; Hindenburg Line; Canal du Nord; St Quentin Canal; Beaurevoir; Courtrai; Selle; Sambre; France and Flanders, 1914–18; *Struma;* Macedonia, 1915–18; Helles; Landing at Helles; Krithia; Suvla; Scimitar Hill; Gallipoli, 1915–16; Rumani; Egypt, 1915–16; Gaza; El Mughar; Nebi Samwil; Jaffa; *Palestine,* 1917–18; Archangel, 1918–19. Dyle; *Defence of Escaut;* St Omer-La Bassee; *Odon;* Cheux; Defence of Rauray; Caen; Esquay; Mont Pincon; *Aart;* Nederrijn; Best; Scheldt; *Flushing;* Meijel; Venlo Pocket; Roer; Rhineland; Reichswald; Cleve; Goch; *Rhine* — Uelzen; Bremen; Artlenberg; *North-West Europe,* 1940, '44–45; *Gothic Line* — Marradi; Monte Gamberaldi; *Italy*, 1944–45; South-East Asia, 1941; Donbaik; *Kohima;* Relief of Kohima; Aradura; Shwebo; Mandalay; *Burma,* 1943–45.' (Michael Brander, *The Royal Scots (The Royal Regiment)*, Cooper, London, 1976).

The battle honours in italics are those borne on the Colours. The official description of the Colours is 'The Royal Cypher within the Collar of the Order of the Thistle, with the Badge appendant. In each of the four corners the Thistle within the Circle and motto of the Order, ensigned with the Imperial Crown.' (Brander, 1976.)

The Scottish troops on continental service in the 17th century fought under their national flag and so it is safe to assume that from the first the Colours were roughly similar to the earliest extant description recorded in 1680. This states that they were a white Cross of St Andrew on a blue ground, with a thistle and crown in the centre circumscribed by the motto 'Nemo Me Impune Lacessit'. The first major change occurred with the Union of the Crowns in 1707 when the Cross of St Andrew was replaced by the Union Flag, the combination of the crosses of St Andrew and St George. By that time, also, the Royal Cypher was at the centre of the Colours and the thistle and crown at the corners, from where they pointed inwards, a distinction unique to the regiment. (Also unusual at this time, amongst Royal regiments, was the Union Wreath.)

In 1801 this distinction was removed when wholesale alterations were ordered. The thistles in the corners were set upright and surrounded by the Circle of St Andrew, with the motto 'Nemo Me Impune Lacessit', while the collar of St Andrew replaced the Circle as the circumscription for the Royal Cypher in the centre. The Colours then needed only minor modifications to emerge in their modern style, described as 'The Royal Cypher within the Collar of the Order of the Thistle, with the badge appendant. In each of the four corners the Thistle within the Circle and motto of the Order, ensigned with the Imperial Crown.' In addition, the Colours bear 'The Sphinx superscribed Egypt' to commemorate the conquest of Egypt in 1801, as well as the regiment's other battle honours. (Brander, 1976.)

At the outbreak of the Great War, The Royal Scots had expanded the regiment from 11 to 17 battalions, as well as two garrison battalions. Fifteen Royal Scots battalions served as active front line units. During the Great War, more than 100 000 passed through the regiment of whom more than 11 000 were killed and 40 000 wounded. The casualty list is estimated as being greater than that of the entire British Army during the Peninsular War. The 4th, 5th and 7th Battalions fought heroically at Gallipoli.

Only two Royal Scots battalions, the 15th and the 16th (2nd City of Edinburgh Battalion), were involved in the initial phase of the first great Battle of the Somme. As part of the 34th Division they attacked together the formidable fortifications of Scots Redoubt and Wood Alley, near the village of La Boisselle. After taking these points, despite a heavy crossfire from La Boisselle, the Royal Scots held them until the night of the 3rd, when they were relieved. By that time their reputation was more than established, but at the cost to the 15th Battalion of 628 casualties, and to the 16th of 482. On 14 July, both battalions took part in an attack on the village of Longueval with the 2nd Battalion; the Royal Scots, moving up on their left. The first stage of the attack was carried out very skilfully and successfully, but the second phase, the capture of the village itself, met with very strong opposition and eventually became bogged down in costly street fighting. Later the 15th Battalion was engaged in the fearsome High Wood sector of the front during which battle Lew Nott was wounded, and was twice mentioned in dispatches. By October the summer offensive was bogged down in mud and the 15th and 16th Royal Scots were 'holidaying' at Armentieres, regrouping and regaining their strength.

Appendix III

Extract from the Unit Record

The unit record consists of daily entries made by the officer commanding the battalion. The following extract encapsulates the great offensive through the eyes of one man, the Commanding Officer and is an interesting contrast to LWN's July correspondence. Official records published after the war show that the 15th Battalion lost 19 officers and 494 men on 1 July and was one of 32 battalions to lose more than 500 casualties on that single day. The 10th West Yorks lost a total of 710 officers and men.

July 1st 1916
Z Day. Zero Hour 7.30 A.M.

TRENCHES — JUMPING OFF POSITIONS

Exactly on time the 15th Royal Scots grouped forward to the attack — (1st and 2nd waves had moved out to No Mans Land some minutes previously). The men left with great heart & in grand form, not least hesitation or staleness — 3rd and 4th waves got severely handled when quitting front line parapet — mostly from M.Guns, one of which was in the bank astride S. end of Boisselle, another believed to be higher up the Sausage Valley.

Advanced moved slightly more to the right than was intended but this Mag gun fire naturally forced the left flank over a bit — this left flank was 'in the air' as 10th Lincolns on our left were not timed to assault until some minutes later than the 15th R.S. This undoubtedly caused considerable loss first to the 15th R.S. & later on to 10th Lincolns & 11th Suffolks: as M.Gun could afford to play on each at separate times: from the start there can be little doubt all the Units of the 101st Brigade started off to the right too much.

News came back that at 7.48 A.M. that 'Scots Redoubt' was crossed — & about 3 P.M. that 'C' Coy (our right flank Coy) had made Peake Trench — but at the same time the runner Pte Quin on being questioned said he had seen a few Suffolks & some 12 men of the 16th R.S. in with our men in Peake Trench — other news coming in from wounded returning & another runner from 'C' Coy (who delivered his note and returned), that the whole attack had been forced on to the extreme right of our objective: also doubted later if 'Scots Redoubt' had actually been crossed astride. The left of attack no doubt clipped the S. end; not a single man I questioned ever saw any of our troops to the left of our 'C' Coy, which as pointed out was now on extreme right of our Area; neither did those in Peake Trench see any troops pass over them towards Contalmaison; I heard that some 12 or so of the 16th R.S. some Suffolks & 1 Lincoln & a few Tyneside Irish had been in Peake Trench, but after holding same for an hour or so were driven back some 200 yards to S. Corner of the Horse Shoe, also heard enemy were attacking on Peake Trench from the left front & M.Gun fire was strong [as] soon as any extension to the left was attempted. Major Slack (reported wounded and is now missing) reformed his line on the road some 300 yds or so in front of Peake Wood — no troops were then on this left — indeed I know portions of B Coy & D Coy, (our extreme left) were among his men and I believe came in with other Units of 101st Brigade showing that all got pushed over to the extreme right.

I feel sure that only the extreme right of the 15th R.S. made their objective, namely Peake Trench; they were however in touch with the 21st Div — (The East Yorks) it was this block which prevented the enemy from rolling the left up still further. The East Yorks, I heard from several men, gave the men of the 15th R.S. extraordinary praise for the fight they were putting up; (R.S.M. Porteous was one of the men who told me). The later events are naturally more or less known now — with the exception that no men holding the most advanced position known to have been held by Maj. Stocks 15 R.S. namely Peake Wood ever saw any British troops go through them or troops fighting in their front — as they were themselves counter attacked & driven back to the Horse Shoe would seem to establish the truth of this, no doubt when Advance is pushed forward the truth will be established beyond any question of doubt.

1st, 2nd & 3rd. Losing practically every Officer (except Lieut. Robson) makes it somewhat difficult to get as much information as one would like but some of the men are very clear — indeed extraordinarily observant in every small details & there is no variation as to where they got & what they saw in regards to essentials. The 15th R.S. casualties amounts to 18 Offs. and 610 O.R. so far as one can judge at the moment.

July 4th
Long Valley Camp

Battalion withdrew from enemies position which had been held by them since the morning of the 1st July.

July 6th
Helencourt Wood

Turned over command of 15th R.S. to Major Rose.

ARCH. G.B. URMSTON, Lt. Col.
Comding. 15th Royal Scots.

Appendix IV

Extract from 'The Scotsman' 3 July 1916

This newspaper extract was in print only 48 hours after the offensive commenced, and seems fairly accurate, although no mention is made of the horrendous casualties.

British Army's Greatest Battle

'Appalling Concentration Of Artillery'

Opening Of The Offensive

(From the Press Association's Special Correspondent)

British Headquarters, France, July 1

The secret has been well kept. The weeks of essential preparation and concentration have passed without attracting the least degree of suspicion that anything beyond the normal was in progress, so unobtrusively and even stealthily has the immense task been carried out. Down to quite lately I had heard officers seriously discussing the improbability of an offensive of any sort by our Army this year, and I confess I found some good reason for agreeing with them. Then about ten days ago London was startled by a rumour which spread like wildfire to the effect that Lille had been taken, and prisoners who ultimately swelled to a total of 80,000 had fallen into our hands. This extraordinary report was passed around with unreasoning credulity. When news was received that a great bombardment was in progress along the whole length of the British front it was realised that a great struggle had commenced. And so the mind of the nation was fully prepared for the news that will have flashed around the world before this dispatch can appear in print.

Three Times Bigger Than Loos

The offensive, which is now in progress, is roughly on a scale about three times the magnitude of the battle of Loos, the previous greatest British effort. The concentration of artillery is literally appalling, every species of weapon, from the gigantic 15-inch Howitzer to the quick-rattling Stokes trench mortar, pouring thunderous avalanches upon the enemy positions.

The work of the men at the benches is at last nobly supporting the efforts of their brothers in the trenches. The opening moves in the terrific drama had been played with great strategic skill. Periodical intense bombardments all along the line, any one of which might have been the preliminary to a great offensive, left the Germans doubtful as to where the real blow would fall.

For many days past in the whole zone behind the front, there has been so much activity that it was very difficult to determine that any particular movement of troops implied a concentration for attack at a given spot.

Nervous Germans

That the enemy had been for some time past in a state of nervous tension all along the line was sufficiently evidenced by his exceptional vigilance and the incessant spasmodic outbursts of firing. Undoubtably the success of a number of raids carried out by our infantry had much to do with this result.

At six o'clock this morning I stood upon the brow of a ridge overlooking the much 'strafed' town of Albert. The sun had not yet risen high enough to eat up the dawn mists which hung on the slopes and in the valleys. July was being ushered in with true summer tenderness, a deep azure sky delicately mottled with fleecy traceries and a soft warm breeze coming from the west, the quarter which makes the Boche regret that he ever started importing the use of gas into warfare at all.

Several kite balloons already floated placidly on high, whilst others were leisurely climbing away from the earth, trailing their great, bead like communications after their bloated shapes. The drone of many aeroplanes hummed athwart the wind. Even as I stood there, with the larks singing overhead and the cattle browsing in the foreground as unconcernedly as though nothing else on earth mattered, the desultory crackling of the guns began to take a more rapid and deeper note.

With amazing rapidity the devastating chorus swelled, for the timetable of the momentous day had now been reached, until from horizon to horizon the uproar rolled in a ceaseless rataplan of thunder.

500 Shells a Minute

Several times I tried to count the pulsations of this inferno, but it was a hopeless task. I do not think I exaggerate in the least when I state that the shell-bursts often reached 500 in one minute along the length of the front my view commanded. From the slow, deep crash of the great howitzer to the malignant treble of the trench mortar, which showers its projectiles at a rate of one every two seconds, the overture to the mightiest battle which the British Army has ever yet fought, rolled its deafening diapason, and apparently this performance by the 'contemptible little Army' was all its own, unaccompanied, that is to say, by any echo of defiance from the foe, for, as far as I can gather, the German batteries made virtually no reply to this opening bombardment.

To say that I saw this stage of the battle is but a mere figure of speech. What I really beheld was the slow settling away of a dense fog of vapour which, like a waterfall, was always receding without growing less. Countless scarlet eyes winked mistily out of this waxing and waning cloud. At moments a rift would open in it, and dimly reveal the spire of Albert Cathedral, with its drooping Virgin, a factory chimney on the opposite skyline and a clump of fire-blasted trees and the like.

The sun drew off the morning haze, and shot with carious streaks the evil looking smoke banks which it had no power to dispel. High above the sky became gradually splashed with the lingering flecks of 'Archies' and I noticed that the German anti-aircraft shells gave off much darker smoke than our own. After about an hour and a half the fury of the bombardment appreciably slackened, and by the creeping into view of the battle foreground I knew that the range of our fire had lifted and that now our infantry were getting to death grips with the foe.

Promising Situation

Writing this as I am, a few hours later than the opening of the offensive as to catch the only means of transmission which exists for a dispatch too lengthy for the overburdened wires, I cannot pretend to present anything approaching even an elementary narrative of the battle as far as it has yet gone.

It takes days to collect and piece into a coherent whole the story of such a far-flung struggle. All that is possible to a war correspondent under such conditions in his wish to satisfy the earnest public's desire for news of the progress of our arms, is to send frequent short messages as intelligence becomes available. What we cannot tell you is only what it would be bad to impart to the enemy, and the delay in getting through the news from the time of gathering it is only to be measured by the congestion of the cable.

The British offensive which was launched this morning extends over a front of about twenty miles north of the Somme.

Of the coordinated French attack south of the Somme I cannot speak, beyond saying that I have heard that it was delivered with irresistible élan and brilliant success. It is a narrative that falls to other hands to record.

Whilst at the moment the situation looks promising, it is well not to carry satisfaction to the point of too great expectations. We are fighting a strong, determined, and resourceful foe, and although he has now been smitten harder than at any time before by the British Army, it would be very unwise to underrate his powers of resistance, particularly in the face of a highly menacing position.

A Definite Objective

The present offensive has a definite objective, and if this is attained, and it is not an unduly sanguine claim to predict that it will be, the British Army on the Western front will have satisfactorily fulfilled the role expected of it for the present.

On the other hand nothing is certain but the unexpected in warfare, and if under the pressure now being thrown by our Army upon the enemy and by the French on our right, the assaulted front crumbles, then great events may follow. But let us wait for these before clearing our throats preparatory to shouting. We have grown not to attach too much significance to the statements of prisoners out here, more particularly when these are of the 'wish being father to the thought' order. But it is an undeniable fact that all those who were taken in the storming of the front line showed a remarkable willingness to surrender, and complained that they had been virtually without food for some days, not because of any shortage of supplies in the rear, but because the deadly character of our almost ceaseless barrage during the past week rendered it so difficult to maintain transport.

Admirable Work By Airmen

It seems not improbable that the comparative feebleness of the German artillery response was due to a shortage of available ammunition from a similar cause.

The work of the British airmen during the fight was admirable beyond praise. They sailed about, often amid a perfect storm of shells, with indomitable unconcern, and their reconnaissance and observation work was of inestimable value. Incidentally, during the course of the morning a squadron of our aeroplanes swooped over Lille and heavily bombed the railway station, in the sidings of which the Germans had collected a lot of war material, returning safely in spite of being attacked by twenty of the once redoubtable Fokkers, of which two were brought down in flames.

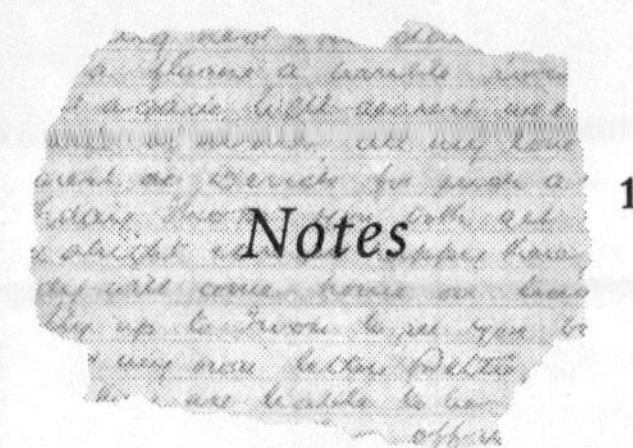

Notes

January

1 The port was Le Havre. The 15th Battalion, the Royal Scots (18 officers, including LWN and his horse, and 600 other ranks) arrived in company with the 16th Royal Scots, part of the 34th Division, and the 17th Royal Scots destined for the 35th Division. Three steamers were used: *Princess Henrietta*, *Empress Queen*, and *Australind*.

2 No 1 Camp.

3 The train trip took the regiment about 300 km from Le Havre to Blondecques, a French rail head 6 km south of St Omer. The men then marched about 6 km to the billets at Renescure.

4 Captain R.B. Greig.

5 Lieutenant-Colonel Archibald G.B. Urmston.

6 15th Battalion, The Royal Scots (1st City of Edinburgh), was one of the battalions raised by Kitchener and formed part of the New Army. LWN was adjutant of this battalion and spent 1916 in France with it. Further mentions of 'the Battalion' refer to the 15th Battalion.

7 Probably Captain C. Anderson.

8 Major H. A. Rose, second in command, 15th Royal Scots, promoted to Lieutenant-Colonel and became the CO of the 15th Royal Scots on 6 July 1916.

9 Mrs McOmie, friend, helper to Doris, nurse, confidante, live-in help, adopted aunt for Derick.

10 The 15th and 16th Royal Scots formed, with the 11th Suffolks and 10th Lincolns, the famous 101st Brigade, which, with the 102nd (Tyneside Scottish) and 103rd Brigades, comprised the 34th Division commanded by Brigadier-General H.G. Fitton, until his death later this month after a sniper's bullet inflicted mortal wounds, and later by Major-General Sir E.C. Ingouville-Williams, who was in command for the Big Push.

11 A popular cigarette.

12 The battalion was about 2 km west of St Omer.

13 A most prophetic remark, for 1916.

14 The first born, Frederick, known as Deckie or Derick was born on 6 February 1914.

15 Small seaside town in Ayrshire, on the Firth of Clyde, 48 km north-east of Glasgow. Mrs Wallace, Fanny, lived there with her daughter, Nancy.

16 A/g Captain Wilfred J. Lodge, one of LWN's best friends.

17 French slang for bad lot, rascal or German. Thought to be a shortening of *tete (de) boche*, meaning hard skull or hard head. Earliest form of a Picardy word for cabbage (*Oxford Dictionary of English Etymology*).

18 Probably the noise made by a small firecracker, in contrast to the noise of the ground artillery. The machine guns in the aeroplanes would sound quite faint but quite clear on the ground.

19 By 1918 there were 1680 German planes on the British front and 367 on the French. There are three named Taubes: the *Kondor* machine, tiny, 100 hp Mercedes engine, with a hole cut in the wing to facilitate observation; the *Krieger Taube*, of a prewar design, sleek tubular fuselage rather like a cigar, with a Benz Bz I or Bz II engine; and the *Jeannin Taube*. This aeroplane was sometimes known as the *Rumpler Taube* and was a famous scout plane. It is most probably the one mentioned here.

20 A type of fragmentation bomb designed by Lieutenant Henry S. Shrapnel, British Army, in 1784. The projectile was timed to burst towards the end of its flight, whilst still in the air, discharging a large number of fragments or balls over a wide area.

21 Reference to either General Joffre or Sir Douglas Haig.

22 Near Warminster, on Salisbury Plain.

23 The battalion *returns* include all the paperwork needing to be done each day by the adjutant and his assistants, including the ammunition used, stores and supplies needed, casualties, attendance at sick parade, the status of the unit's horses and so on.

24 *The Times* of Monday, 24 January 1916 described the death of the Brigadier as follows: 'Brigadier-General Hugh Gregory Fitton, CB, DSO, ADC who was Director General of Recruiting and Organisation at the War Office from September 1913 to November 1914, died of wounds on January 20th. He was born 1863, entered the Army in 1884, saw service in the Sudan and distinguished himself in the Dongola and Nile Expeditions. He also served in the South African War, and was decorated many times. He was ADC to the King from 1907.'

25 Field Marshal Sir Douglas Haig, 1st Earl, born 19 June 1861, died 29 January 1928.

26 General Joseph Jacques Césaire Joffre, born 12 January 1852, died 3 June 1931. Commander-in-Chief of the French Armies, he earned the title 'Victor of the Marne'.

27 It costs 1.25 a bottle and it's good enough for the soldiers, my darling. Since we will be in this town for some time I have decided to perfect my command of the native language!

28 22 January 1916.

29 Captain R.R. Russel.

30 Marched from Renescure to Morbecque, a village about 10 km south of Hazebrouck.

31 The Army Services Corps later became the NAAFI.

32 General Pulteney, G.O. C. 3rd Army.

33 Anthony Henry Gerard Fokker (born 6 April 1890 in Java, died 23 December 1939), a pioneer aircraft manufacturer, designed over 40 types of aeroplanes during the Great War. His revolutionary invention of the geared system, which linked the crankshaft of the engine to the trigger mechanism of the machine guns, made it possible to fire a machine gun through the propeller arc.

34 The Slingsby case and the pride of Herr Fokker got a great deal of coverage in the January *Times*, which was delivered to the front the day after publication throughout the war and seemed to have been the Army's main source of information. The Slingsby case was a *cause célèbre* of the day and grabbed headlines in all the papers in spite of the war raging across the Channel. Charles Edward Eugene Slingsby, aged 4, petitioned to the courts that he was the legal son of his mother and father and was thus in line to inherit great wealth, the Slingsby estates in Yorkshire. His uncles and aunts, also with an eye on the estate, attempted to prove he was the illegitimate son of an American couple, in San Francisco. The first hearing found in the boy's favour, but the relatives appealed on the grounds that Mrs Slingsby went to California and advertised in the 'Wanted' sections of the San Francisco *Examiner* for a baby boy!

35 Hazebrouck.

36 Sir George Houston Reid, 1845–1918. Elected to NSW State Parliament in 1880. Premier of the State, from 1894 to 1899. Prime Minister 1904 to 1905. In 1916, after some years as Australian High Commissioner in London, he entered the British Parliament. He retired in 1918.

37 Kaiser Wilhelm II (born Frederich Wilhelm Viktor Albert on 27 January 1859, died 4 June 1941), German Emperor, 1888–1918, cousin of King George V.

38 The battalion marched from Morbecque to Vieux Berquin, and then via Croix du Bac to the Erquinhem area, billeting in Hallobeau and Jesus Farms, a total distance of about 25 km.

39 Lieutenant D.G. Shields (17 June 1915).

40 Hallobeau and Jesus Farms, about 4 km west of Armentieres.

41 Doris was born in 6 February 1893. She was expecting her 23rd birthday. Derick was born on her 21st birthday.

FEBRUARY

1 Probably Vieux Berquin.

2 Camps No 5 and 6, at Morbecque.

3 Official Battalion records stated: 'Erquinhem 28th Jan. very heavy art. bombardment, all night, and again at 9.30 am to 12.30 pm and more in the evening. Total casualties 13th DLI (Durham Light Inf.), 10th NF (Norfolks) & 15th RS about 30 to 40, 15th RS 1 killed and 5 wounded, very small loss considering amount of artillery fire.'

4 The London 'season' had already started: six Zeppelins raided six English counties (Norfolk, Suffolk, Lincolnshire, Staffordshire and Derbyshire) on the same night, 2 February, with 54 persons killed and 67 injured. It was estimated that the Zeppelins dropped 220 bombs.

5 Probably Armentieres.

6 Hallobeau and Jesus Farms do straddle the main road to Armentieres. Erquinhem is probably the town referred to on the left, whilst the village of Lys is on the right.

7 Armentieres.

8 Probably Vieux Berquin, a small hamlet 14 km east of Armentieres on the edge of the Foret de Dieppe.

9 The Royal Engineers, 23rd Division.

10 LWN was born on 12 February 1886; he was approaching his 30th birthday.

11 The popular Australian weekly news magazine. It was founded in 1880 by J. F. Archibald and J. Haynes as a literary magazine catering for Australian and overseas writers. Its editorial policy was radical, republican and fairly socialist, with a motto of 'Australia for Australians'. It became steadily more conservative, but maintained the famous Red Page with its high standard of literary criticism. Taken over by Australian Consolidated Press in 1962, it remains a very successful weekly news magazine.

12 Earl Horatio Herbert Kitchener (born 24 June 1850, died 5 June 1916). Field Marshal, Imperial Administrator, conqueror of the Sudan, Commander-in-Chief during the Boer War and Secretary of State for War in 1914. Organised the New Army on a scale unprecedented in Britain. Kitchener died at sea off Orkney Islands some four months after the inspection described by LWN.

13 Steenwerck, about 6.5 km east of Camps No 5 and 6, about 3 km west of Armentieres.

14 The 4th Army, under General H. Rawlinson, consisted of the III, VIII, X, XIII and XV Corps. In the III Corps, commanded by Lieutenant-General Sir W. P. Pulteney, there were three divisions: 8th Division, (Regular), Commanded by Major-General H. Hudson; 34th Division, (New Army), Commanded by Major-General E.C. Ingouville-Williams, consisting of: *101st Brigade* — 15th Royal Scots (1st Edinburgh City), 16th Royal Scots (2nd Edinburgh City), 10th Lincolns (Old Chums) and 11th Suffolks (Cambridge); *102nd (Tyneside Scottish)* Brigade — 20th, 21st, 22nd and 23rd Northumberland Fusiliers (1st, 2nd, 3rd and 4th Tyneside Scottish); 19th (Western) Division: commanded by Major-General G. T. M. Bridges.

15 LWN was trying to beat the censor, hoping this would be a clue as to the regiment's whereabouts.

16 Probably a Bleriot monoplane, as the British Army was operating at least two squadrons of this swift French machine.

17 St Omer.

18 The children of Millicent Mary Aspinall, Doris' cousin.

19 The battalion's next responsibility in the line was to take over the Bois Grenier section. The HQ was at La Rolanderie Farm.

20 Reference to Gallipoli.

21 104th Field Ambulance.

22 Moved up to Vieux Berquin on the 20th and then straight to Hallobeau, La Rolanderie, taking over the Bois Grenier section from the Durham Light Infantry, with the HQ at La Rolanderie.

23 Children of LWN's elder brother, Archibald (*m.* Hilda). Colin was aircrew in the Royal Australian Air Force. He was the pilot of the Walrus amphibian on HMAS *Perth* and lost his life in World War II, when the *Perth* was sunk by the Japanese on 28 February 1942.

24 In-laws of LWN.

March

1 Second Lieutenant J.L. Brough.

2 Captain D.G. Shields.

3 Second Lieutenant J.R. Devine.

4 Armentieres. The battalion is still in the La Rolanderie area.

5 Garrison town in north-east France, on the river Meuse. In the Great War, Verdun became in Winston Churchill's words, 'the anvil upon which French manhood was to be hammered to death'. In an attempt to take the German pressure away from Verdun in mid-1916, General Sir Douglas Haig opened the great Somme offensive on 1 July, instead of Haig's preferred date in late August when the British forces would have been better prepared. The city was completely destroyed in the Great War.

6 Reference to the battalion records states: 'March 8th, Enemy's Art. is very fine, hit exactly where they intend to — ranged to a yard, but such spots must have been given them by observers far forward.'

7 'C' Battalion area.

8 Divisional reserve billets at Hallobeau.

9 Via Fleurbaix, to Trenches N.10.5, relieved the 11th Royal Sussex.

10 Fleurbaix, about 4 km south-west of Rolanderie, along the Rue Delpierre.

11 Foray Farm.

12 Major-General E. C. Ingouville-Williams, 'Inky Bill', General Officer Commanding of the 34th Division.

13 Lieutenant-Colonel Sir George McCrae, Kt., Volunteer (Officer's) Decoration, Commanding Officer of the 16th Royal Scots (2nd City of Edinburgh).

14 Captain W.B. Robertson.

15 16th Royal Scots.

16 Fleurbaix.

April

1 Trenches N. 10.5–N. 6.1.

2 It was a very accurate rumour, as both the 15th and 16th Royal Scots moved out for exercises and rest within the next few days and left for the Somme in the first week of May.

3 2nd Division, Australian Imperial Force.

4 Not long after LWN left Maryborough Grammar School, in Queensland, he studied at the Ballarat School of Mines, Victoria,

graduating as a mining engineer, with the object of moving back into the family company in Bundaberg, Queensland, to set up a gold mining and prospecting company. It was not his bent and after a brief period he enrolled in the Faculty of Medicine at Sydney University. He had completed the pre-clinical years when he and Doris were married in 1913, and LWN decided to complete his course in Edinburgh, at the Medical School, and the Royal Infirmary.

5 Lieutenant C. Anderson.

6 Captain R.R. Russel.

7 The 24th Battalion, Australian Imperial Force, was moved up to Sailly to train with the Royal Scots. This famous Australian unit fought with distinction at Gallipoli. After the retreat from that operation the battalion, consisting of 25 officers and 947 other ranks, went via Egypt to France, arriving in the early part of 1916. The commanding officer, Lieutenant-Colonel William W. Russel Watson, Volunteer (Officer's) Decoration, was awarded the OBE in 1918 for distinguished service in France, at Pozieres in 1916. The battalion was at La Creche on 1 July, and by the end of July was at Pozieres.

8 Sailly sur la Lys.

9 Eperlecques.

10 From the front, the battalion marched through Sailly, then to Raverskerque and on to Roquetoire in company with the 16th Royal Scots, and then on to Eperlecques via Tatingham on their own.

11 Kut. Sir Charles Townshend, the British commander in Kut, was cut off and surrounded by the Turks, during the first few months of 1916. Several heroic efforts were made to relieve Kut, all failing. Nearly the last and most desperate attempt was made by the 3rd and 13th Divisions, delivered on the right bank of the Tigris, over flooded land and in dreadful weather, between 13 April and 22 April. It was driven back by a Turkish counter-attack and failed. Finally, the steamer *Julnar*, commanded by Lieutenant Firman, R.N., made a heroic but forlorn attempt to get supplies through the blockade to Townshend, but struck a cable about 8 miles from Kut and surrendered. Townshend surrendered on 29 April, going to a POW camp on the Island of Prinkipo. So ended the second and disastrous phase of the Mesopotamian campaign.

12 Trebizond is a strategic port situated on the Black Sea, and possesses an excellent harbour. It was essential for the Russian advance to capture

Trebizond, which they did after a very bloody and tenacious resistance from the Turks on 18 April.

May

1 Graham Atlee-Hunt, a very close cousin.

2 The in-laws.

3 Lieutenant N.B. White joined The Royal Scots on the same day as LWN.

4 Captain G.L. Pagan.

5 Another effort to foil the censors. Almost certainly a reference to Albert, north-east of Amiens. Albert was to be a most important town in the coming years, as well as providing shops, bars and hairdressers for the troops.

6 Lieutenant W.A. Hole.

7 The Albert trenches.

8 The only Black in the battalion roll at this time is Lieutenant W.C.G.

9 The CO and 24 officers moved up into Albert trenches, arriving at 10 pm, in company with the 26th Northumberland Fusiliers 1 (3rd Tyneside Irish) who relieved that night the 24th Northumberland Fusiliers (1st Tyneside Irish).

10 Long, horizontal tunnels, dug with great care and secrecy, towards and sometimes under the enemy lines, then packed with up to a ton of high explosive, to be detonated remotely.

11 The battalion spent the next few days in and around the town of Albert.

12 Colonel Archibald G.B. Urmston left the battalion for recuperation. His wife, referred to as Mrs U, was apparently sick and could not cope with separation, which added to the stress being experienced by the Colonel.

13 To relieve the 16th Royal Scots.

14 The Lovat Scouts.

June

1 General Officer Commanding 34th Division, Major-General Sir Ingouville-Williams.

2 Eight inch Howitzer fire directed on to a trench mortar emplacement in the village of La Boisselle; the battalion record notes: 'The shooting was good, but 50% of the shots were duds. Set fire to a cookhouse in La Boisselle.'

3 About 15 km west of Glasgow, in Strathclyde.

4 The battalion pulled out after the action reported in this letter, assembling on the railway crossing on the Albert–Amiens road. After breakfast, the men proceeded to billets in Bresle.

5 The unit records describe the heaviest bombardment sustained by the battalion on 2, 3, and 4 June.

6 LWN was recommended for the Military Cross for his role, which was recognised by a MID by Sir Douglas Haig. The battalion record describes the action: 'About 1.10 am. very heavy bombardment with all calibre of shells. After about 10 minutes line to Bn. HQ from signal dugout was cut also forward lines to Coys. Communication maintained throughout. Bombardment maintained for an hour and information very difficult to receive and transmit. Runners and A Coy did magnificent work in getting messages between Coy and Battalion HQ and signal station.'

7 Relieved by the 21st Northumberland Fusiliers.

8 The 'scrap' referred to is the Battle of Jutland on 31 May 1916. It was to be the first and only major sea battle of the Great War.

9 Reference to Lord Kitchener who put to sea from Scapa Flow on 5 June aboard HMS *Hampshire*, en route to Russia. The *Hampshire* ran into bad weather but pressed on, and at 7.40 pm struck a mine which had been laid some days before by the German submarine *U 75*. The *Hampshire* sank in 2 minutes, 2.5 km from land between the Brough of Birsay and Marwick Head. Lord Kitchener, his whole staff and almost the entire complement perished, with only 12 survivors.

10 A fairly common diminutive for the *Bulletin*.

11 La Houssoye.

12 Sir William Robert Robertson (born 29 January 1860 at Welbourne, Lincolnshire, died 12 February 1933), Field Marshal, rose from a private to become Chief of the Imperial General Staff, a position he held for most of the war. He supported Sir Douglas Haig in the dangerous and bloody policy of concentration of manpower in the Western Front.

13 Probably the 17th Highland Light Infantry (Glasgow Commercials).

14 G.O.C. 101st Brigade.

15 Relieved the 21st Northumberland Fusiliers.

16 Austrian HQ. The Austrians reoccupied the city in October 1914, the Russians having captured it on 14 September. The Russians recaptured the city in June 1916, after a lightning campaign masterminded by General Lechitski. Czernowitz was retaken by the Austrians in August 1917.

17 Sir George Cathcart, FRCS, Senior Surgeon at the Royal Infirmary, Edinburgh, a pioneer British surgeon. LWN was his surgical dresser when a medical student in the first part of 1914 and again in the latter part of 1917 after he graduated in Medicine.

18 Dernancourt, about 5 km south of Albert.

19 Lieutenant Colonel Sir George McCrae.

20 In a field near the village of La Boisselle is the Glory Hole Sector, where the British and German trenches were so close, a few hundred metres north of Sausage Valley which was an important landmark in the 1 July offensive. Sausage Valley was to prove to be a deadly place, where on the opening day of the Somme offensive the Grimsby Chums, the Cambridge Battalion and the two City of Edinburgh Battalions (15th and 16th) suffered horrendous losses.

21 The official battalion record's account of the preparations between 21 and 30 June noted: 'Working parties Whole Battalion employed carrying pit-props from 9 pm to 6.30 am. Heavy work parties sent up to trenches with stores. Heavy thunder storm, men very wet. Marched to trenches. Roger attack, only small amount. Heavy shelling, 1 killed, 1 wounded. Busy getting all wire between rear trenches cut and ready for troops moving across the open. Also 'slants' in wire in front of fire trenches along whole Brigade front. Repairing damaged trenches in the night hours. Heavy shelling. Roger attack, gas was seen to move splendidly, but wind too light. 29th–30th. Marched up to trenches, cut more wire. 30th. Settled last details, cut all wire in front of fire trenches. 2 am began to move Companies into 'jumping off' trenches. Men magnificent. Total Casualties of 15th R.S. since arrival in France up to Z day Off, 1 wounded, O.R. K.24 103 wounded. Arch. G.B. Urmston. Lt. Col.Comding 15th R.S.

July

1 The fierce five-day bombardment leading up to the opening of the offensive on 1 July is regarded as one of the heaviest artillery bombardments in history. A French correspondent, writing from the Somme on 1 July said that the bombardment of Thursday, 29 June, was the most violent day of all. In some parts of the line, notably near Thiepval, north of Albert, shells were being fired by the British at a rate of 16 per second. The correspondent made the mistake, also made by the Allies, of believing that the methodical shelling was bringing about the complete destruction of the German defences. The major offensive was made along an 30 km front, using 455 guns, one heavy gun every 62 metres. In the bombardment culminating in the 1 July push, the Allies fired 4 million shells.

2 The battalion, as D, B and C Companies, were opposed by crack German units: the 2nd Prussian Guard and the 202nd–209th Bavarian Infantry. The three companies of the 15th Royal Scots were supported on the left by the 32nd Division, 101st Brigade, Lancashire Fusiliers and on the right by the 21st Division, East Yorks. The great offensive, spearheaded by the Royal Scots, commenced about 600 m south of La Boisselle and about 500 m north–east of Bécourt, along Sausage Valley, so named from the German sausage-shaped observation balloons often seen flying in this valley. By 10.20 am on 1 July, they had advanced to Peake Wood, 1500 m from their starting point.

3 Only two Royal Scots battalions, the 15th and the 16th (2nd City of Edinburgh Battalion), were involved in the initial phase of the battle. As part of the 34th Division they attacked together the formidable fortifications of Scots Redoubt and Wood Alley, near the village of La Boisselle. After taking these points, despite a heavy cross-fire from La Boisselle, the Royal Scots held them until the night of the 3rd, when they were relieved. On 14 July, both battalions took part in an attack on the village of Longueval with the 2nd Battalion, the Royal Scots moving up on their left. The first stage of the attack was carried out very skilfully and successfully, but the second phase, the capture of the village itself, met with very strong opposition and eventually became bogged down in costly street fighting.

4 Lieutenant Robson, LWN, the CO and two or three others were the only officers in the battalion to survive after the push of 1 July. The battalion lost 18 officers and over 600 other ranks killed, wounded or missing on 1 July. The 16th Royal Scots lost three officers killed, three wounded and three missing, and over 400 other ranks killed, wounded or missing.

5 LWN likely fatigue explains his repetition of the details from his previous letter.

6 This draft was the remains of 6th Battalion Royal Scots, fresh from Egypt. 'Very good draft, but absolutely no bombing experience.'

7 Major Robert Joseph Taylor, Captain John Claude Harper, MC, Major Walter Jacques Stack, DSO of the 4th Battalion, all of the Australian Army Medical Corps, commenced studying medicine at Sydney University with LWN in 1911.

8 Training day, bathing, live bombing at Millencourt, about 5 km west of Albert.

9 Major-General Sir E.C. Ingouville-Williams, CB, DSO, 'Inky Bill' was the commander of the 34th Division and was a much-loved and respected commander.

10 LWN recommendation (5th July 1916) was as follows:

Action for which commended: In very difficult circumstances, getting in touch and information with front line and helping to keep up connections with Brigade signal exchange, wires being cut in the first few minutes of the attack. Recommended by: Arch. G.B. Urmston, Col. Commanding 15th The Royal Scots. Honour or Award: Military Cross.

11 Two officers from the 14th Royal Scots (2nd Lts. Carmichael and Lowe), 54 other ranks, chiefly from the 3rd and 4th Royal Scots, and 10 of the 15th Battalion men who had been slightly wounded and were returning.

12 July 28 1916 is their third wedding anniversary.

13 Lieutenant Dudley A. Townley, 13th Australian Light Horse.

14 Manning was at the Edinburgh Royal Infirmary with LWN, and they joined up together.

15 The battalion moved up from Henencourt by motor bus to Fricourt Farm, bivouacking in Becourt Wood. On 31 July, the battalion moved out to trenches via Fricourt Farm at the north end of Mametz Wood.

AUGUST

1 Lemberg, Austria. Captured by the Cossacks in an action described as the Brusilov offensive, after the Cossack general of that name, it was probably the last really effective military effort by Russia. The offensive commenced on 5 June 1916, with 38 Russian divisions matched by 37 Austrian divisions. Initially the Russians had great success, but the campaign fizzled out due to some woolly Russian planning. However, the campaign compelled General Erich von Falkenhayn to withdraw seven divisions from the Somme, and lead Rumania to enter the war on the side of the Entente, with disastrous effect. Brusilov won a Pyhrric victory, capturing 350 000 prisoners but losing over 1 million men by prolonging the offensive after losing the initiative.

2 'Quadrangle' Trench.

3 Bazentin le Petit.

4 Bécourt.

5 General Cadorna with Colonel Badoglio, the CO of the Italian 74th Regiment, conducted a very careful and exacting preparation to capture Gorizia. Badoglio personally supervised the trenches and communication trenches, which enabled a most efficient attack, starting on 4 August. They captured the hills, including Monte San Michele (important in World War II) and surrounded the stronghold. By 8 August the attack on Gorizia commenced and was eventually successful.

6 First cousin to LWN, on his mother's side of the family.

7 Colonel Thomas Gordon Ross, DSO, from the 12th Australian Field Ambulance.

8 They moved up into the front line, under the 112th Infantry Brigade, leaving Bécourt at 12.45 pm. The battalion relieved the 10th Loyal North Lancs, under Lieutenant-Colonel Cobbold.

9 Relieved by the 10th Gloucesters under the command of Lieutenant-Colonel Sutherland of the Black Watch.

10 In association with the 10th Lincolns, the attack was directed at a German trench on the left of the line. The raiding party consisted of 60 picked bombers led by Second Lieutenants Hay and Mein who were to make a frontal attack while another party under Second Lieutenants Watson and Hodgson attacked along the trench. The attack was supported by two Stokes guns and a 101/4 trench mortar battery. The attack, which commenced at 10.15 pm, was fierce and resulted in a gain of 50 m but with heavy casualties. Watson was killed and Hodgson and Ross were seriously wounded. Another attempt the next day was also repulsed. 'Had to be content with holding old position.' On the next day they were ordered to try to take the German trench again, but again were repulsed by a ferocious German counter-attack and again had to 'be content with holding the old position'.

11 Full packs weighed over 60 pounds (about 25 kg), which did not include weapons, tin hat, gas mask, etc.

12 Franvilliers.

13 The battalion marched to Mericourt, entrained to Longpere and then marched to Liercourt. Entrained at Pont Remy, journeyed via Etaples, Boulogne, St Omer to Bailleul, then marched to Erquinghem, then to Bois Grenier.

14 Probably Liercourt.

15 Gordon Beresford Alford was the only child of Charles Gordon Alford and Elizabeth Crofton Nott and a second cousin of LWN. He was born in 1895, was married to Clara, had two small sons and died of wounds close to his 21st birthday in 1916.

16 Herbert Henry Asquith, 1852–1928. British Liberal Prime Minister from 1908. Protracted trench warfare culminating in the losses at the first battle of the Somme and other domestic political woes saw his resignation in 1916.

17 This was not so; Stocks was killed during the initial days of the offensive.

18 Reference to William Morris Hughes, 1862–1952. Australian Labor and Nationalist Prime Minister between 1915 and 1923.

19 On 15 July 1916, a German submarine, the *Deutschland*, claiming to be a Merchantman, arrived in Norfolk, Virginia, in the United States of America, from Bremen, Germany, with a cargo of goods and mail. The US authorities allowed her to load nickel and rubber, both in very short supply in Germany and critical to their war effort. This was the first occasion a submarine had been used to carry cargo. It was sufficiently serious to provoke the Allies to propose that neutral nations be forbidden to allow belligerent submarines use of their ports. The United States refused to forbid German submarines entry or trade and in October 1916 another submarine, *U 53*, which refuelled at Newport, then set about sinking six Merchant vessels—three British, two Dutch and one Norwegian.

20 Count Johann von Bernstorff, German Ambassador to the USA.

21 Son of LWN's Aunt Rebecca Norris (née Blair).

September

1 Lieutenant-Colonel Rose takes temporary command of the 101st Brigade, whilst Major Clark became temporary CO of the battalion.

2 To relieve the 16th Royal Scots in Bois Grenier Line.

3 Major Hugh Rayson, MC attached to the 57th Battalion and Major Charles Kingsly Parkinson, both medical graduates apparently from Sydney University, appear in the Nominal Rolls at the Australian War Memorial. Major Keith Henry Grieve, who was also in the Australian Army Medical Corps was awarded the MC on 3 August 1916. Packer cannot be found, but the name may be incorrect due to difficulty in reading the pencilled original.

4 A famous bookshop in Amiens, run by Madame Carpentier and her daughter, did a brisk trade in stationery as well as the very naughty *La Vie Parisienne*, whose risque cut-outs adorned many dugouts and trenches.

5 Probably Canal de Douai, 1 km south of Erquinghem, a popular spot for illicit and somewhat dangerous bathing.

6 Into action.

7 As many of the senior officers of Kitchener's New Army were non-professional soldiers it was not uncommon for some men to maintain business and professional interests such as Colonel Rose, by nipping back to England for company board meetings.

8 By next Saturday, the battalion will be out of the line and back at La Rolanderie Farm. The La Lys River passes through Sailly, then winds through the very flat countryside, past L'Hallobeau Farm, alongside and through Jesus Farm (mentioned previously), and then through Erquinghem. The battalion, resting at La Rolanderie, is about 1 km from the river, and the flat floodplain of the river would certainly offer a great place for the horse race.

9 Relieved by the 11th Suffolks. The battalion returned to La Rolanderie for some rest and peace.

10 To relieve the 16th Royal Scots, in the right sector, right sub-sector.

11 On 15 September 1916 the British 'tank' made its first appearance.

October

1 Second Lieutenants D.H. Petrie and G.E.P. Hamilton from the 7th Royal Scots and Second Lieutenant R.G. Murray from the 5th Royal Scots.

2 Captain Wilfred J. Lodge, who was acting CO during October.

3 Back in the billets on Rue Delpierre.

4 The battalion was relieved by the 16th Royal Scots and returned to the billets on Rue Delpierre.

5 Geoff Failes came through the war, and after returning to Australia, married Vera, who was one of Doris's best friends at Sydney University and a bridesmaid at their wedding in 1913. Geoff Failes was tragically drowned in 1935, whilst fishing with LWN on the Bingee Bingee rocks on the far south coast of New South Wales.

November

1 The battalion moved up from Rue Delpierre relieving the 16th Royal Scots in the right sector of the line.

2 From the battalion records: 'The objective of the raid was to kill Germans, damage their trenches and to obtain identification. A concrete bunker was found by Selby, which had a strong concrete door, which resisted all efforts to open, until one of the Germans opened the door to throw a bomb, but was shot. Captain Selby went a few yards further down a communication trench, came upon 3 Germans who he shot. The raid was judged to be very successful. 13 Germans, excluding those killed outside the barricade were killed, a machine gun emplacement and a trench mortar destroyed, and much damage to their trenches. Our casualties were light, 1 killed and 7 minor wounds.'

3 Herbert (Mick) Aspinall, one of Doris's cousins. He returned from the war and was a prominent solicitor in Sydney until his death in the 1970s.

4 Relieved the 16th Royal Scots again.

5 Suburbs in the southern part of Edinburgh.

6 By the 16th Royal Scots, and returned to Billets at La Rolanderie.

7 The injury to LWN's left ear was quite a deal more serious than he made it sound, as he was left moderately deaf in that ear for the rest of his life.

8 The return ride from La Rolanderie to Steenwerck and back is 25 km.

9 The battalion relieves the 16th Royal Scots.

10 Second Lieutenant Eric Sandison died of wounds in the British War Hospital, Boulogne, on 18 November 1916.

11 On this occasion, the battalion was relieved by the 11th Suffolks.

December

1 Relieved the 16th Royal Scots.

2 Cluny Gardens and the Dell are both south of the City of Edinburgh, near Colinton.

3 Rue Delpierre.

4 Near the City Hospital, in the Braid area of Edinburgh.

5 Little Rolanderie.

6 Probably searching for the British guns near Jocks Joy and Water Farm.

Bibliography

Books

Allen, Kenneth, *Big Guns of the Twentieth Century*, Firefly Books, Hove, East Sussex, 1976.

Arthur, Sir George, *Life of Lord Kitchener*, Macmillan, London, 1920.

Brander, Michael, *The Royal Scots* (The Royal Regiment), Cooper, London, 1976.

Chamberlaine, Peter, *Machine Guns*, Macdonald and Jane's, London, 1974.

Chasseaud, Peter, *Topography of Armageddon*, Map Books, Lewes, East Sussex, 1991.

Ellis, John, *The Social History of the Machine Gun*, Ayer Co Publishers Inc, USA, 1975.

Ewing, John, *The Royal Scots 1914–1919*, Oliver and Boyd, Edinburgh, 1925.

Gibb-Smith, Charles H., *The Aeroplane — an Historical Survey, HMSO*, London, 1960.

Gray, Peter and Thetford, Owen, *German Aircraft of the First World War*, Putnum, London, 1962.

Gwynn-Jones, Terry, *Farther and Faster*, Allen & Unwin, Sydney, 1991.

Hammerton, Sir John, *The Great War*, The Amalgamated Press Ltd, London, 1934 *circa*.

Hart, Liddel, *The History of the Great War*, Papermac, Division of Pan Macmillan Ltd, London, 1992.

Hutchinson, Lt. Col. Graham S., *Machine Guns, Their History and Tactical Employment*, Macmillan & Co., London 1938.

Ide, Arthur, *Royal Canberra Hospital*, R. & B. Pedigree Publishing, Canberra, 1994.

Jane's Fighting Aircraft of World War 1, Jane's, London, 1990.

Jane's Historical Aircraft, 1902–1916, Jane's, London, 1972.

Kerr, John, *Southern Sugar Saga*, Bundaberg Sugar Company, Bundaberg, Queensland, 1993.

Macdonald, Lyn, *The Somme*, Penguin, UK, 1993.

Middlebrook, Martin, *The First Day on the Somme*, 1 July 1916, Penguin, 1984.

Morris, Chant, Johnson, Willmott, *Weapons and Warfare of the 20th Century*, Octopus, London, 1976.

Nash, David, *German Artillery, 1914–1918*, Almark Publishing Co., London, 1970.

Shepperd, G.A., *Arms and Armour*, 1660–1918, Rupert Hart Davis, London, 1971.

Weaver, Lawrence, *The Story of the Royal Scots* (The Lothian Regiment), Country Life and George Newness Ltd, London, 1916.

Other Sources

Official Records, 15th Battalion, The Royal Scots (The Royal Regiment). Supplied by Major R.P. Mason.

Scientific American, September, 1894.

Sir Douglas Haig Supplement to the London Gazette, *The Times*, 4 January 1917.

The Scotsman (Edinburgh) various, January–December 1916.

The Times (London), various, January–December 1916.